Implementing Business Intelligence in Your Healthcare Organization

Edited By
Cynthia McKinney, MBA, FHIMSS, PMP
Ray Hess, MSA, RRT, FHIMSS
Michael Whitecar, MIS, LCDR (ret.), MSC, USN

HIMSS Mission
To lead healthcare transformation through effective use of health information technology.

For more information about HIMSS, please visit www.himss.org.

About the Editors

Cynthia McKinney, MBA, FHIMSS, PMP

Cynthia McKinney is a Senior Managing Consultant, Strategy and Transformation, at IBM (International Business Machines). Prior to joining IBM, Ms. McKinney served as the Director of Management Engineering and Decision Support for a 15-hospital system in Kansas City, MO. Ms. McKinney has an extensive background in project management, analytics, system selections, and strategic and operational planning and optimization of work-flow processes in both clinical and financial departments. Ms. McKinney received her bachelor of science in Accounting and a master's degree in Business Administration in Operations Management Healthcare from the University of Missouri. She has been an active member of HIMSS since 1987 and achieved Fellow status in 1999. She obtained her PMP certification in 2010. Ms. McKinney has been a frequent speaker at HIMSS on topics such as business intelligence, process improvement and cost containment. In 1997, she organized a local chapter of HIMSS (Heart of America) in Kansas City. In 2001, Ms. McKinney was elected to the HIMSS Board of Directors on which she served until 2004. Since 2005, Ms. McKinney has been an active leader/participant in the Management Engineering-Process Improvement Committee. For the past four years, Ms. McKinney has led the Executive Dashboard/Business Intelligence Work Group. Ms. McKinney has been recognized by HIMSS for her active participation in the health IT industry, having recently been recognized with the Distinguished Fellow Award (2010); the SIG Leadership Award (2007); the Spirit of HIMSS Award (2006); and the HIMSS 2004 Board of Directors Award.

Ray Hess, MSA, RRT, FHIMSS

Ray Hess is Vice President for Information Management at The Chester County Hospital in West Chester, PA. Mr. Hess' information management and process improvement experience includes having overseen decision support services for 16 years, health information management for six years and workflow automation/clinical decision support efforts for more than seven years. Mr. Hess is a Six Sigma Green Belt. He is a Registered Respiratory Therapist and has clinical experience, which includes more than 10 years in patient care and cardiopulmonary rehabilitation. Mr. Hess has more than 25 years of management and administrative experience, including overseeing cardiology services for four years. He holds bachelor degrees in Behavioral Science and History and a master's degree in Healthcare Administration. Mr. Hess has spoken frequently at the Annual HIMSS Conference & Exhibition and to audiences throughout the United States and internationally. He has published multiple articles and book chapters. He is a Fellow of HIMSS and is actively involved in multiple communities and projects. He has been involved with the HIMSS Management Engineering-Process Improvement Community since 2005. Hess has received multiple awards and recognitions. These include the WARIA US Gold Award in 2006; a CIO Top 100 Innovator Award in 2009; a Healthcare Informatics Innovator Award in 2010; and becoming a Computerworld Laureate in 2011.

Michael Whitecar, MIS, LCDR (ret.), MSC, USN

Michael Whitecar is currently the President and Chief Executive Officer (CEO) of ANGLE PROOF, Technologies LLC, providing healthcare organizations and businesses with a framework to achieve operational excellence. This is achieved by optimizing every ANGLE of the organization with people, process, and technology in the context of business strategy. Prior to ANGLE PROOF Technologies, Mr. Whitecar served as President and CEO of The Chief Information Group, Inc. for six years, and also served as Chief Operating Officer (COO) of Park City Solutions, Inc., serving federal healthcare. Before entering the corporate sector, Mr. Whitecar served an exemplary 20-year career in the United States Navy as a Medical Service Corps officer, retiring as a Lieutenant Commander. Mr. Whitecar's naval career included submarine operations during the Cold War; service as Program Manager, Department Director, Consultant to the Navy Surgeon General; and a Chief Information Officer of the US Naval Hospital, Naples, Italy. Mr. Whitecar earned a bachelor's degree in Computer Science from Park University in Parkville, MO, and a master's degree in Management Information Systems from the Naval Postgraduate School, Monterey, CA. He also is a graduate of the Naval War College, Newport, RI. Additionally, he completed CIO graduate-level courses/seminars at Case Western University, Cleveland; and Software Engineering at Central Michigan University, Mount Pleasant. Mr. Whitecar is a frequently published author, most recently in journals published by HIMSS, the Society of Research Administration (SRA) and the Navy Medicine Institute (NMI).

About the Contributors

Eric Adjei Boakye, MA, is a Business Intelligence Analyst at Mayo Clinic. Mr. Adjei Boakye has five years of experience in requirement gathering, design and testing of business intelligence systems, such as data warehouses, OLAP (online analytical processors), dashboards/scorecards and reports. Mr. Adjei Boakye is a member of HIMSS, the American College of Healthcare Executives (ACHE), the Lean Enterprise Institute and the HIMSS ME-PI Business Intelligence Work Group. He has published articles in the local newsletter of the ACHE.

Michael G. Brooks is a specialist leader in the healthcare information management practice of a global professional services firm where he advises healthcare providers on information management, business intelligence, analytics and other IT strategy solutions. Mr. Brooks has more than 25 years of experience in health IT and business intelligence. He is a frequent speaker and writer on issues related to information technology and business intelligence. Mr. Brooks is a Certified Business Intelligence Professional (CBIP), Certified Professional in Healthcare Information and Management Systems (CPHIMS), as well as a member of HIMSS, the American Informatics Association (AMIA) and the Boulder Business Intelligence Brain Trust.

Anna Fredricks is a Senior Market Manager for IBM's global healthcare focus in Systems and Technology Group. Ms. Fredricks has more than 30 years' experience in business strategy and market development in industry, brand and client organizations. She brings extensive experience working with clients in other industries into her work in healthcare, including a major Customer Resource Management (CRM) initiative in financial services and modeling an extended enterprise as part of IBM's partnership with a major aerospace client. She participates in local HIMSS Chapter meetings and is a member of the Phi Kappa Phi Engineering honor society.

Robert Jablonski serves as Director of Business Development for the West Region of Beacon Partners, a Weymouth, MA-based healthcare consultancy. Mr. Jablonski also has served as President of the Washington Chapter of HIMSS and Chairman of the Small and Independent Consultants Special Interest Group. He presented at the Annual HIMSS Conference & Exhibition in 1993. He has spent 25 years consulting with clients throughout the United States in IT selection, deployment and management, as well as supply chain management and process redesign and re-engineering.

Prashant Natarajan is a Senior Product Manager with Oracle. He has been involved in data integration and warehousing, business intelligence, embedded analytics and transaction system analysis and design for healthcare providers and payers for more than a decade. Previously, he worked as a project manager, systems analyst and technical communicator at Siemens, McKesson and Healthways. Mr. Natarajan is a member of the HIMSS ME-PI Committee and has previously been a submissions reviewer for the Annual HIMSS Conference & Exhibition.

Susan D. Noack is the Worldwide Industry Executive, Healthcare for IBM Business Analytics. She has spent her entire career in the healthcare industry, including the last 30 years within health IT and enabling strategies. Ms. Noack's experience includes working within the hospital provider market, evolving health information exchange initiatives and with large physician organizations and payers. Responsible for the Healthcare Industry for IBM Business Analytics, she continues to be an advocate for information technology and advanced analytics as enablers to improving quality of care, and transforming care delivery systems.

Jonathan Rothman, MBA, is the Principal of Emergency Medicine Business Intelligence (EMBI), which he founded in 2010 after building and running a business intelligence practice for a multi-site emergency department group practice of more than 360 physicians. Mr. Rothman has more than 20 years' hands-on development of healthcare business intelligence and operational systems in multiple inpatient and outpatient healthcare settings, and in 1991, he obtained an MBA in Risk Management from Temple University in Philadelphia.

Rich Temple is an Executive Consultant at Beacon Partners, a well-respected healthcare management consulting firm. Mr. Temple works with all different types of providers to help them navigate through the challenges facing the healthcare industry today. Prior to Beacon Partners, Mr. Temple served as a Chief Information Officer for multi-facility healthcare organizations in New Jersey. He is a former President of the New Jersey Chapter of HIMSS and is a blogger for Healthsystemcio.com. Mr. Temple also has spoken at many industry events, as well as authored articles on many aspects of healthcare in several different periodicals.

Joyce Zerkich, MBA, MSBIT, PMP, CPHIMS, is a Project Manager at Trinity Health, located in Farmington Hills, MI. Ms. Zerkich received several quality and leadership awards for her extensive global experience implementing projects as the program manager for information technology and business initiatives in healthcare, finance, insurance and automotive. She attained the HIMSS Certified Professional in Healthcare Information and Management Systems (CPHIMS) certification in 2009.

Table of Contents

By Cynthia McKinney, MBA, FHIMSS, PMP; Ray Hess, MSA, RRT, FHIMSS;
and Michael Whitecar, MIS, LCDR (ret.), MSC, USN

Section I: Business Intelligence within a Healthcare Organization

By Michael G. Brooks

By Michael G. Brooks

Section II: How to Get Started

By Michael Whitecar, MIS, LCDR (ret.), MSC, USN

By Michael Whitecar, MIS, LCDR (ret.), MSC, USN

By Jonathan Rothman, MBA

By Eric Adjei Boakye, MA

By Eric Adjei Boakye, MA

By Michael Whitecar, MIS, LCDR (ret.), MSC, USN

Acknowledgments

The authors wish to thank the following individuals who provided subject matter expertise in the preparation of this book:

- Marion J. Ball, EdD, Senior Advisor, Healthcare and Life Sciences Institute, IBM Research
- Krista J. Casey, MBA, Clinical Quality Specialist, Lehigh Valley Health Network
- Basit Chaudhry, MD, PhD, Healthcare Analytics, IBM Research
- Karen Fairchild, President, Fairchild Consulting, Inc.
- Karen Green, CIO, Brooks Rehabilitation
- Brenda Mollohan, MHA, JD, PMP, Executive Consultant, Beacon Partners
- John Neider, Marketing Manager, Siemens Medical Solutions Health Services
- Daby M. Sow, PhD, IBM Research

Dedication

This book is dedicated to Cynthia McKinney, MBA, FHIMSS, PMP, for the hard work and leadership she has provided to the HIMSS Management Engineering – Process Improvement community since 2005. This book and many other tools are available as a result of her dedication to the healthcare industry.

Introduction

By Cynthia McKinney, MBA, FHIMSS, PMP; Ray Hess, MSA, RRT, FHIMSS; and Michael Whitecar, MIS, LCDR (ret.), MSC, USN

There is much discussion of the use of intelligence, both clinical and business, in healthcare. There is a spectrum of users: some organizations have implemented business intelligence (BI) to some degree, and others are still considering beginning to explore the world of business intelligence. What all organizations learn through this process is that implementing BI is a journey that is rarely ever "completed."

Our goal in writing this book is to prepare readers for using BI capabilities as a way to combine and exploit their information assets. Data alone are not helpful. However, when data are turned into information, they provide an organization with the power to change. The key driver to successful BI is applying the five "Ws" to this process:

- What do I need to know?
- Why do I need the information?
- When do I need the information?
- Where (or how) am I going to view the information?
- What am I going to do with the information?

BI requires an array of knowledge and resources—executive-level sponsorship, clinical and operational expertise and technical staff—to build data-driven applications. To provide readers with a comprehensive approach, we designed this book to draw knowledge from myriad individuals experienced in BI within a healthcare environment and attempted to develop chapters independent of any single position within the healthcare organization. Thus, technical jargon is translated into laymen's terms; business scenarios are reflective of executive management's needs; and requirements from a clinician's perspective are addressed in a format that is easy to understand.

How to Use This Book

As you read the book, you will find some information duplication. Our goal is to enable you to either read the book from cover to cover or delve into specific chapters. When applicable, chapters are referenced to other chapters for ease of locating additional information. At the end of each chapter, high-level checklists have been developed to help an organization through all the "To Dos."

If your organization has started using BI, this book will provide new ideas on how to extend or build upon previous investments. For organizations new to business intelligence, this book will help accelerate the learning process by providing an overview of the technology and real-life examples of how other organizations have achieved results and insights in the future potential of BI.

Section and Chapter Review

Section I explores business intelligence within a healthcare organization, beginning with an introduction to BI and how it operates within healthcare organizations; a structured process for assessing current capabilities and developing a BI strategy; and the major catalysts for BI value realization. Chapter 2 examines BI across the continuum of healthcare delivery, providing examples of applications based on their general relevance to the acute care and ambulatory care environments.

Section II begins by discussing how to get started with BI. Mid- to large-sized healthcare organizations facing imminent change, and therefore having to cope with the requirements of an evolving environment, will find what is needed in the BI foundation discussed in this chapter. Additionally, this chapter will establish the BI foundation by setting the standards leveraged through the benefits of creating a BI governance structure. Chapter 3 is intended to further stimulate thought from a governance perspective, but not overwhelm any BI initiative with preliminary requirements. The objective is to share a recommended approach that should be tailored to the environment.

The contents of Chapter 4 are most often overlooked as prerequisites to a successful and sustainable BI implementation. To assess an organization's environment in preparation for developing the BI infrastructure, a complete asset inventory of the environment is required. The inventory must not be limited to IT resources, but must also include governance, policy, culture, people and business processes.

Chapter 5 explains why technical staff requires use cases as the first step in determining what and how data will be used. This chapter will define the need for and show how metadata are used. Finally, the importance of integrating the process with use cases and metadata will be shared.

Chapter 6 explores the technical considerations an organization may face upon deciding to build rather than buy their business intelligence solution. BI applications can be complex, and there are many moving pieces to put in place, including software applications, technology, data, processes and sponsorship.

To explore the process of designing, developing, testing and deploying a BI system, Chapter 7 will introduce the assessments and high-level strategy and architecture documents that have been developed to point the path to the technical design, development, testing and deployment of the system.

Chapter 8 presents a perfect-day scenario to address post-implementation. Additionally, we will revisit the models presented in Chapter 4 with expectation that the team has addressed the findings, whether through organizational change or simple modifications to processes and resources. Following this assessment of the environment, we will examine important tasks to ensure the BI implementation is sustainable.

In its most fundamental form, business intelligence requires change and an organizational change management strategy. Chapter 9 discusses change management and how to assist an organization through the change process. Change may be a new process, new people or new technology. Any type of change in an organization needs to be delicately crafted to meet the needs of the specific organization. It must consider the organization's culture, the speed of change they are willing to adopt and the tools needed to help them through the process. This chapter will focus on the various elements of change specific to business intelligence and how to gain organization adoption.

In Section III, we begin with Chapter 10 by focusing on the use of dashboards, the first component to address results. Based on the overwhelming literature written about dashboards, it is clear there is a dashboard for just about every purpose that may be needed. While this chapter will cover the different types of dashboards, its purpose will primarily focus on understanding what dashboards can do for an organization, what they cannot do and how dashboards support the use of advanced business intelligence.

Chapter 11 discusses key aspects of a robust reporting system, including examining four levels of BI reporting capabilities that may exist or need to be developed in the healthcare enterprise to achieve robust reporting. Each level will be presented with its characteristics, advantages and disadvantages. This chapter will also present a rationale for why an organization ought to consider a comprehensive Level-4 enterprise reporting strategy along with recommendations for best practices. Additionally, this chapter will focus on how the BI project team can develop and leverage existing resources and skill sets to implement the desired highest Level-4 reporting capability that encompasses strategic, tactical, operational reporting requirements, as opposed to the more limited efforts that are usually sufficient to achieve capability in Levels 1, 2 and 3. Case studies will be provided by organizations that have successfully implemented a robust BI reporting system.

To further extend a robust reporting system, Chapter 12 will introduce further data diagnosing capabilities with drill-down capabilities. Drilling is a technique that enables a BI user to quickly navigate various levels of data, finding the answers to the questions facing the healthcare organization. Depending on one's needs, drilling can be used to view the data in deeper detail, or in contrast, drilled up to a higher summary level.

Healthcare organizations need a commitment to excellence and a means of measuring that commitment and its results. Chapter 13 digs deeper into benchmarking, which has the potential to significantly improve the efficiency, cost-effectiveness and quality of healthcare services.

Advanced components of BI will be further discussed in Section IV, beginning with Chapter 14. This chapter will review the use of thresholds, triggers and alerts as part of a BI system. It will look at the value they bring to an organization and go over considerations associated with setting up these tools. The chapter will then look at these same tools in the clinical and business context and show that they too are part of a comprehensive BI system. The chapter will then change focus to consider workflow management and process automation from a BI perspective. Ultimately, the chapter will challenge the reader to look beyond the traditional boundaries of BI and seek to drive outcomes rather than just report them.

Chapter 15 continues with advanced components of real-time monitoring and management. When configured properly, the real-time monitoring system can yield truly concurrent data. These data can then be used to feed the traditional BI system databases with rich and accurate datasets. This chapter will focus its examples primarily on the clinical arena. It is the area of focus in many of the new regulations, including value-based purchasing and accountable care organization legislation.

Modeling, simulation, forecasting and predictive analytics will be presented in Chapter 16. For most organizations, migrating to data-driven decision making is not only an evolving competency, it is becoming a necessity for staying competitive and efficient in today's healthcare industry. Business intelligence supports this need, and for every successful project completed, the requests for new information and more sophisticated analysis grows.

The contributing authors are all participants of the HIMSS Management Engineering-Process Improvement Committee. The authors have written several guides on executive dashboards and have provided numerous webinars on dashboards and BI. These authors possess a wealth of knowledge on the topic of business intelligence. Our goal was to provide a book that will help your organization begin or continue its journey with business intelligence.

SECTION I

Business Intelligence within a Healthcare Organization

CHAPTER 1

Why Does Your Organization Need Business Intelligence?

By Michael G. Brooks

This chapter will provide an introduction to the role business intelligence (BI) plays in healthcare organizations; a structured process for assessing current capabilities and developing a BI strategy; and the major catalysts for BI value realization. In many cases, BI strategy is viewed as an information technology (IT) project or the implementation of a reporting tool rather than as a change agent. It is critically important that senior executives, management, clinicians, analysts and other stakeholders be involved and committed to the improved use of information in driving business value. The successful implementation of BI technology represents the beginning of an ongoing value realization process where IT and business/clinical users work together to deliver business results.

What is it that enables one health system to deliver care at lower costs than another, one hospital to deliver better outcomes than another hospital, one physician group to obtain higher patient satisfaction ratings than their peers or one department to achieve significant improvements? In most cases, the better performing organization has developed a capacity for doing the right thing, the right way, at the right time and in a consistent manner. Accomplishing this feat may involve organization-wide initiatives or a combination of micro-level adjustments that are difficult for outsiders to recognize.

The healthcare industry is experiencing a period of rapid change with evolving applications, new data sources, innovative business models and a growing population of information-hungry "knowledge workers" who demand instant results. The web, social media, electronic health records (EHR), health information exchanges (HIE), patient medical home, genomics, proteomics, informatics and other developments are contributing to this challenge by generating more data in different formats faster than end users can effectively comprehend. In contrast, traditional healthcare applications (e.g., patient accounting, payroll systems, computerized provider order entry [CPOE], etc.) are designed for a specific function—to optimize the execution of a specific process or transaction. The result is often a gap between the data used to perform day-to-day transactions and the information clinicians and managers need to make informed decisions.

Technology is often not the only determinant of success. Many organizations fail to optimize their capabilities while other providers achieve outstanding results with fewer resources. Senior executives and clinicians frequently indicate that while existing systems capture plenty of data, they are unable to get the information they need in a useful manner. Specific BI products do not necessarily seem to be the key differentiator, as all major vendors have customers that can demonstrate varying degrees of successful deployments.

The use of BI and analytics is often overlooked as a strategy, process and/or capability that can contribute to the organization's efforts to improve care and patient outcomes, reduce costs, gain market access and obtain competitive advantage. The key to successfully using information as a strategic asset involves adopting an "intelligent" mindset that values and optimizes the use of this resource. This mindset includes how information is created, organized, maintained, analyzed, shared and acted upon. This mindset does not come from simply acquiring technology in hopes of achieving results. It requires top management vision, commitment, resources and perseverance, with the recognition that not every project will yield the optimum answer the first time. Achieving this mindset is a journey of continuous discovery, actions and course corrections, with the ultimate goal of improving the way organizations deliver patient care, treat their employees, optimize their suppliers and pursue operational excellence.

THE STATE OF HEALTHCARE INFORMATION

Health IT has been around for roughly 40 years. Changes to healthcare information systems (IS) in the United States have been largely influenced by changes to reimbursement, the need to manage cost, availability of new technology and other factors. Healthcare information systems initially evolved as independent billing-centric applications to support transaction-based concepts such as patient, test, encounter or claim. Such systems were developed independently on various proprietary vendor platforms while interoperability and data standards took a back seat. As a result, it has become increasingly difficult for organizations to access, organize and analyze information across multiple systems for complex decision making.

Beginning in the 1960s, EHRs began to evolve as landmark systems such as the Problem-Oriented Medical Information System (PROMIS), the Regenstrief Medical Record System (RMRS) and Summary Time-Oriented Record (STOR).[1] In the years that followed, diagnosis-related groups (DRG) were established and clinical systems increased in sophistication and ease of use. As clinical systems advanced, the number of other data sources (ancillary systems, bedside terminals, hand-held devices, diagnostic equipment, etc.) proliferated.

During this time, healthcare providers struggled with the challenge of getting various vendors' systems to interface with each other. To facilitate billing and other administrative activities, limited standards (i.e., International Classification of Diseases [ICD], Health Level Seven International [HL7], Systematized Nomenclature of Medicine–Clinical Terms [SNOMED CT®], Logical Observation Identifiers Names and Codes [LOINC®], etc.) evolved. These standards were important steps in the right direction, but still left providers with an expanding landscape of fragmented systems. Getting those systems to interface effectively required a substantial amount of costs and manpower, resulting in integration costs and maintenance becoming a major portion of an IT department's operating budget.

The 1990s saw the widespread, commercialized use of the Internet, made possible by flexible browsers, search engines, new programming languages (HTML, Java, etc.) and high-performance networking technology. These developments provided organizations with new channels for interacting with other providers, their patients, payers and other parties. The Internet also provided new channels for accessing medical literature resources such as MedLine, running marketing campaigns, sharing provider benchmark data and other uses. Soon providers and patients were able to share structured and unstructured information with other organizations more efficiently and, in the process, new data sources (web usage, social networks, market information, news, etc.) quickly expanded.

As technology advanced, so did concerns about privacy and data security. In 1996, the Health Insurance Portability and Accountability Act (HIPAA) required the creation of national standards for electronic healthcare transactions (e.g., eligibility, claims, payments, etc.) and national identifiers for providers, health plans and employers. Since then, additional regulations have been released related to electronic data interchange (EDI), privacy and security, which impacts the ability of organizations to access, analyze and publish patient-related information.

In 1999, the Institute of Medicine's (IOM) report, *To Err is Human: Building A Safer Healthcare System*, estimated that as many as 98,000 deaths occur annually from errors in hospitals.[2] Two years later the IOM followed this report with a second report, *Crossing the Quality Chasm: A New Health System for the 21st Century*, which documented the failure of the healthcare system to translate medical knowledge into practice and apply new technologies safely and effectively.[3] As a result, there was an increased awareness of the need to improve the use of technology and information to achieve better clinical outcomes. This awareness was supported by numerous other initiatives such as the Leapfrog Initiative, National Commission for Quality Assurance (NCQA) reporting and the Physician Quality Reporting Initiative (PQRI), as well as individual payers choosing metrics by which to base their payment structures to providers. Many of these initiatives shared a common theme of requiring healthcare providers and health plans to report standardized clinical quality indicators and other metrics.

In 2009, President Obama signed the American Reinvestment and Recovery Act (ARRA) into law, which included the Health Information Technology for Economic and Clinical Health provisions (HITECH Act). The ARRA/HITECH Act established a program that involved the use of incentives and penalties to promote meaningful use. Under this program, eligible providers must use certified EHR technology, exchange electronic information and report various clinical and non-clinical measures to the Centers for Medicare and Medicaid Services (CMS). The ARRA/HITECH Act provided the impetus for healthcare organizations and vendors to accelerate the transition from unstructured to structured data and compliance with various vocabulary and content standards. Finally, ARRA/HITECH requires that eligible providers implement new systems and capabilities, such as clinical quality measures reporting, clinical data repositories and HIE over the next few years.

The Patient Protection and Affordable Care Act (ACA) of 2010 contained numerous provisions that were directed at payers, government programs and consumers. While the overall implications of this law are beyond the scope of this book, it is important to note that ACA emphasized the use of accountable care organizations (ACO) in an effort to promote better care for individuals, better care for populations and lower growth of Medicare expenditures through improvements in care. ACOs contain elements of both the payer and provider models in that they assume responsibility for treating a defined population of Medicare beneficiaries. As a result, HIE and new reporting and quality metrics will be required by management and the government to achieve this mission. It will be important for ACOs to establish the framework for collecting, organizing and reporting information to the government, various participating providers, the community and other organizations.

So, how does the state of health IT relate to BI? Today, healthcare executives and clinicians find themselves facing the challenge of needing to sift through massive amounts of data at many different levels (enterprise, department, population, physician, diagnosis, patient, etc.) to answer complex questions. These data may come from many different sources, delivered in many different formats and at different points of time, all of which increases the difficulty of analysis for end users. It is through meeting challenges such as these that BI has evolved.

WHAT IS BUSINESS INTELLIGENCE?

As big and complex as the world of health IT is, the BI sector may now be a close rival. Gartner estimates the size of the global BI market at $10.8 billion and is projected to grow at double digit rates through 2014.[4] The term "business intelligence" has been around for about 50 years and has continually evolved due to changing business requirements, new technologies and methods of analysis. As a result, there are many definitions for BI, often coming from different points of view (data warehouse, analytics, software, traditional reporting vendors, etc.), which has made it increasingly difficult to understand exactly what BI is. This fragmentation has led to a confusing array of terms—business intelligence, analytics, data mining, operational business intelligence and dozens more.

People normally associate BI with data warehouses, reporting tools and dashboards. Actually it's much more, and there are many ways to deploy the technology. In one of the most conventional definitions, "business intelligence" is defined as a broad category of application programs and technologies for gathering, storing, analyzing and providing access to data to help enterprise users make better business decisions.[5] Initially, the technologies associated with BI platforms were primarily focused on data warehouse, query and reporting functions. As technology evolved, the range of applications referred to as BI expanded to include a variety of other technologies required to address an expanding range of data types (web, text, image, geospatial, etc.) and ever-broadening range of strategic needs. Gartner identifies several technology capabilities in the broad category of BI such as[6]:

Integration
- BI platform infrastructure: The underlying framework of capabilities (e.g., security, metadata, administration, portal integration, etc.) to promote a consistent and effective user experience.
- Metadata management: Common metadata (the data about the data) that enables administrators and power users to search, capture, store and publish metadata objects such as data hierarchies, dimensions, measures, metrics and report parameters.
- Development tools: Programming-oriented tools and a development environment to support the creation of BI applications.
- Collaboration: Capabilities that enable BI users to share, discuss and manage metrics and supporting commentary via discussion threads, chat, annotated notes and other methods.

Information Delivery
- Report writers: Capabilities to develop and publish formatted and parameter-based reports.

- Dashboards: Ability to publish web-based, interactive displays of information using a variety of visual displays.
- *Ad-hoc* query tools: Provides users with the ability to submit their own inquiries without IT intervention and includes some ability to navigate authorized data.
- Microsoft Office integration: Ability to access data in Excel and export published reports in Microsoft Office products (PowerPoint, Word, Excel, etc.)
- Search-based BI: Applies a search index to structured and unstructured data with the ability to map such data into a defined dimensional data structure.

Analysis

- Online analytical processing (OLAP): A capability that provides users with the ability to quickly run queries, complex calculations while providing the ability to perform slice-and-dice analyses, and multi-dimensional drilling against a pre-selected set of data.
- Interactive visualization: Features that support the interactive, graphical display of information using a variety of graphics functions (line charts, bar charts, bullet graphs, etc.) with the ability to filter, drill up/down/across, apply alerts and other functions in order to deliver information in a meaningful context.
- Predictive modeling and data mining: The capability to apply sophisticated mathematical, statistical and other analytical methodologies to identify hidden facts and develop projections that support decision making.
- Scorecards: Capabilities to display key performance indicators and other metrics in a manner that aligns with strategic objectives or supports the use of performance management and process improvement methodologies such as Six Sigma, balanced scorecards, etc.

Underlying these capabilities is a foundation of other components of a BI architecture. The best known of these components is the enterprise data warehouse (EDW). An EDW is a central repository of granular data that is stored in a relational database format and contains detailed information that may be used by other BI tools and processes. Another key component involves data staging capabilities, collectively referred to as extract/transform/load (ETL) tools, which supports data extractions from source systems, the transformation of data from the source systems format to the destination format and the routines to handle the loading into the enterprise data warehouse.

While the definition just presented focuses on the technology associated with BI, successful BI strategies require consideration of a variety of other components such as data governance, business and clinical processes, change management, policies, procedures, staffing and capabilities. This leads to a modified lifecycle view of BI based on the work of The Data Warehousing Institute (TDWI) to include the processes, technologies and tools needed to turn data into information, information into understanding and understanding into actions that drive the desired business results and provide a basis for ongoing improvement.[7] (See Figure 1-1)

Effective business intelligence environments represent those deployments that are successful in improving the overall operations and results of their organization. Such deployments have occurred at a variety of levels, including strategic (enterprise), tactical (division, departmental or product/service) and operational (departmental- or process-focused). Regardless of the level of the deployment, commonly shared characteristics include:

Strategic focus. Many healthcare organizations have acquired more than one of these technologies to supplement clinical and financial application systems and meet various internal and external reporting requirements. A BI strategy is distinguished from merely having a

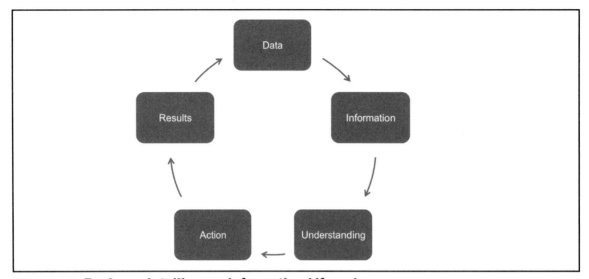

Figure 1-1: Business Intelligence Information Lifecycle.

"tool" to having a definitive purpose that guides what business or clinical purpose that tool will be used for and guidelines for what constitutes success. In addition, executive sponsors and stakeholders are defined to support that strategic focus with clearly defined roles and accountabilities.

Governance model. One of the distinctive advantages of BI lies in its ability to bridge various functional departments, systems and data sources to deliver relevant information in a useful context. As a result, an effective governance model is imperative in developing and coordinating the guidelines on who has access to what information, how decisions regarding data standards and information strategies interact with other enterprise initiatives, how resources will be allocated and other key functions.

Standards. Healthcare has long suffered from differences in data standards. Inefficiencies in collecting, processing, storing, reporting and analyzing information have a major impact on care delivery quality, patient safety and costs. Effective data standards improve the efficiencies and effectiveness of clinical and non-clinical data normalization to enable decision makers to speak the same language, which increases confidence in the data and supporting IT services.

Capabilities. To deliver information in a meaningful form to the ultimate decision makers, organizations must commit the requisite amount of staffing resources with the appropriate skills and supporting processes in order to support the management and delivery of information resources to the end-user decision makers. Driven by the BI strategy, the size of the organization, complexity of services and other factors, it is the quality of the capabilities of the organization that continues to be the biggest contributor to BI effectiveness.

BEYOND BUSINESS INTELLIGENCE

In recent years, many vendors and consulting firms have sought to differentiate themselves from the traditional reporting- and data warehouse-centric definitions by offering capabilities and solutions characterized as "analytics." This can be confusing in an era of mergers and acquisitions and where many of the vendors that have traditionally been categorized as BI are now attempting to rebrand themselves as "business analytics."

The difference between BI and analytics often lies in the sophistication of the techniques, the technology involved in processing data, how the information is presented and how the results are used. Imhoff and White define business analysis as "the process of analyzing trusted data with the goal of highlighting useful information, supporting decision making, suggesting solutions to business problems and improving business processes. A business intelligence environment helps organizations and business users move from manual to automated business analysis. Important results from business analysis include historical, current and predictive metrics, and indicators of business performance. These results are often called analytics."[8]

At the end of the day, many organizations in healthcare and other industries have applied BI and analytics to address a wide variety of complex problems in areas such as supply chain optimization, marketing strategy, risk management, fraud detection and social network analysis. In some cases, industries outside of healthcare are farther along in their deployments of BI due to the availability of data standards, less restrictive legal provisions regarding data sharing, level of IT spending and other factors. However, through the combination of legislative mandates, need to reduce costs and changing reimbursement models, healthcare organizations are increasingly looking to BI for answers.

WHERE HEALTHCARE AND BI CONVERGE

Healthcare is often viewed as a data-rich environment that is constrained by challenges such as disparate systems, paper-based processes, inconsistent terminology, structured and unstructured data and other factors. With the current initiatives such as Meaningful Use and ICD-10, the industry is making substantial progress in addressing many of these issues, which creates some attractive possibilities for healthcare organizations needing better reporting and analysis solutions. As pay-for-performance and value-based purchasing become more prominent in the healthcare market, the need for this convergence is imperative.

For organizations beginning to think about BI, it is important to consider some of the similarities and differences between traditional health IT applications.

Similarities
- Executive sponsorship is critical to the successful implementation and benefits realization of both clinical information systems and BI applications.
- Workflows must be addressed both in the deployment of clinical systems and BI. Healthcare organizations depend on so many sources of clinical data and metrics that are often in unstructured form, collected at various points in the care process, vary in definitions or with varying degrees of frequency. It is important that the workflows capture the data necessary to support the data model and the needs of the ultimate decision maker.
- Adoption. Obtaining user acceptance and participation are as important in BI as in the use of clinical information systems. Gaining credibility with decision makers and other stakeholders will impact the degree to which BI becomes embedded in the organization's culture and daily practices.

Differences
- Focus. Traditional health IT applications contain data that are designed to support specific transactions or tasks. Data captured within the data warehouse are typically organized by subject area.
- Integration. Data contained in health IT applications represent specific functions of that source system. Data warehouses and BI applications often deal with integrated data combined from multiple source systems to support analysis and decision making.
- Usage. In many cases, system usage for traditional applications will be consistent during certain periods, such as month- or year-end. The data warehouse environment must have

the capability to handle large upward spikes in demand when running complex queries or other processes involving large amounts of data.

- Data access. Data contained within health IT applications are frequently accessed and updated one record at a time, on an ongoing basis or driven by events. Data contained within a data warehouse are frequently loaded, but rarely subject to updates by end users.
- Time orientation. Health IT applications often contain the most current data values for a particular record and store data for a limited period of time (often for two to three years). Data warehouse environments store data for a much longer period of time, include multiple versions or snapshots of the records and always contain an element of time in the key structure.

CASE STUDY 1-1

The following case study illustrates how business intelligence has evolved from its initial development to become a powerful enabler for positive change at Intermountain Healthcare. This interview was conducted by the editors with Lee Pierce, Director, Business Intelligence and Enterprise Data Warehouse, Intermountain Healthcare.

USING BUSINESS INTELLIGENCE TO DELIVER EXTRAORDINARY CARE

Intermountain Healthcare (Intermountain) is a not-for-profit organization that operates 23 hospitals and more than 160 medical care clinics throughout Utah and southern Idaho. Intermountain offers the full range of healthcare services and is widely recognized as one of the premier delivery systems in the United States. Intermountain's leadership in the use of advanced clinical information systems began with its first deployment of electronic health records in the 1970s. As part of its strategy to become an information-driven, integrated healthcare system, Intermountain initially deployed its enterprise data warehouse (EDW) in 1995. Since then, Intermountain has made substantial progress in achieving a vision that demonstrates the value that better information can deliver to patients, physicians, employees and management.

Business Need

Through its early foray into electronic health records, Intermountain quickly understood the importance of collaboration between clinical teams, business leaders and technical staff to effectively organize and deliver clinical and financial data that promote improved care coordination and clinical outcomes. As their business intelligence vision has evolved, Intermountain recognized the need for data consistency and a set of technical and analytical capabilities that enabled better decision making and strategy execution across various operating groups. Finally, to handle routine and ad-hoc queries that involved combining data across a growing number of data sources, the information systems organization recognized that such a strategy must be robust to handle the performance, scalability, and wide range of requests. Today, the EDW contains more than 10 terabytes of data and supports more than 150 million queries per month by thousands of information consumers from all areas of the organization. But while this environment seems large by many standards, it is Intermountain's ability to quickly access and deliver high-value, focused information to decision makers that makes the difference.

Solution

In one example, Intermountain recognized the importance of improving outcomes for its colon surgery patients. The General Surgery and Pain Management development teams of Intermountain's Surgical Services Clinical Program identified the problem of post-operative ileus (POI) and researched industry literature for evidence-based best practices for this medical condition. Once a best practice was identified, physicians and clinical project leaders worked closely with the EDW team to combine data from various sources (electronic medical records [EMR], enrollment and financial systems) in the EDW and systematize evidence-based measurements that would enable clinicians to engage patients in the care process. As a result of this initiative, the Surgical Services Clinical Program realized $1.2 million in year one savings, and length of stay was decreased from 8.44 days to 6.75 days while maintaining or improving quality outcomes.

Benefits

At Intermountain, BI and the EDW are recognized as key elements of its success. However, as Lee Pierce, Director of BI and EDW points out, "Successful business intelligence is only achieved by an ongoing collaboration between clinical teams, business leaders and information systems staff to identify and solve significant problems." While Intermountain has had dozens of other success stories and received a variety of awards for its achievements, they recognize the importance of challenging conventional thinking and doing what works best for its patients, physicians and the rest of the organization. Its investment in clinical systems and business intelligence capabilities provide a platform for supporting future improvements in care delivery and management for years to come.[10]

BUILDING THE BUSINESS CASE FOR BI

In many respects, healthcare has benefited from the developments in BI technology in areas such as ease of use, ability to accommodate different data types, improved performance, scalability and analytics sophistication. Healthcare executives must look for new ways to leverage their information resources in the face of growing pressures from government, payers, competitors, capital markets and suppliers. To do so, each organization must develop its own strategy and supporting business case to meet its unique market challenges.

In a 2009 study on the use of BI in healthcare, the Aberdeen Group found that the majority of healthcare providers characterized as best-in-class had implemented BI technologies and operational practices to better manage staffing costs, medical supplies cost and revenue cycle effectiveness.[9] An important distinction is that the value of BI in these examples came from improved access and willingness to act on information to drive results.

Every industry has examples of organizations that achieve outstanding results, and other organizations with the same technology that fall short of meeting expectations. Whether the organization has a BI solution, is considering various initiatives or trying to determine what the strategy should be, it is important to establish a clear understanding of precisely how BI adds value to the organization. The key to determining BI value is the understanding that while the lack of effective BI can hold an organization back, technology alone is not sufficient to achieve value. Several key steps can help determine the incremental value and business case for BI in an organization. These steps are briefly touched on next and are elaborated in the remaining chapters of this book.

Step 1: Understanding Preliminary BI Requirements

Whether the organization is beginning to use BI or is considering taking their BI strategy to the next level, the first step involves determining the potential BI value opportunity within the organization by answering four key questions:

1. What are the organization's strategic priorities and operational needs (clinical and non-clinical)?
2. What must be done to achieve those needs?
3. Who are the key decision makers and stakeholders?
4. What questions must be answered in order to take appropriate action?

These questions define the opportunity, information requirements, customers and other factors that will determine the value and priority of investments in process improvement and supporting BI capabilities. In addition, the strategic priorities and targets should be the bold goals that represent the yardstick for success. For example, if the organization's priority is to improve the quality of care delivered to its ACO patients, then executives and clinical leaders will need to address questions related to identification of the population and its subsequent care needs and/or disease states, resource utilization, patient satisfaction, quality measures and other factors. The answers to these questions provide input into decisions regarding investments, staffing, resource allocations, process improvements and other areas.

Step 2: Developing the Strategy

Once the strategic priorities and operational information needs are identified and current capabilities are assessed, the next step is to identify the overall vision for the use of BI. Components of this vision include high-level data architecture, BI applications (how it will be used), major technology components (back office and front office), governance models, organization components (people, skills, processes, culture, etc.), high-level process improvement areas and key stakeholder groups. Each organization is different, and it is possible that there may be multiple starting points within the organization (e.g., finance is served by a data warehouse containing financial and revenue cycle information, while no similar resource exists for clinical data). The vision should then be documented, thoroughly vetted and approved before proceeding.

Step 3: Identify Estimated Total Cost of Ownership (TCO)

There are many ways to implement BI capabilities, and each will have a different mix of costs. In some instances, the costs of BI initiatives will be more easily captured and tracked within the IT organization. In other cases, costs such as management time, clinician involvement, source system upgrades and other elements will not be as clearly associated with BI. Typically these costs fall into three main categories:

1. One-time costs: Often referred to as capital costs, these costs include hardware and software, implementation and other one-time expenditures.
2. Annual recurring costs: These costs include items such as hardware and software maintenance costs, IT staffing salary and benefits costs, subscription to external data sources and communications costs.
3. Opportunity costs: There are trade-offs in every project. This category represents the foregone benefits of the alternatives not chosen.

Once cost components are identified and calculated, it is helpful to capture them in a TCO model that will provide the flexibility to roll-up various initiatives in the BI project portfolio and model various deployment scenarios. This approach also provides the documentation with underlying assumptions for future reference.

Step 4: Identifying Expected Benefits

Business intelligence initiatives provide valuable support to quality improvement initiatives that can lead to benefits such as improved clinical outcomes, increases in productivity, utilization, patient satisfaction, increased revenue and cost reduction. These benefits often come in the form of hard dollars (increased revenue, lower costs) and soft dollars (cost avoidance). Fundamentally, BI capabilities contributed value in several key ways such as:

- Improved performance (productivity, utilization, cost savings, etc.)
- Improved efficiencies (easier access to reports, better communication, better use of management time, etc.)
- Better analysis and business and clinical decision making (from more accurate data, analytic tools, etc.)

- More timely data (integrated metrics generated from reports from the EDW and other source systems).
- Access to historical data (trend analysis, treatment patterns, etc.)

SUMMARY

Understanding what drives an organization to implement business intelligence is the key component to achieving success. Whether it is regulatory requirements and reporting, operational improvement or a strategic initiative, an organization must go through all the steps of discovery, success, failure and re-discovery. Some projects will lead to new opportunities and unexpected benefits, while other projects may stall or fall short of expectations. The important thing is to do what fits the situation and learn from the experiences of other healthcare and non-healthcare organizations that have implemented similar business intelligence strategies.

Table 1-1: Chapter 1 Checklist—Why Does Your Organization Need Business Intelligence?

Item	Completed (Y/N)
1. Understand the key drivers specific to your organization.	
2. Create awareness and the overall value of improved information among key executives and stakeholders.	
3. Develop consensus on the key information requirements to support the organization's priorities.	
4. Assess the organization's business intelligence readiness.	
5. Develop a shared vision and strategy for the role of business intelligence.	

REFERENCES

1. Hoyt RE, ed. *Medical Informatics: A Practical Guide for the Healthcare Professional.* 3rd ed. Raleigh, NC: Lulu.com; 2009.
2. The Institute of Medicine. *To Err Is Human: Building A Safer Health System.* Washington, DC: The National Academies Press; 1999.
3. The Institute of Medicine. *Crossing The Quality Chasm: A New Health System For The 21st Century.* Washington, DC: The National Academies Press; 2001.
4. Moore S. Gartner projects global business intelligence market to grow 9.7% in 2011. Gartner [web site]. February 18, 2011. Available at: http://www.gartner.com/it/page.jsp?id=1553215. Last accessed November 2011.
5. Gartner Group; 1989.
6. Gartner. Magic Quadrant for BI Platforms. Stamford, CT: Gartner Inc.; 2011.
7. Loshin D. *The Data Warehousing Institute Faculty Newsletter, Fall 2002 as cited in Business Intelligence: A Savvy Manager's Guide.* Maryland Heights, MO: Morgan Kaufman Publishers; 2003.
8. White C, Imhoff C. Advanced analytics and business intelligence: term abuse? BeyeNetwork; May 18, 2010.
9. White D. *BI in Healthcare—A Prescription for Good Financial Health.* Boston: Aberdeen Group; 2009.
10. Pierce L. [Interview.] April 26, 2011.

Chapter 2

A Case for Business Intelligence across the Continuum of Care

By Michael G. Brooks

There are many ways in which business intelligence (BI) capabilities can be used and deployed to drive the success of healthcare organizations. Each organization must identify areas and how such capabilities will be implemented to drive the best results. The examples presented and discussed in this chapter will be used to explore how BI enables decision makers at all levels to carry out continual improvements within their organizations with the ultimate goal of achieving clinical and operational excellence.

Once the organization's vision for BI is established, the next step is to identify specific initiatives that must be implemented to realize significant value. In defining and managing the implementation of the BI strategy, it can be helpful to take a portfolio management approach where related projects are grouped together based on similar departments, technology requirements, stakeholder needs and other factors. This approach can be helpful in evaluating, prioritizing and implementing BI initiatives to quickly meet users' needs, while building a robust information environment.

This chapter provides examples of applications based on their general relevance to the acute care and ambulatory care environments, which are organized based on the functional area to which they apply. In some cases (meaningful use, accountable care organizations [ACO], etc.), overlap is highlighted to illustrate the flexible nature of BI.

BUSINESS INTELLIGENCE IN THE ACUTE-CARE SETTING

Managing the delivery of healthcare in the acute-care environment has few rivals in terms of operational and information complexity. For years, hospitals have invested in enterprise and departmental applications that were designed to perform a specific set of tasks. Such applications resulted in an environment where there are often siloed data sources with "multiple versions of the truth." When making decisions, clinicians and managers often had to supplement data from these systems with manual reporting processes, externally generated data or educated guesses. Implementing a properly configured BI solution enables organizations to reconfigure their data flow in order to get information in a useful format. Therefore, the situation frequently leads to discussions on BI technology. However, BI is more about meeting information needs and supporting decisions (function) than just technology (form).

There are many ways to deploy BI within an acute-care organization (desktop, departmental, enterprise, etc.), each with their own inherent strengths and weaknesses. For example, within a single organization, there may be multiple configurations, such as an enterprise data warehouse (EDW) containing financial and claims data accompanied by various independently developed data marts containing specialized information (call center data, referral data, quality reporting metrics). The good news is that regardless of the architecture that has been implemented, there are many different types of uses of BI that can yield significant value to the organization.

Financial Performance

In 2009, the Aberdeen Group surveyed top-performing healthcare organizations in terms of revenue margins, revenue-cycle performance, staff turnover and business intelligence capabilities.[1] This survey indicated that BI contributed to success in staffing productivity, billing and coding effectiveness and supply chain spending by improving visibility into key activities that drive financial success.

While decision makers in all areas of the organization rely on financial data to some degree, the finance department's needs are among the most wide-ranging and complex. To complicate matters, the American Institute of Certified Public Accountants (AICPA), government and other regulating bodies are increasingly asking for more financial and non-financial performance measures. As a result, the types of questions related to financial performance cover an expanding spectrum, including staff turnover, revenue cycle, new services, patient demographics and supplier performance.

One challenge financial decision makers face is that the data they need are often found in bits and pieces across multiple systems. Financial decision makers rely on data from patient management, patient accounting, enterprise resource planning (ERP) and other systems to get a better picture of the organization's current and projected performance. Furthermore, many organizations face a proliferation of data marts, spreadsheets and manual reporting systems containing data that have already been massaged based on the individual user's needs, preferences and assumptions. Such a situation can lead to conflicting information, often resulting in "multiple versions of the truth," inefficiencies, suboptimal decisions and wasted time. Managing this situation requires an appropriate balance of data governance processes, standards and other controls to maintain consistency and accuracy across the many sources.

Once the issue of data management and quality is addressed, users have access to a wide variety of desktop or web-based BI tools, as well as a growing list of specialized analytic applications. By combining data from multiple sources and applying sound statistical and data-mining techniques, decision makers can benefit from new insights through the use of cost and revenue analyses, trending, forecasting, service line analysis, claims analysis, value-based pricing/purchasing, compliance reporting and financial reporting. Examples of successful finance-related initiatives include:

Reducing insurance denials. Ohio-based Cleveland Clinic serves hundreds of thousands of patients and employs more than 1,600 physicians. The Clinic needed a way to identify and address problems associated with denied insurance claims. It developed a denials database containing claims data on more than 200 relationships. Initially, analyzing and researching the database was a cumbersome, time-consuming process. To address this challenge, Cleveland Clinic determined the need for more timely analysis, allowing managers to quickly identify potential denial issues and identify specific improvement opportunities in individual departments. The Clinic implemented Tableau Software's data visualization and BI solution to analyze payment denials, detect patterns and streamline reporting to key decision makers. As a result, the clinic estimated that in the first year they saved $20 million in denials and, in the process, improved patient satisfaction.[2]

Monitoring physician activity and preference item cost. Baptist Health South Florida determined it needed a better way to track physician activity and manage the cost of implants. Using Dimensional Insights' ETL technology, Data Integrator, data were combined from multiple systems and analyzed using Diver, an online analytical processing (OLAP)-based business intelligence solution. Baptist Health implemented a variety of applications that included physician scorecards for each of its seven hospitals. Physician practice patterns, implant usage rates and costs were analyzed, which led Baptist Health to reduce the number of different products used, consolidate vendors and renegotiate rates to reduce supplies costs.[3]

Controlling supply chain costs. Mount Sinai Medical Center is a 955-bed, not-for-profit hospital located in Miami. In 2008, the Medical Center lost $15.7 million in operating margins. Management realized a more evidence-based approach to supply chain management was needed. They implemented Premier's MySpend software and other analytic tools with integration to multiple-source systems. This strategy allowed the organization to compare usage, contract terms, pricing and benchmark data to support more informed decisions with vendors and the physician community. As a result, Mount Sinai realized a net surplus of $14.5 million in 2009, attributing much of its improvement to the use of analytics to control spending.[4]

Operations Performance

Similar to financial reporting, users of operational data extend to all major parts of the organization. At the highest level, the chief operating officer and his or her direct reports are responsible for a wide variety of decisions in areas such as supply chain management, human resources, facilities management and capital management. Operational questions include:

- Are we on track to meet our goals?
- Where is the waste in our organization?
- What is the impact or realized value of our improvement initiatives?
- Where should we be allocating our resources?

BI can help improve operations by supporting analysis of areas such as performance, productivity, resource utilization and customer satisfaction. Analytic-enabled activities include compliance reporting, efficiency and cost control, continuous process improvement initiatives (LEAN, Six Sigma, etc.) and market outreach.

A major challenge is the breadth and depth of decision-makers' information needs and often requires manually generated data and domain expertise in areas such as clinical informatics, supply chain, human resources, departmental workflow and information technology (IT). Operational analyses may also involve coordination with third parties (suppliers, affiliated physician groups and related subsidiaries such as transport, durable medical equipment providers, etc.) to incorporate and/or share data, findings and resources.

When it comes to connecting bits of data across multiple systems, applying rules logic, filtering techniques and delivering information in a relevant context saves time and enables management to focus on the areas that need immediate attention. With the growing volume of data, complexity of decisions and the potential business impact at stake, healthcare providers can no longer operate without a BI strategy if they are to be successful in the future. Examples of successful operational BI applications include:

Staffing management. St. Thomas Elgin General Hospital (STEGH) is a 166-bed facility that serves St. Thomas, Ontario and the surrounding community. STEGH implemented a single data repository using Actuate's open source Business Intelligence Reporting Tools (BIRT) and Performance Soft Views dashboard technology to improve operational reporting. In one particular area, STEGH identified an issue with excessive sick time that correlated with periods of high occupancy. Overall STEGH created more than 50 projects in 30 departments, which resulted in savings of $3.1 million improved patient satisfaction and enhanced workload management.[5]

Lab utilization/turnaround time (TAT). Children's Hospital of Philadelphia's (CHOP) Department of Pathology and Laboratory includes more than 300 technologists and pathologists to process more than 1 million samples and specimens per year. In 2007, concerns about employee productivity and service led CHOP to implement a reporting and analytics scorecard capability using Microsoft SQL-Server, Excel, Visio and other software components to improve visibility into key performance measures such as lab volumes, cycle times and TAT. Within 10 weeks of implementing the solution, CHOP reduced lab result turnaround time by 50 percent, improved employee accountability and streamlined communications.[6]

Performance management. Nemours (a non-profit for children's health) implemented enterprise performance management programs for several financial and clinical areas. Using a Microsoft business intelligence platform, Nemours tracked metrics, including actual vs. budget performance, patients likely to recommend the organization, number of employees completing prescribed training programs and the number of patients that had a Body Mass Index (BMI) captured. Since implementing this program, Nemours has seen its gross margins improve significantly each year.[7]

Clinical Performance

Using clinical BI to support patient care, quality management and other functions involves a continuous, iterative discovery process that often involves investigation of historical data, comparison with external benchmarks and forward-looking predictive analysis to help information consumers gain a more thorough understanding of the facts. To do this, clinicians have historically had to overcome a number of barriers such as unstructured data (e.g., text, voice and image), paper charts, incomplete or inconsistent data, manual processes, complex regulations and non-standard medical terminology.

The responsibilities of the clinical leadership team span a variety of care delivery, administrative and strategic activities and often extend beyond the acute-care setting. Major functional areas of responsibility include clinical services, quality management, safety, patient and provider satisfaction, physician recruitment/retention, credentialing, risk management, strategy development, medical informatics, research studies and regulatory compliance. As a result, the information requirements and types of analysis are diverse. Definitions of reporting requirements vary, are subject to change and often require data from multiple sources. To meet these needs, it is not unusual to have analysts with deep domain expertise residing in clinical departments who can work with data architects to get the information they need.

To support these functions, clinical analysts must perform a variety of routine and *ad-hoc* analyses to identify and understand clinical outcomes by medical condition, treatment plan effectiveness, variations in practice/treatment, physician referral patterns, trending and resource utilization. In some cases, such analysis may be as simple as a dashboard with key performance indicators or reviewing a routine exception report. In other instances, such analysis may involve sophisticated statistical analysis or data-mining efforts involving data from a range of months or years.

Frequently, it is the availability of "good" data that is the biggest obstacle. Data requirements for clinical BI applications have included patient demographics, problems, diagnosis, treatment patterns, medications, outcomes and other factors. Typically, such information is organized by patient encounter within a specific care setting and provides only a narrow view of the patient's medical history. Health information exchange (HIE), ACOs and other initiatives involve the aggregation and use of information from multiple settings of care to help providers understand the bigger picture or the continuum of care. In addition, technology advancements such as genomics, remote wellness monitoring and other areas increase the likelihood that the amount and type of information to be analyzed will continue to grow.

The developments in clinical information pose both a challenge and an opportunity for clinicians who need access to the best available information, in many instances in real-time. The amount of information managed by organizations is estimated to double every 18 months.[8] In addition, new data standards and reporting requirements are emerging from a variety of regulatory bodies, payers and other industry organizations. With these challenges, healthcare providers must develop more effective approaches to managing data quality, growth, governance and performance, while being vigilant regarding the security of sensitive personal health information.

BI offers an invaluable view of clinical data before, during and after a patient encounter and ensuring access to information from one or many clinical systems is no longer a barrier to providing superior patient care. BI provides the tools to improve patient safety and quality of care by trending, comparing clinical data to standard benchmarks and offering information about how treatment plans could be improved based upon evidence-based guidelines. It can also support pay-for-performance efforts by highlighting gaps in quality measurements and calculating potential incentives if those gaps are addressed.

Several healthcare organizations have applied BI strategies in the clinical setting to improve care delivery processes and safety, while also striving to manage overall costs such as:

Improving treatment care plans. H. Lee Moffitt Cancer Center's Total Cancer Care Survivorship Initiative combines the use of an Oracle data warehouse, Oracle Enterprise Healthcare Analytics, Microsoft SQL Server, Microsoft Amalga and other analytic tools to analyze historical data, patient treatment results and other data to identify patient-specific treatment recommendations. Prior to their implementation, researchers had to review data from 25 different information systems. By leveraging the data warehouse and analysis capabilities, Moffitt is increasing the speed by which researchers can identify the most effective cancer treatments and improve clinical trial recruitment.[9]

Quality, safety and risk management/adverse drug events (ADEs). Duke University Medical Center uses an integrated data warehouse, safety reporting system and automated ADEs Surveillance System to collect, store and analyze clinical information related to its quality initiatives. BI tools provide unit leaders with real-time access to aggregated patient safety data and support analysis at the health system and service level. As a result, targeted quality improvement initiatives were implemented helping to prevent an estimated 157.8 potential cases of nosocomially-acquired C difficile colitis per year, which led to improved patient outcomes/patient safety rates and reduced hospital costs.[10]

Chronic-disease management registry. Denver Health and Hospital Authority integrated clinical lab data into an existing financial data warehouse to create a registry to track chronic disease patients and deliver timely, complete patient information to physicians. As a result, physicians can monitor high-risk clinical indicators and help patients keep their medical conditions under control. Microsoft BI tools helped the organization monitor process changes, while significantly reducing medication turnaround times.[11]

In view of the demand, growth and complexity of clinical information needs, BI technology serves two important functions. First, it allows providers to turn the traditional patient encounter/claim-centric model on its side to analyze information from different perspectives (e.g., by medical condition, medical practice unit, population segment, etc.). Second, it allows providers to quickly zero-in on the information that matters to find the proverbial needle in a haystack. Whether the issue of the day is measuring outcomes, reducing unexpected readmissions, preventing ADEs or finding new ways to improve care, BI offers clinicians and researchers the ability to explore and act on information from new perspectives. This capability will grow in importance as new data sources and types emerge (genomics, proteomics, image, etc.).

BUSINESS INTELLIGENCE IN THE AMBULATORY SETTING

Medical groups and other organizations that are primarily involved in providing care in the outpatient setting face many of the same high-level issues (revenue cycle, productivity, physician performance, outcomes, etc.) as their acute-care counterparts. Beyond that, several key differences often exist, including organization structure, culture, fewer systems, availability of skilled IT resources and access to capital.

Standard reporting from practice management, ambulatory electronic health records (EHR) and financial systems has traditionally focused on transactions and audit trails with limited flexibility for *ad-hoc* analysis and data manipulation. In recent years, there has been a trend toward increased transparency (physician claims, outcomes, quality, satisfaction and other metrics). Programs such as Meaningful Use and Physician Quality Reporting Initiative (PQRI), as well as third-party benchmarking services such as HealthGrades, are collecting and publishing a growing number of metrics. Savvy clinicians and medical group administrators must continually monitor such data and investigate any significant variances to protect the medical group's reputation and obtain reimbursement.

While larger academic faculty practice plans and clinics may be able to afford a centralized data warehouse, smaller organizations can still benefit from BI by using data marts and web-based and desktop analysis tools that provide more flexibility and insight than traditional practice management systems. Such uses include physician scorecards, trending reports, utilization forecasts, productivity reports, practice patterns and other *ad-hoc* analysis, as illustrated in the following example:

Analyzing clinical delivery outcomes and performance. Southeast Texas Medical Associates (SETMA) uses IBM/Cognos to identify hospital readmission patterns based on patient demographics, medical history, treatments and other information. By analyzing this information SETMA is able to adapt its post-hospital care plans to address a patient's post-discharge care needs. As a result, SETMA has reduced unnecessary hospital readmissions by 22 percent annually.[12]

BI tools in an ambulatory setting can also help providers see a full patient continuum when the patient has received services at participating (in the BI tool) hospitals or labs. Use of the BI tool may enable the provider to see the full, aggregated care of the patient across more than one care site. As the ACO model moves forward, this continuum will be most effective in managing patient populations and in coordinating care for bundled payment scenarios.

Although BI is more commonly found in the acute-care setting, its use in the ambulatory environment continues to grow as a result of increased reporting requirements, increasing sophistication of self-service BI technology and growing acceptance of hosted software-as-a-service (SaaS) analytics offerings.

BUSINESS INTELLIGENCE AND REGULATORY REQUIREMENTS

ARRA/HITECH Act provisions set the stage for one of the biggest transformations in the history of health IT. Through a combination of incentives and penalties, eligible hospitals and professionals must meet an evolving set of complex criteria that include reporting on various clinical quality measures, volume and attestation requirements, adoption and workflow changes. These criteria are being announced in three stages over several years. The evolving nature of the criteria creates challenges for vendors and providers to develop software products, design data models and implement systems in the absence of a complete understanding of the ultimate design.

As mentioned earlier in this book, healthcare has historically relied heavily on the use of unstructured data, often not stored in electronic format, which involved conflicting codes and ambiguous descriptions. Meaningful Use Stage 1 criteria begins to address these issues by focusing on the electronic capture of health information in a structured format, using that information in the care coordination activities, compliance with specific coding structures (i.e., ICD-10, Logical Observation Identifiers Names and Codes [LOINC], etc.), submission of clinical quality measures and other data to Centers for Medicare and Medicaid (CMS), and other requirements. Stage 2 builds upon Stage 1 efforts by focusing on the use of health IT in the continuous improvement at the point of care, the electronic exchange of health information, emphasis on structured data, expanded reporting and other requirements. Stage 3 focuses on promoting improvements in quality, safety and efficiency, leading to improved outcomes, leveraging decision-support capabilities, providing access to comprehensive patient data and other capabilities.[13] Each stage involves a progression of more complex data management, analysis and reporting requirements that emphasizes the importance of an effective BI strategy.

CMS indicates that the certified EHR capabilities and Meaningful Use criteria represent the minimum requirements for realizing incentives and avoiding penalties. And while CMS has indicated that certified EHR systems must electronically generate the basic data for Meaningful Use reporting, such capabilities are insufficient for managing hospital and physician group clinical performance. As a result, providers must coordinate systems changes and reporting strategies with other internal needs, EHR and feeder systems software upgrades and external requirements.

From the standpoint of published Meaningful Use requirements there are generally three types of measures that must be tracked. The first type relates to the volumes of Medicare and Medicaid patients treated by the eligible providers. These volume data are commonly generated by most patient accounting systems and help determine the organization's eligibility and amount of the incentive payments.

The second type of measures involve tracking the level of Meaningful Use requirements using calculated denominator and numerator values based on the total number of unique patients, the number of patients involved in a particular activity or other criteria. Examples of activities tracked include computerized provider order entry (CPOE), electronic prescribing and medication lists. Producing these measures may require additional modification to clinical and non-clinical source systems as future criteria are defined.

The third type of measures relate to attestation requirements where a provider indicates that the criteria have been implemented and are being used. Examples of attestation-related criteria include clinical decision-support rules, drug-drug/allergy alerts and privacy/security controls. Attestation requirements also include the ability to electronically report attestation to CMS. One of the attestation criteria involves the reporting of clinical quality measures related to high-priority chronic conditions and health screening/prevention. These measures are based on PQRI, National Commission for Quality Assurance (NCQA) and other programs and involve complex rules to produce the specific calculations.

Based on the guidance CMS provided, there are several business intelligence-related implications:

EHR certification. CMS has indicated that if data warehouses are used to generate the required measures that they will be subjected to Meaningful Use certification criteria. Providers who rely on data warehouses to meet current and future requirements must monitor regulations and maintain their BI platforms in accordance with CMS compliance regulations.

Data management. Business intelligence professionals must develop controls to manage data definitions, patient data privacy and security. As source applications are upgraded, coding requirements change (ICD-10) or as mergers occur, effective change management and data governance programs will be increasingly important to support trending, analysis and reporting consistency.

Coordination with other reporting initiatives. Providers are required to meet reporting requirements from a variety of governmental and industry programs (Medicare cost reporting, PQRI, NCQA, Leapfrog, The Joint Commission, etc.). In some instances, different departments may be reporting similar data to multiple organizations. Business intelligence capabilities can improve the efficiency and consistency of the various compliance reporting efforts.

Strategic positioning. ARRA/HITECH Act legislation is designed to promote the use of advanced clinical information technology to improve care delivery, achieve better outcomes, and reduce Medicare and Medicaid costs. CMS' intent is to link reimbursement, cost, utilization and outcomes data to drive future pay-for-performance reimbursement models. As reimbursement models evolve, BI can provide decision makers with the information they need to manage outcomes, customer satisfaction, pricing and costs.

As Meaningful Use requirements evolve, many vendors and providers are faced with the challenging prospect of how to satisfy reporting requirements that have not yet been announced. To be recognized as a certified EHR, the vendor must provide the capability to generate the required metrics. Other NCQA and PQRI indicators, as well as the reporting requirements of ACOs and other federal initiatives, may provide clues that could prove helpful in architecting a BI environment. To get the greatest benefit, healthcare providers should look beyond compliance reporting and develop the capabilities that concurrently address external requirements, internal quality reporting, process improvement efforts and decision-making needs.

Meaningful Use is just one federal program with major BI implications. Other concurrent federal mandates (ICD-10, ACOs, value-based pricing, comparative effectiveness, bundled payments, etc.) must be coordinated to maintain the integrity of the organization's information architecture. As a result, BI will grow in importance as providers strive to balance their internal priorities with external reporting needs.

BUSINESS INTELLIGENCE AND EMERGING BUSINESS MODELS

Cost pressures and increased competition are driving consolidation, affiliations and emerging business and care delivery models such as ACOs. The Patient Protection and Affordable Care Act (ACA) defines an ACO as "an organization of healthcare providers that agrees to be accountable for the quality, cost and overall care of Medicare beneficiaries who are enrolled in the traditional fee-for-service program who are assigned to it."[14] The program is designed to address three chief aims: better care for individuals, better care for populations and lower growth in Medicare expenditures through improvements in care. Under this program, ACOs that are successful in meeting CMS's performance goals receive federal "bonus sharing payments" in addition to their regular fee-for-service payments.

To be successful under this program, ACOs must excel at delivering measurable quality care that meets federal guidelines, achieve high levels of patient satisfaction, manage costs, expedite information sharing among participants and manage various administrative functions such as billing, quality management, bonus-sharing payment distribution and reporting. Just as EHR and HIE are essential to capturing and sharing clinical data among providers, BI provides the insights to explain the past, interpret the present and model the future at the patient, population and network level.

Historically, providers have been limited to data contained within their own systems. Obstacles ACOs must overcome include ability to seamlessly support multiple points of entry into the ACO network, analyze data from multiple sources while preserving privacy, manage variations in provider practices and preferences, and comply with complex reporting requirements while accommodating growth in patient volumes and data. The nature of orchestrating a network of participating providers requires looking at information from new perspectives (service line, medical condition, population segments, etc.) that are beyond the reach of most acute, ambulatory and payer systems.

As a result, BI can support the ACO model in a variety of ways including:

Care delivery management
- Modeling care programs to test alternative ACO models and treatment plans.
- Enabling other reform initiatives such as medical home.

Population care
- Planning and managing beneficiary population health needs, patient involvement and outcomes.
- Modeling resource requirements, costs and utilization patterns.
- Supporting quality improvement efforts.

Provider participation
- Monitoring provider utilization and practice patterns.
- Orchestrating care delivery and management across care venues, inclusive of pharmacy and ancillary testing sites.
- Managing customer service and physician satisfaction.
- Supporting various reimbursement and bonus payment distribution models.

Operational, compliance and quality reporting
- Satisfying public and private reporting requirements.
- Reporting on quality and process measures in areas such as diabetes, hypertension, coronary heart disease, heart failure, high-risk pregnancy and preventative care.

To meet these demands, CIOs must provide a robust information systems environment that includes the capabilities necessary to support the diverse day-to-day and impromptu data needs required by clinical and administrative ACO decision makers. It important to recognize that successful BI also requires the commitment of non-IT executives, including chief medical information officers (CMIO), chief financial officers (CFO), chief operations officers (COO) and their management teams, who bring the functional domain knowledge that does not exist with IT. While IT can lead the planning, development and provisioning of a BI environment, the involvement of clinicians and other non-IT stakeholders is essential in identifying and exploiting improvement opportunities that maximize the value to the organization and its customers.had

CASE STUDY 2-1

With much of the attention on technology, processes and data, it is easy to forget that the primary mission is the care of the patient and that business intelligence is an enabler for better outcomes. As the following case study illustrates, with a proper focus on achieving high levels of patient satisfaction and quality outcomes, business intelligence can be a key ingredient of a successful clinical excellence strategy.

STRIVING FOR BUSINESS INTELLIGENCE EXCELLENCE

Poudre Valley Health System (PVHS) is a locally owned, not-for-profit organization that provides care to the residents of northern Colorado, Nebraska and Wyoming. With three hospitals representing 500 beds and affiliated physicians, PVHS offers a full range of healthcare services, including emergency/urgent care, intensive care, medical/surgical care, maternal/child care, oncology care, orthopedic care and other services. For several years, PVHS has had an organization-wide focus that leverages key performance indicators and BI to drive continuous quality improvement with the emphasis on providing an outstanding patient experience.

Business Need

For several years PVHS has demonstrated an ongoing commitment to clinical and operational excellence as demonstrated by its selection as a 2008 Malcolm Baldrige Award for Quality winner. But the health system isn't satisfied with that achievement and is constantly looking for ways to further improve clinical outcomes, patient satisfaction and operations in areas such as medication errors, falls, bedside medication verification rates and clinical adoption.

Solution

Several years ago, PVHS implemented a health system-wide balanced scorecard program. Key performance indicators (KPIs) were defined that aligned strategic goals and objectives from the health system to the individual employee level. To support this program, PVHS uses Information Builders' WebFocus solution to access data from MEDITECH, Allscripts and other data sources. KPIs are published for decision makers at all levels using the WebFocus dashboard. At this time, PVHS is in the process of producing its third generation performance dashboard in order to use web technology and other features to improve the quality and delivery of KPIs to end users.

Benefits

According to Russ Branzell, PVHS Chief Information Officer, "It's not good enough to be above average, we need to keep asking, 'How do we keep getting better at improving patient care and satisfaction?'" As a result of the efforts just described, key benefits PVHS has realized include:

- Everyone at PVHS understands that the priority is on delivering the best possible patient satisfaction and care.
- The emphasis of all activity and business intelligence capabilities is on enabling better decisions to improve customer experience.
- When everything works as it should, clinicians are more able to focus on what's important—treating the patient.[15]

    As further proof this approach works, PVHS continues to win high marks for ongoing improvements in outcomes, patient satisfaction, revenue growth and profitability.

SUMMARY

There are many ways in which business intelligence capabilities can be used and deployed to drive the success of an organization. Each organization must decide in what areas and how such capabilities will be implemented to drive the best results. Based on the examples discussed in this chapter, BI enables decision makers at all levels to make continual improvements with the ultimate goal of achieving clinical and operational excellence.

Table 2-1: Chapter 2 Checklist—A Case for Business Intelligence across the Continuum of Care.

Item	Completed (Y/N)
1. Identify specific opportunities or problem areas where better information will significantly improve business and/or clinical results.	
2. Engage clinician and management champions.	
3. Identify and enlist the support of key stakeholders, subject-matter experts and other participants needed to address the problem/ opportunity.	
4. Determine what BI information and capabilities will be needed to determine the root cause and evaluate alternative solutions.	
5. Conduct analysis of current state and alternative solutions.	
6. Evaluate analysis results and implement preferred alternative(s).	
7. Evaluate results for validation and implement continuous improvement results where appropriate.	

REFERENCES

1. White D. *BI in Healthcare–A Prescription for Good Financial Health*. Boston: Aberdeen Group, December; 2009.
2. Fierce Health Finance. Cleveland Clinic earns back $20 million in denials in one year using IT-recommended software package. Fiercehealthfinance.com. Available at: http://www.fiercemarkets.com/misc/ebook_previews/ebook_rev_cycle.pdf. Last accessed November 2011.
3. Baptist Health monitors physician performance and healthcare spending. Available at: www.yglworld.com/templates/yglworldcom/userfiles/doc/di/cs/DI_CS_Baptist.PDF. Dimensional Insights; 2009.
4. Minich-Pourshadi K. Health business analytics: elevating the spend analysis. Health Leaders Media; January 13, 2011.
5. St. Thomas Elgin General Hospital manages costs and improves health needs of community with actuate performance management solution. BeyeNetwork; November 12, 2009.
6. Hospital uses business intelligence to save time and gain insight from data. Microsoft; April 2008.
7. Business intelligence for healthcare: the new prescription for boosting cost management, productivity and medical outcomes. Business Week Research Services; February 2009.
8. IDC: digital data to double every 18 months. *Inform Manag J*. September 1, 2009.
9. Goedert J. Bringing analytics to the treatment level. *Information Management Magazine*; Sept/Oct 2009.
10. Ferranti JM, Langman MK, Tanaka D, et al. Bridging the gap: leveraging business intelligence tools in support of patient safety and financial effectiveness. *J Am Med Inform Assoc*. 2010 Mar-Apr;17(2):136-43.
11. Business Week Research Services. Business intelligence for healthcare: the new prescription for boosting cost management, productivity and medical outcomes. New York: McGraw-Hill; 2009.
12. Laskowski N. Cognos BI software at crossroads of technology, hospital readmissions. SearchBusinessAnalytics.com; April 13, 2011.
13. Meaningful Use, Stage 3 criteria. 45 CFR Parts 412, 413, 422, and 495; p. 44321; July 28, 2010.
14. Patient Protection and Affordable Care Act, Section 3022.
15. Branzell R. [Interview.] April 15, 2011.

Section II

How to Get Started

CHAPTER 3

Getting Started within Your Organization

By Michael Whitecar, MIS, LCDR (ret.), MSC, USN

As organizations face the challenges discussed in the first two chapters, it is evident that business intelligence (BI) can be a supporting aid for grasping these challenges and overcoming them. This chapter will show how to get started creating a BI foundation by gaining an understanding of the inner workings of each preliminary key component and how to strategically orchestrate them into a set of focused actions. This will establish a guide for the project team to use in implementing an effective BI structure.

Mid- to large-sized healthcare organizations facing imminent change to cope with the requirements of an evolving healthcare environment will find what is needed in the BI foundation discussed in this chapter. This chapter will establish the BI foundation by setting the standards leveraged through the benefits of creating a BI governance structure. For scenarios that are considered smaller in size and scope, or for independent (departmental) initiatives, this chapter should not be viewed as a one-size-fits-all solution. Instead, this chapter is intended to further stimulate thought from a governance perspective but not overwhelm any BI initiative with preliminary requirements. The chapter's objective is to share a recommended approach that should be tailored to the environment at hand.

HOW TO GET OFF THE GROUND

The first consideration of any BI initiative, large or small, is that this is a long-term project that does not end. As a project, there should be a manageable level of oversight, various types of action plans, expectations of results and the availability of resources (staff, technologies) to launch the initiative and sustain it over time. The ideas and philosophies behind BI must be embedded and must resonate within the entire organization. If the processes that support the collection of data originate from third-party entities, they too should adopt the organizational mindset to transparently support the BI initiative.

The BI mindset should be driven from the top down and adopted within the culture of the hospital. This will be discussed in more detail in Chapter 4. The BI mindset must be woven into and must become an integral part of existing and future initiatives that require data resources to support sound business decisions. By focusing on this first thought of adoption, initial organizational observers will provide tremendous insight into the readiness for BI, the substantial commitment and the necessity for various types of resources. This insight will help managers and staff to identify and monitor where change management is needed; it will also facilitate continued observation of the effectiveness of those changes. This entire organizational observation will provide the initial temperature and momentum required to establish the foundation for a solid BI structure.

STEP 1: DEFINING GOVERNANCE

The first key to a successful BI initiative is to establish a governance structure. Governance includes a set of activities that is an integral part of supporting a holistic approach to the adoption of BI. These activities must be aligned with the strategic goals and objectives of the organization to ensure such activities are objectively evaluated with respect to organizational priorities. BI governance is about specifying the decision rights and accountability framework to encourage desirable behavior in the use of BI. Solid governance harmonizes decisions about the management and use of BI with desired behaviors and business objectives. The behavioral side of BI governance defines the formal and informal relationships and assigns decision rights to specific individuals or groups of individuals. The normative side defines mechanisms formalizing the relationships and providing rules and operating procedures to ensure that objectives are met. Therefore, the initial approach to implementing effective BI governance will begin with addressing "what decisions must be made, who should make them and how will these decisions be made and monitored?"

A dedicated team to address governance should be established early on. This may take the form of a BI governing body or committee derived from the executive management team. The committee should contain a mix of skills and knowledge that will contribute to the initial launch of the BI program, to executing the overall plan and to sustaining and monitoring the BI system throughout its lifecycle. Thus, to meet the ever changing needs of the organization and BI, the committee may be required to interchange membership in order to adapt to the needs of the organization.

The committee should be governed by a charter. A charter is the grant of authority or rights, stating that the granter (in this case the executive management team) formally recognizes the prerogative of the committee to exercise the rights specified. In addition to rights, the charter must clearly identify the BI needs of the organization. These needs may be found in the annual strategic business plan or in both internal and external influences that instill pressures to comply with authoritative regulations.

The charter should also establish a mechanism for the BI committee to properly classify and prioritize BI requests or requirements coming from the business, operations or clinical entities of the organization. Depending on the size of the organization, it may be necessary to create sub-committees. Either way, the committee should oversee the process and make sure all areas within the organization have adequate representation when deciding which BI projects to fund, execute or terminate. Thus, turn to governance for:

Resource validation. A prioritization mechanism by which BI projects can be approved, rejected and sequenced based on specific criteria.

Guidelines/rules/recommendations. Traditionally, the information technology (IT) department has been solely responsible for defining the architectures, standards and best practices to follow. However, as healthcare organizations start to realize the significant impact that these decisions may have on BI projects, there may be need to make these topics part of the BI governance process.

Definition of roles and responsibilities for both IT and stakeholders. As BI projects are by nature highly complex, establishing the proper interaction and outlining areas of responsibility between the IT department and stakeholders becomes critical for a project to succeed. Setting boundaries between both sides will most likely challenge paradigms known today. Setting boundaries should be recognized as an opportunity to think outside the box and delegate more involvement to those functional leaders, process owners or knowledge workers.

Initiating a governance program may lead to additional challenges and the need to overcome skepticism. A frequent reason given for an organization not to adopt a BI governance process is the perception that implementing BI governance is a costly and complex exercise that does not provide value. While it is true that an executive management team should possess a general understanding of the priorities of the organization, and how the business strategies translate into a series of BI initiatives, establishing a BI governance process will provide the necessary framework by which the proper resources can be aligned to the priorities. In order for the BI initiatives to be successful, they need to be actionable.

An active BI governance process will establish proper change management (CM) and training methodologies that facilitate user adoption and promote overall use of BI, minimizing the potential for fear and resistance to new behaviors and technologies.

Establishing the Governance Committee

To establish a BI governance committee, identify a project manager to manage the overall effort. The project manager must be an individual who can manage a technical project while maintaining strong relationships with the business owners. Next, identify the stakeholders. This group will include those from within the organization and those external to the organization with interests and who can impact the outcomes. A stakeholder can be defined as someone with "skin in the game." Stakeholder members may be defined as follows:

Departments of concern. Representation on the committee should include a mix of two types of members:

- Standing members: Members who are part of the core BI committee.
- *Ad-hoc* members: Members who attend as needed to represent their department or division.

IT department. IT personnel, including the chief information officer (CIO) can provide a wealth of knowledge about the technical requirements and supporting infrastructure. The need for IT specialists can change based on the direction of the BI project. For example, if a "build vs. buy" decision is made favoring in-house development, there will be additional stakeholder roles that should be represented as a whole on the committee, including data modelers, data integrators and enterprise architects. The intent is not to overstate a need for an IT presence, but to increase the awareness of what type of IT resources may be required and further supported. Potential IT roles are further defined in the next section. While not all of these individuals are part of the BI committee, they may be involved in the BI initiative.

Finance department. Aligned with fiscal guidance, BI projects will be considered strategic in nature, however, depending on the implementation, cost can easily escalate. It is recommended for the BI committee to have a direct link or at least representation to the controller/

chief finance officer (CFO). This will facilitate the prioritization of projects through fiscal responsibility and availability of funding. Furthermore, financial data and information is a key element of any BI system. The financial and revenue cycle complexities will be represented by this group as well.

Nursing informatics. This discipline has been rapidly evolving over the past several years and, if welcomed as a member of the committee, can provide real and succinct knowledge in the general practice of healthcare delivery.

Physicians. Probably the most strategic seat to fill is that of a physician or preferably, the chief medical information officer (CMIO). The CMIO is responsible for supporting the development of clinical information systems that assist clinicians in the delivery of patient care. CMIOs represent the needs and requirements of the physician community and serve as an advocate of management in promoting the use of IT in the clinical setting. Like the nurse informaticist, the CMIO works in partnership with IT department's design and implementation teams to translate clinician requirements into specification for new clinical and research systems.

Operations. The chief operations officer (COO) and or designee(s) are needed to provide insight into the operation of the organization. The input and buy-in of this executive will be a critical factor in successfully implementing a BI structure.

Quality/process improvement. In today's healthcare environment the rate of change and requirements are increasing exponentially. Various organizations use different functions to address these changes. There needs to be representation from the Quality or Process Improvement departments to increase the awareness of change and express how to address that change.

External affiliates. Depending on the complexity of the organization, there may be various continuums of care sectors that are included in the roll-out of an enterprise-level BI system. These may include rehabilitation, psychology, long-term care, visiting nurse/home care, ambulatory clinics and physician offices. The BI charter should define the scope of the BI structure and whether these areas need representation or not.

The early selection of stakeholders will enable equal representation across organizational boundaries and external entities. Representatives will be responsible for sponsoring particular BI projects for their division/department, demonstrating to the committee benefits of the initiative, identifying people in their functional areas to support BI efforts and communicating significant information within their departmental domains. BI committee members are expected to take an unbiased view when deciding on initiatives that are the most advantageous to the organization. Additionally, a level of subject-matter expertise (SME) from their specific area will be available to the BI committee for department-specific knowledge.

Along with the governance committee, there is also a need for an implementation team. Depending on the size of the organization, there may be overlap between the two groups. The implementation team is charged with the implementation of the system based on the directives that come from the governance committee. The governance committee will provide the strategic direction, while the implementation team accomplishes the tactical work.

Business Intelligence Technical Team Membership

A typical BI implementation team may include the following members from the IT department:
- **Business analysts** will work closely with stakeholders to gather requirements, document requirements and oversee the change control process.
- **Data architects and designers** will design the data models, database structure and provide how information will flow through the various BI elements.

- **BI infrastructure architects** will ensure that all the software modules work together and that hardware is in place to handle the BI solution.
- **Developers (extract/transform/load [ETL], semantic layer, report, online analytics processing [OLAP], etc.)** will be responsible for the processes that affect how data move from the source systems to the target environments or for the end-user environment, depending upon the type of developer; **Database administrators** (DBAs) will turn the logical models from data architects into the physical model, the actual database tables.
- **Data analysts** (DA) will be responsible for identifying and analyzing operational data sources and developing a process to bring the data together with the help of ETL developers and DBAs.
- **Testers** will perform quality assurance checks for both front-end, reports, and back-end ETL processes. Note that testers include a mix of IT and non-IT representatives.

  There are also non-IT team members and they include:

Subject-matter experts, who are normally experts in a field of focus. They have full knowledge of a specific business function and how it fits into the overall business model; they can provide insight into how to interpret data.

Users. The users of the front-end tools are part of the team too; however, not all of them will be engaged at all times. The users play a large role in defining the needs. The users can be classified as:

- Power users—those who will utilize the BI tools to their fullest capabilities (using the advanced features). They go beyond using canned reports; they take advantage of power users during design by getting their input on how they are going to use the analytical tools. Some of these users will also serve as SMEs.
- Business users—the broad user group (main users) normally about 60 percent to 75 percent of users in most organizations. They are unlikely to use the advanced features, but will primarily rely on canned reports and content. These users will provide input about functionality, accessibility, appearance and user-friendly features to help create standard reports.

There will be other team members who may require membership on an as-needed basis such as security experts, network administrators and data stewards. Even core team involvement will vary. Some will work on the BI project full time while others will supply their expertise on an as-needed basis, like SMEs and the other users. Organizations should note that they can utilize one person for more than one role—e.g., a data analyst could perform integration testing.

STEP 2: UNDERSTANDING WHO NEEDS WHAT AND WHY?

After gaining insight into the organization's high-level goals and objectives, a clearer understanding of what is needed for a BI implementation should develop. Understanding who needs what and why they need it is an important and legitimate approach. Most likely, there will already be established parameters that have defined the reason for the BI committee and a governance process. Thus, further clarification may be all that is needed.

If such parameters are not clear in definition, further research may be necessary. The BI committee members should start by reviewing prioritized departmental needs and strategic goals. This will include conducting interviews with each department head and staff members to determine what their informational needs are. To determine what is important, identify what the department is trying to accomplish and how it expects to measure the success through the use of key performance indicators (KPI). KPIs are commonly used by organizations to measure and evaluate their progress toward a particular measure of activity. Realization can be defined as making progress toward certain strategic goals, such as developing KPIs for monitoring meaningful use of EHRs under the Centers for Medicare and Medicaid's (CMS) incentive program. However, in most cases, each department may not be at this level of BI maturity.

KPIs define a set of values used to measure activities which are deemed to be mission critical. These sets of values, called indicators, are used to feed the BI system (i.e., tools) for summarizing information. The BI committee and stakeholders may need to identify indicators that will feed into or become KPIs if KPIs are not already established. Indicators identified as potential KPIs can be categorized into the following sub-categories:

- Quantitative indicators are represented as numbers.
- Practical indicators interface with existing organizational processes.
- Directional indicators specify whether an organization is improving.
- Actionable indicators are used to control the organization's effect on change.
- Financial indicators are used in performance measures.

KPIs represent objectives that will add the most value to the various divisions and departments interviewed. During a discovery process, the established KPIs may or may not be aligned with the overall direction of the organization. This finding is a perfect opportunity to recommend how to achieve alignment. Identifying and understanding these KPIs, or the need for a KPI, will help the BI committee determine what needs to be collected and what is the source of truth for support of the organizational strategic objectives.

Assuming the first agenda item for the BI committee is to conduct interviews with various departments and stakeholders, it will be helpful to create a matrix portraying the author of the requirement and exactly what is needed. This two-fold approach will provide the BI committee with the ability to align common needs among departments and stakeholders and reduce duplicative efforts. To further define the need for information, discovery should include the location of the data, the data owners and the processes required to obtain the data. An interesting observation of discovery may be the existence of disparate data repositories that are either grouped in one entity or available across other departmental boundaries. The disparate data repositories represent information needs that are not being met by existing systems, users are unaware of data and users do not have access to the authoritative source of data. The evaluation should include what type of representation the needed information needs to take to support the end user optimally. Options are discussed later in the book and may include a dashboard (Chapter 10), reports (Chapter 11) or one of several other methodologies.

The needs discovery matrix, depicted in Table 3-1, should be created with a minimum of two sub-divided descriptive sections such as clinical and administrative. It may be further sub-divided into as many sections as needed to meet the organization's requirements. Understanding the immediate needs will help identify the low-hanging fruit that can serve as quick wins to garner support for the implementation of the BI program.

When creating the matrix, it is important that all BI committee members agree on how the criteria and each initiative will be weighted. When scoring, simply multiply the initiative weight by the criteria weight. For instance, meaningful use had an initiative weight of three. The organizational impact was considered medium (two), resulting in the organizational impact weight of six (weight of three times rating of two). The total calculated score of 24 is the sum of each of the weighted criteria for the meaningful use initiative (6 + 9 + 3 + 6 = 24). Using the matrix will help the BI committee prioritize initiatives for the organization. Once each initiative is scored, the results and recommendations from the governance committee should be presented to executive management for final approval.

Table 3-1: Needs Discovery Matrix.

	Criteria					
	Organization Impact	Source of Data	Complexity	Legal/ Political Requirement	Total Score	
Initiative	Weight	1- Low 2- Med 3- High	1- Manual 2- DIs Data 3- Rec	1- Low 2- Med 3 - High	1 – No legal or political 2 – Political Req 3 – Legal Req	Sum of total scores
Meaningful Use	3	6	9	3	6	24
CPOE Utilization	3	9	9	9	3	30
Third-Party Billing Rejections	2	6	6	6	6	24

Key: Rec=Record (System of Record); Req=Requirements; DI=Directional Indicators.

The real heavy lifting of the BI committee will come in the form of prioritizing the BI requirements for the organization. This will require each committee member to present his or her division/department's BI requirements and the overall value that their particular BI initiative will bring to the organization. The organization may already have a process for prioritizing projects that can be leveraged by the BI committee if the criteria to measure each are similar in scope.

When presenting the results to executive management, each stakeholder representative should be present or available to provide background information, if requested. The BI committee should clearly explain the weighting criteria used in the matrix and why the criteria used were selected. Then each initiative can be clearly and logically presented for final ruling. The committee should also present and recommend the use of existing or needed KPIs.

Understanding the challenges of change may impact approval of the recommended findings by the BI committee; it would be best served if executive management can approve at least one low-hanging fruit in order to show the organization's commitment, the need and adoption. Additionally, identifying one low-hanging fruit will serve a need to begin identifying costs for both development and sustainment.

STEP 3: MANAGING THE PROJECT

Activities performed within the BI committee should be reflective of those performed under the auspices of program management. The entire BI initiative should be managed as a large project with sub-activities as required (KPIs, as sub-parts intertwined with other sub-parts). It will be essential to establish the position of a BI project manager (PM) as soon as the project begins. The PM will initiate the project. Using industry best practices such as the Project Management Institute's (PMI) *Project Management Book of Knowledge* (*PMBOK®*) is recommended to manage the BI project. Some healthcare organizations may have instituted a Project Management Office (PMO). If the BI PM is an outsider to the PMO, the PM is encouraged to leverage the PMO's services and work collaboratively.

Whether the PM of choice is the *PMBOK®* or other best practice methods, the BI PM needs to follow and monitor the process closely. Based on *PMBOK®* teachings, the BI PM should possess a working understanding of project initiating, planning, executing, monitoring and closing. The management activities needed to contribute to the overall project include initiation, scope, time, cost, quality, human resource, communications, risk and procurement.

Again, this information is not emphasized for every BI project. The size, scope and complexity will determine how the project should be managed. The information presented here is to merely reinforce the need to recognize BI as a project and to utilize industry best practices to manage it. With the intent not to duplicate the guidelines set forth in the *PMBOK®*, the remainder of this chapter highlights a few significant key activities that will serve as a PM baseline.

Project Initiation

Project initiation, as the step implies, is the first phase of the project. It's during this initial time the project goal is established. The BI PM will work hand-in-hand with the project's stakeholders to fully determine how to measure the success of the project. This allows the BI PM and project team (or committee) to agree on the project scope. The project scope will include project goals, budget, timelines and any other variables that can be used for measuring the status of the project.

Typically, the team will have a project kickoff meeting led by the BI PM. It is common for a member or members of executive management to attend this meeting to enforce the importance of the BI project to the organization. During the kickoff meeting, the team will review team introductions, the contents of the committee charter, BI goals, project communication, roles and responsibilities and the project's timeline. Depending on the size of the BI project, the initiation phase could last a week or more.

Project Planning

The next activity is BI project planning, whereby the committee or project team will create a specific list of tasks that need to occur for a successful BI implementation. Project tasks may be created using manual methods, such as engaging in brainstorming sessions or having the team use sticky notes to actively and openly post their thoughts. After there are sufficient written tasks, display them in the order the team thinks they will logically occur during the project. This type of format allows tasks to be rearranged if needed and to visually observe the entire project. Another method for determining tasks is to refer to past projects in which similar steps needed to be taken. If the organization has a PMO, ask it to review and comment on the various tasks that have been identified. Tasks should be clear and simply stated. If a task cannot be described in a sentence or two or completed between two hours and two weeks, it may be necessary to break it up into two or more smaller tasks.

There are many proposed formulas for calculating a task's estimated duration, and many PMs calculate time estimations by hand. However, there are handy PM software applications that will automatically make these calculations. Even at this early stage, tasks can be entered into a PM program, allowing the software to do the heavy arithmetic. Based on the tasks' estimated time, a calendar may be used to determine when the work should begin and how long it should last, followed by listing the resources need to complete each.

Executing and Monitoring

Executing and monitoring go hand-in-hand. At this stage, everyone on the team should have a clear understanding of their roles, responsibilities and those tasks assigned to them. When tasks are completed, team members will inform the BI PM and provide any deliverables, such as documentation, data dictionaries, data sets and software program source codes. Weekly project status meetings should be conducted to ensure the team is making progress according to the project plan and timelines. If risks are identified, mitigation strategies should be developed and executed to overcome unforeseen problems. Weekly meetings will ensure all team members and stakeholders are aware of the latest status, communicate any risk and possible mitigation strategies and determine resource utilization. The BI PM should also provide and/ or present a monthly status report to the BI committee. As the BI project grows, compliance with governance may require the committee's attention and decision making to ensure both new and current requirements remain aligned with the strategic goals of the organization.

Depending on the size and complexity of the BI project, during sustainment, governance may have established a Configuration Control Board (CCB). The CCB is responsible for managing new requirements or change requests. Establishing a CCB may seem like overkill, but when BI projects get too large in number or scope, having additional resources will ensure continued momentum.

SUMMARY

By now, it should be evident what may or may not be needed to get started. Emphasizing scope and size of a BI project will determine the complexity and involvement of stakeholders, resources and funding. The larger the BI project, the more information the committee will need to fulfill its charter obligations. Thus, it may be necessary to further observe the inner workings of the entire organization from knowing the available resources, documenting and flow charting business processes, to understanding the expectations of how information flows through the organization and how it will impact the BI project. The closing of this chapter is a perfect segue into lifting up the hood or looking below the iceberg's surface, which is presented in the following chapter.

Table 3-2: Chapter 3 Checklist—Getting Started within Your Organization.

Item	Completed (Yes/No)
1. Know the definition and development needs of establishing a BI committee governed by a charter formulated by executive management.	
2. Establish the appropriate level of governance for your BI project.	
3. Identify stakeholders and BI champions and seek for committee membership.	
4. Define the inner workings of business and clinical processes utilizing tools, such as the discovery matrix, to assist with prioritizing initiatives and recognizing low-hanging fruit.	
5. Establish and institutionalize industry best practices supporting project management and identify a project manager.	

CHAPTER 4

Assess Your Environment

By Michael Whitecar, MIS, LCDR (ret.), MSC, USN

In its most basic form, business intelligence (BI), the essence of knowledge management, is a strategy, not a purchased software product. Knowing upfront how to manage and leverage knowledge assets within the organizational environment can significantly enhance the use of information and the direct results of a BI initiative. A strong understanding of how people think independently or in groups, interact with one another and work together is needed to achieve success.

This chapter will discuss how to assess an organization's environment in preparation for developing the BI infrastructure. A complete asset inventory of the environment is required. The inventory must not be limited to information technology (IT) resources, but also include governance, policy, culture, people and business processes. The concept behind this chapter is to stimulate thought-provoking ideas by providing many preliminary questions before beginning the process of assessing the environment. While some examples of tools to use are being offered, similar tools may already be available that are capable of doing the same type of required analysis.

The contents of the inventory will provide an assessment of how the organization is going to use the newly discovered information. To gain a quick understanding of why this chapter is so important, ask the following questions: What impact will this information have on the original owners of the data? If there is change in the data, what communication processes are in place to ensure the calculation will either be or not be affected by the change? What is the process to share the results? If someone has a question about the results, who do they contact? Who is going to be in charge of keeping track of the requests?

Information comes in many forms with the ultimate state of providing a message to the individual or group who will then interpret the transmission and make an informed decision. Note the word "interpret." Each entity that receives a message from the outcomes of BI will in turn interpret the message differently from one another. Many factors will contribute to the decision, and how it is made will include the culture of the organization, the people and the overall operational environment and tempo. Thus, it cannot be assumed once the BI initiative is launched everyone and every business process will understand the message the same way and make the expected decision.

Figure 4-1 depicts the entirety of the BI initiative as an iceberg. The preparation activities are below the water line and the outcomes of the BI initiative are above it. The end result most likely will be in the form of an executive dashboard. Most BI implementations assume what lies above the water line is all that is needed. Many software vendors present their wares without referring to the hidden elements below. It is these elements, along with determining a business readiness state, that can make or break the BI implementation.

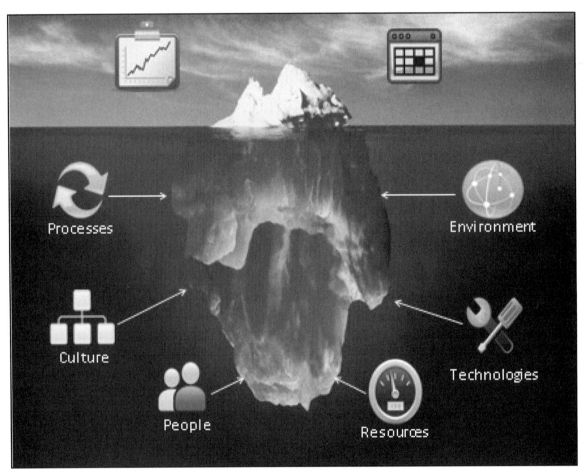

Figure 4-1: The Entirety of the Business Intelligence Initiative.

THE APPROACH

To begin the environmental asset inventory, each entity below the surface of the iceberg, as illustrated in Figure 4-1, will be addressed. Significant emphasis will be placed on the technologies that are available to address up front informational and technical requirements. Within the technologies entity, it will be examined how information flows in, out and between each of the assets: How fluid is the information? Will it be able to travel, receive transformation and finally be ready to be analyzed?

To inventory the technologies entity, a framework that is a results-driven diagnostic tool will be used to provide a unique business process approach to improving the access, flow and value of organizational information. The outcome is an in-depth view of how information is created, stored, shared, presented and analyzed. The outcome formulates a BI strategy and execution plan. The strategy can be aligned with process innovation. This will enable the development and testing of new ideas, while ensuring the processes and technologies operate predictably, reliably and independently.

Processes

A collection of business processes is individual steps that govern the operation of a system. A system is referred to as a set of interacting or interdependent components forming an integrated whole. In the case of BI, there will be many diverse systems with many processes that will either work independently or together in a collective environment. From a technical view, these systems include data gathering, data transformation and data analysis. Speaking functionally, it is intended to look at systems a healthcare organization is prepared or able to adapt that will support the BI infrastructure and the impact of the outcomes. Infrastructure may include data-gathering systems that retrieve data from multiple and disparate health information systems (HIS); outcomes will most likely have an impact on the operations of the organization and will require modification or creation of new processes to respond to a new level of informational awareness.

In support of ensuring processes and technologies operate predictably, reliably and independently, initial focus needs to be a gap analysis of the business processes currently in place. These processes may include the existing movement of data through the organization and the delivery of patient care, the use of existing HIS's that are expected to benefit from the BI implementation or directly support it and those processes that support feedback mechanisms or inquiries to data analysis.

When discovering and recording current processes, use this time to examine and determine the owners of each process, how well it is optimized and used and what will require modification to support the BI implementation. It may be discovered that new processes need to be established or, in some cases, underutilized processes removed. During the gap analysis, it is vitally important that the BI implementation project manager (PM) relinquish control to those who understand how the organization operates. These people live and breathe the processes every day and realistically make or break BI.

To demonstrate findings, a hospital may have an individual who is responsible to collect data from other parties or healthcare information systems monthly. This person would then manually enter the data into a database for further analysis or input into a presentation for a senior official. Many times, the parties reviewing the data presented may challenge the numbers, as this manual recording and calculation of data could result in typographical errors. It is in this example that we immediately see that a new process doesn't need to be developed. Instead, the existing process needs to be enhanced by automating the input of the data into the dashboard with the calculations already performed.

Some of the most commonly misunderstood processes are those that govern the development, application and use of business rules. For example, a healthcare organization uses glucometers that are able to transfer patient blood readings to a central healthcare information system. If a result report is pulled using the glucometer data and patient diagnosis data from the HIS, it must be understood how the information is calculated and then retrieved for the dashboard. It would be most beneficial when retrieving the authoritative data if the relationship or association with other data is known. This way, based on dashboard results, it could be understood how the impact relative to other numbers is affected and vice-versa. This fundamental process is probably one of the first that needs to be understood and approved by all involved stakeholders.

To further demonstrate the significance of this type of required process, consider a hospital that is calculating quality measures for diabetics. One of these calculations uses glucometer data and reports that diabetic patients are showing a marked improvement in their blood glucose levels. But one of the clinicians responded that she thinks this is overstated. Upon further investigation, it is determined the correct diagnosis codes were not retrieved from the HIS. The correction was to perform the calculations on the full patient population instead of using diabetic patients only. The lesson learned is that there was not a process in place to check with the stakeholder's expectations, only assumptions that, if not caught in time, it could be costly.

During post-BI presentations and dashboard reviews, it is recommended to leverage participating stakeholders' knowledge to help define and implement a process to forecast and explain findings. A feedback mechanism is essential so the responsible presenter can ensure metrics are being retrieved, calculated and displayed correctly. If the presenter is not able to provide an answer, he or she must know where to turn for assistance. This way the stakeholders will gain a better understanding of the organization, its processes and the positions required to have the knowledge to make the metrics and calculations work.

To ensure the orchestrated processes are working independently and producing the expected outcomes, it may be of interest to extend the gap analysis. The scope should include determining if the healthcare organization has an established governance policy that will ensure the processes are followed as designed. If found, a governance approach will ensure clear communications, correct project direction and contribute to the overall outcomes and impact of the BI implementation.

Governance processes may also support how the dashboards are presented, the frequency of presentation and the buy-in from executive leadership, who may be assigned responsibilities based on the outcomes. In most cases, it may be required to establish governance processes. Each process could be as simple as a policy to agree when and how the goals (dashboard outcomes) should be presented. Additionally, it is crucial that stakeholders agree on how the goals are going to be presented. This may sound trivial, but if expectations are not established in the beginning, people will naturally produce their own.

Supporting Process Discovery and Identification

During the gap analysis of business processes, diagram the steps to show their sequence and how they relate to each other. A box and arrow diagram with a brief description is helpful to describe each step.

An example of this stage might be the development of a flowchart with processes that support the entire system of how data should be transmitted to a central repository, such as a data warehouse. The processes may include manual interventions, the execution of batch information system processes or the automation of an internal script that is executed at a certain time. For each process, further the discovery by extracting sub-processes or steps and provide a sub-number to drill-down into sub-processes.

Finally, when certifying the needed process, identify, by title rather than name, who will be accountable for the system as a whole and for each of the steps. Positions to be identified may include individuals with overall accountability, participating positions such as functional representatives, and in-house, contractual or technical staffing.

Processes are what make the delivery of healthcare and the operations of an organization function. It is these processes that need to be discovered, analyzed and addressed for the BI implementation to work successfully during pre- and post-deployment. Determining what the current processes are and what will be needed in the future will provide additional support to keep the iceberg floating above the surface.

Culture

Culture is an interesting area to inventory, as the significant need for BI deployment may not be certain or evident. Experience has shown numerous times that a dysfunctional culture can be just as disastrous as one in which broken technologies have been implemented.

When starting to look at culture, think about a time when walking into an office building, a restaurant or even a supermarket for the first time. As humans, we tend to look around and take notice. For instance, in a supermarket, we might notice the way physical things are put into place and organized, whether a greeting at the front door was received or the attitude of the staff. What organizations may not understand is that information is like money. It can provide power; it can become a bargaining tool, and if used wisely, can be an investment based on sound decisions. It is intended that a BI implementation will raise the level of awareness relative to the information being increasingly or publicly exposed. How are people going to react to this new information? What if frontline employees learn of information before their direct supervisors or chief executive officer (CEO)? Is this a welcoming experience or does the senior staff feel threatened about their positions?

Initiate the cultural assessment by gaining a sense of awareness of the area that will surround the inner workings of the BI deployment. Let's assume the first BI task is to respond to the executive management team. Explore their reaction to the receipt and exposure to new information. Will each board member interact appropriately with one another when information has surfaced? Are there any politically correct issues that will have to be addressed? Are they willing to share their new informational discoveries? How will they want the information to be displayed or presented? Are they willing to take risks? Are they patient? The project team needs to understand executive behaviors and what is conveyed and practiced throughout the organization.

Next, identify key individuals and how to deal with them to make the BI deployment successful. The project team will need to be on good terms with the IT department, since most resources required will come from this department. Determine the overall attitude of the IT personnel. Are they willing to support the requirements? What type of ownership will they assume if an external team is involved in their business? Do they want to get involved far and beyond the initial BI foundation? Is the IT department willing to support troubleshooting of not only the technologies to build the BI framework, but the idea of supporting a help desk to provide staff with informational support? There have been many horror stories that described how IT departments were not helpful, and their cultures did not allow them to support projects that may have been outside their control or understanding.

Now take a look at all of the current, tailored or new business processes. What departments support them? Will these departments be willing to interact with the project team and support the changes the team makes in what they do in order to make the BI initiative successful? Are department personnel acting as team players? If so, is this because they too see a need for what is being done or will they lose their jobs if they don't? Are departments able to be innovative during this process? Will they be rewarded for their contributions? One example of encountering departmental complexities arose in a facility where job descriptions were hidden from public viewing. The BI initiative being deployed required the use of job descriptions. The culture was to maintain the status quo without any retribution and, thus, the entire project failed.

Gaining a sense of the culture will help greatly in the long run. Deploying BI demands a lot of attention from each of the contributing players. They all must interact well together and understand the big picture. Culture is hard to change. If the team determines that the culture will dampen the BI deployment, a change management program may need to be a part of the overall plan; thus, a change manager who can facilitate the cultural change requirements and become an advocate for the changes should be employed.

People

Organizational information will be valued differently among various stakeholders throughout the organization. A piece of information may be highly valued by one user, while disregarded as useless by another. For example, healthcare stakeholders are often interested in patient outcomes, length of stay and financial status, whereas technologists may be more interested in the total cost of ownership (TCO), help desk ticket submissions, or producing a network reliability rate.

So how does the organization identify the value of its information? That is dependent upon its strategic goals and objectives. An organization may define key performance indicators (KPI) to track over the course of the year to ensure it is meeting its targets. KPIs will be highly valued by the executive team, but may not have the same value to employees of the organization. Employees will likely value transactional data that help them perform their duties and make better decisions in serving their customers. This transactional data, when summarized, will likely feed the KPIs of the organization.

This attribute below the iceberg's (in Figure 4-1) waterline could also be classified as part of the culture or environment, which needs to be reviewed on its own merit. People make things work. People interact with other people. People are chosen to fulfill certain positions based on their qualifications, skill sets and experience.

To get started, draft an outline of the processes involved and the results needed to be achieved. For each actionable item, determine what types of people are necessary for the process. What skills will be required? What personalities may be needed? Who can be the champion of the BI initiative? For each major task, record these attributes. Then on the next line, determine what human resources are available. This is another gap analysis based on what types of people are needed and the availability of people to fill those roles.

After each major task/process is recorded with the attributes and characteristics required, plot those that can be identified. For instance, if a champion is required, who can/should fill that role? Is a physician needed? How about a financial manager? Does the champion need to be respected by those involved in the process? Does the champion understand the underlying data? Does the person know how to manipulate the data to create the results that are trying to be achieved? This all depends on what has to be achieved as the direct outcome of the BI efforts.

Now that there are requirements listed, it's time to determine how to fill any gaps. What is missing from the requirements list? Once identified, what is the plan to fill the gaps? Are there people resources onboard to accommodate the needs? Are the missing attributes or characteristics trainable? Do new people need to be hired? Finally, when do these types of people have to be onboard and up to speed?

The end result of this exercise is a people model that supports the BI initiative, listing the required attributes and characteristics, the current level available for use and the outcomes of a gap analysis showing what is still required. From this information, the project team can determine what is needed and when.

Keep in mind that the people category also includes those who may not be directly involved with the BI initiative. Often projects may need to count on people who are part of a critical process that is integral to success. This is important to identify up front as well.

Resources

The previous paragraphs discussed many underlying components that could be considered as resources. There is also a need to look at resources not included in any of those components. Resources are components not directly reflected up front.

Start with the initiation. Do the personnel resources to launch your project exist? The team is going to need those who can support the efforts with discovering processes, recording each of them and if necessary thinking of new ways to operate. With this as the start, are there technical resources to collect, manipulate and share these findings? This may sound trivial, but not knowing how things are going to be communicated or managed is a major landmine. Are there technical resources available, such as a shared network drive or an intranet, where the team can record findings and collaborate? Do things like a list of e-mail addresses to foster communication need to be created? Does everyone have access to these lists?

Other resources may include statisticians, artists and designers. If the team is going to use PowerPoint to display the BI results, does the audience have PowerPoint to receive the reports and view? If using Adobe PDF instead, are technical resources available to convert presentations to PDF?

When it comes to managing the overall BI project, do the tools exist? For example, is there Microsoft Project or another type of tool to manage the project? Is there a classroom or training aide available to teach team members how to use Project or to know how to develop Gantt charts and schedule presentations?

Resources may come in many different sizes and shapes, and oftentimes the team may not even be aware of what is needed. Try to lay out the complete blueprint of the BI project first, and then identify both direct and indirect resources that are going to be needed. This blueprint or overall project plan should be a working document that can be modified as needed, especially with identifying resources. Keeping a working list will help while executing the project and will help identify resources ahead of time. In some instances, resources that are needed and are available will still need to be tailored. This too can include technologies, people or supplies. For example, the organization may have a trouble ticket system in place, but as a resource, can it accommodate troubleshooting business processes or metric evaluation?

During post-BI implementation, there is a need to determine what resources are required. Is there staff to support drill-down capabilities that need to be answered by data or process owners? What is the process to record these transactions? Many people like to print their presentations, especially metrics, so that they can review them at home or another remote location. This may sound minuscule, but are there enough printers to support this need? Are there enough color printers?

Like anywhere else, resources are very important for the BI project; they act as the fuel to make things go. Conducting a full gap analysis of the resources needed, when they are needed and what is currently available will help produce a successful BI deployment. Using models similar to those described earlier to collect this information will assist in this tool requirement.

Another operational consideration to address before starting any BI systems implementation is a review of tools that will be used with the BI application. These will include database management systems (DBMS), data integration tools, querying and analytical tools, reporting and other front-end tools, data profiling tools, change management tools and testing tools. Some questions to ask are: Are all potential end users properly equipped to run the BI tools and applications? What software tools does the prospective user community currently use to perform its analysis? What hardware is available to use with the BI implementation?

Unless someone has previously implemented a BI system in the organization, they are not going to have all the tools needed. That means the team will have to select vendors and products for the BI implementation. Two main things to remember during the vendor and tool evaluation are: 1) business intelligence has to produce insights that are timely, accurate, high value and actionable, so the tools you choose should satisfy these requirements; 2) just like any software vendor, BI vendors will often oversell their products. They will present the illusion that the organization will transform itself overnight if only it buys their products and may claim they have the perfect solution for the organization. It is important to be sure to ask that a healthcare example be used, and not some other industry, if the vendors demo their products. This is because what might work really well for a financial institution might not work as an example for healthcare.

Just as with any software purchase, the organization should evaluate BI vendors based on criteria such as:

- Licensing—concurrent vs. individual users (which concerns whether licenses are interchangeable between people).
- Availability of technical support and willingness to answer questions before and after the purchase is made.
- Vendor stability and longevity.
- Product maturity and reputation in the marketplace.
- The number of analytical and presentation tools in the suite.

When evaluating products, which is a more detailed evaluation than a vendor evaluation, the team can use these criteria (Note: this is not a complete list, but the main criteria):

- Cost of ownership—license costs, ongoing support, training, upgrades.
- Compatibility with existing systems.
- Response time and processing speeds.
- User friendliness (ease of use) that fit the user community. Tools should be user-friendly (since most of these will be used not by non-IT experts or programmers, but by the masses) and should have an intuitive and logical interface.
- Web-based—the querying and reporting tools should offer a web interface that will allow users to access the tool through a common browser.

Environment

The environment is very similar to the culture, except in this case, the setting is the focus. The environment consists of things like the pace of work, geographical location, resource availability, components of culture or the overall interactions one has with another.

First take a look at the pace of work. How rapidly is work completed? Part of answering this question involves determining the technology support workers use to perform their tasks. One question to address is the issue of consistency. Are the providers consistent with how they enter their data? Is there training established, if needed? What is the timeliness of the input needed to accomplish the BI project on time—providers may not always get to their input requirements in a desired time frame.

Next, ask what departmental boundaries will need crossing. Will data come from one source or multiple sources operated by different departments? Do these systems communicate with one another? One way to better understand the environment is to draw a picture with the processes running through it. Draw the departments, the business processes that run through them and the information they gather. This provides a holistic, at-a-glance view for a reviewer to determine the environment of each setting.

In a sense, the environment is about the surroundings and the tempo of operations. In one instance, the environment was chaos. Processes and accountability were mismanaged, and the implementation of a BI initiative was nearly impossible. The environment was managed neither by priorities nor by understanding of progress being achieved. If the BI initiative is going to entail an environment like this, there will be a need for alternative plans. This is where having or building relationships is so important. Players on the sidelines need to be onboard with the project, and the team should use a holistic point of view, so the process or departmental owners can see what the team is seeing. In other words, walking out to the edge of the balcony and taking a look inward allows a person to see the environment from a different angle to determine if there are acceptable attributes and characteristics.

Table 4-1 depicts a few recent issues confronted by a data quality BI implementation at a military hospital. These issues are presented as environmental findings aligned with resolutions. The intent is to illustrate environmental issues that can hinder a BI implementation.

Table 4-1: Recent Issues of a Data Quality BI Implementation at a Military Hospital.

Problem	Resolution
Many data quality (DQ) managers are frustrated with the layout of the DQ web sites, specifically the help desk links.	Redesign web site interfaces to be more consumer-focused and provide easy-to-find services.
Help desk personnel lack training using Remedy. Too many extra steps are being developed that could easily be accommodated with the knowledge of Remedy.	Provide help desk personnel with Remedy training.
Data quality staff appear to be "mission" disconnected. They do not have a view of the big picture behind data quality; therefore, it is evident that some things are being done without knowing why.	Provide monthly/quarterly data quality department meetings outlining the mission, how it's expected to be achieved and who is responsible for each action. In other words, it is critical to bring internal people together to achieve optimal performance and results.
Data quality managers are not always notified about the status of their submitted help desk tickets.	Integrate Remedy into data quality web site so that customers can routinely check the status of their tickets. Also, improve/expand access to Remedy by others within the department, so they too can provide information to their customers.

Technologies

Decisions are based on information. The importance of real-time data and the ability to deliver data in an easily digestible format is well-known. To complicate matters, logical and judicious decisions are constrained by the type and quality of information available. Even with new transactional business systems, healthcare organizations drown in oceans of data, but starve for information in a form that can be quickly interpreted in the context of problem resolution. What some users do not understand is the information they are seeking does not sufficiently flow horizontally, penetrating boundaries; too often information flows are blocked by organizational silos and non-integrated healthcare systems.

One of the most common reasons the implementation of BI fails is because too much information is trying to be deciphered without a supporting infrastructure. The focus should be on providing and explaining the data in a quick glance. There is no one perfect template for any type of BI design. Before considering how to mine information and present the findings, the team must understand their own technical environment. Depending on the audience, efforts may need to be tailored to suit the need. For example, senior healthcare executives are not impressed by fancy presentations; they simply want to take the pulse of their healthcare operations to stay informed and see what, if any, adjustments are needed.

Authoritative data are very important to consider, as a copy of a copy degrades the integrity of the data. Depending on the location of the data, the system will need processes in place to retrieve the information.

The following sections that specifically focus on information knowledge have been saved for last to demonstrate a more holistic approach to evaluating the flow of the information needed from disparate silos and archives to the need for presenting in real-time. As this chapter's objective is to stimulate thought and have the project team ask the right questions, the following will present a more technical view with a laymen's touch. These topics of information knowledge will begin with how one expects the information to be created, followed by how it will be stored and readily accessible. Then the discussion will delve into how the information will be shared among the stakeholders, the entire organization or other third-party external entities and lastly, how the team is going to present the information, followed by the expectation of how the information is to be analyzed. Asking these questions and answering them should provide the bigger picture without getting too technical. These questions are not presented to create fear of moving forward in those not technically savvy, but should be addressed as the team moves forward in communicating with the IT department.

HOW IS INFORMATION CREATED?

This is a fundamental question that deserves a little more attention than most because it is often overlooked. The question of how data/information is created takes a look at the point of entry into the entire BI "system." Where are the data coming from (data can originate from many sources)? Starting with the most obvious, data can come from paper forms, records or reports. It can come from manual data entry into an information system or by using thumb drives and automated transfer methods.

When defining the requirements for the BI initiative, the team must ask specific fundamental questions. Where are the data located, how are they managed and how can they be obtained? Using the military medical facility example from earlier, data sources were well-defined and documented. In the requirements, the systems were identified as being located around the globe, the data elements were defined and the data files were developed. Every day, each file was electronically transferred to a central repository for further processing. Since this was a process that was put into place previously, most would assume it works and is efficient. However, the team should ask how the information is created. In this case, the information is created at the initial entry of a patient into an outpatient clinic. There was no jurisdiction over that part of the process, so the team had to make the assumption that end users entering the patient information were trained. The line of embarkation began when the file left the facility and arrived at the central repository.

Instead of assuming the file was arriving on time and intact, the team decided to develop their first metric and, in this case, a KPI. It was called the Transmission Completion Report (TraCR) program. TraCR displays the completion status of the daily files (i.e., patient appointments) transmitted from military hospitals worldwide to central repositories for data warehouse aggregation. This tool provides military hospitals with peace of mind, knowing their data have made it to the central repository in a complete and timely fashion.

Monitoring file transmissions for both on-time delivery and data integrity has reduced the level of effort in managing trouble tickets and enables military hospitals to validate their transmissions and resolve issues when they occur (instead of two months later).

HOW IS INFORMATION STORED?

Once the team knows where the information is created, the next step is to determine exactly how the information is stored. For example, assume the data need to be immediately available with real-time updates. To retrieve this information, the process may need to be able to identify the system in which the data are located and how long it will take to retrieve. If it is real-time data, the data will most likely be readily available. However, if it is archived data, there may be a waiting period, as the data may be stored on another device or archived in some form of backup media. A variety of backup media could possibly exist, including storage servers, tapes and other hardware types of devices.

Once research has identified the location of the data, there are many other factors that need to be addressed. First, it would be helpful to understand how the data are managed and how they will be distributed. Within the storage environment, is data schema available to identify what fields are available and their names? Who maintains the data? Will there be database administrators (DBA) who can support retrieval of the data? Will the data be available when needed? From a data quality perspective, how accurate are the data? Also, how complete and timely are the data? Asking these types of data storage questions up front will save a lot of time in the future.

HOW IS INFORMATION SHARED?

Sharing does not necessarily mean how to present the results of the dashboard, but how can the data be transparently shared with others from its original origin? Once the information is made available, will it stay dormant in its own silo? How can others use the newly discovered information?

From a technical perspective, there are many ways information can be shared. As discussed earlier, even information extracted from medical servers uses a technical method to transfer (share) its information with a centralized server. When discussing "how is the information presented," it will appear more logical and understandable because it is something the people can see and touch; thus, the idea behind sharing is how to stimulate or further the conversation.

The fundamental question about sharing is asking if the right technologies are in place to accommodate the process. For example, will information be shared via e-mail? If so, does the e-mail support images? This is assuming the dashboard can export the results into an image. When sharing information, is it real-time information? Are there technical skill sets available that can transform the availability of the results using web services? Web service is a technical term for sharing (making available and consuming) individual services to other applications. Does the plan allow others to perform analysis or further calculations? Will the others be allowed to log in using reporting tools? If so, does the team have the manpower and skill sets to accommodate user management requirements? A more efficient and secure method is to make the new information available in what's called a data warehouse, something that is separate from the main source. If choosing this route, how is the process going to transfer the data from one server to the other? Again, ask if the skill sets of a DBA are available in order to establish the connection.

How are security and HIPAA rules followed? If there is a desire to share the information outside the organization, the team will need to ensure they are not transferring private health information (PHI) or any other information that could violate HIPAA policies. Sharing is not much different than presenting; however, when deciding to share, there are many underlying questions that need to be answered and reviewed. This process can ensure the right framework and foundation is in place to support future BI and sharing needs.

HOW IS INFORMATION PRESENTED?

Once new information is ready to be shared and presented with others, who is the target audience? If the audience is an executive board, the choice of an executive dashboard through a software product is possibly a logical choice. If this is the case, are the presentation features known, such as how to minimize too much information, but keep it detailed enough to grab the attention of the right individuals? Are the right skill sets available to operate the presentation software? When presenting information, are the subject-matter experts available to discuss how the information was calculated and how to make corrections where necessary?

Another common way to present information is through the use of slide presentations, such as PowerPoint. Does the organization have the skill sets available and the technology to be able to download the information as images and manipulate into the slide presentation? Will they be able to update the information if the presentation is required again? Looking to the future, wouldn't it be nice if presentations were automatically updated—no more editing of slide presentations? This could be a possibility through the use of web services, but again will require the right skill sets and technologies to accomplish.

Most of the time, information will be made available via the Internet. Many BI tools will provide methods to export the information to the web so that a wider body of users may access it. A review of skill sets and technologies is needed if there is a desire to use the web to display business information; the team will need to address the user management and role-based requirements. For instance, if they decide to integrate new information into Microsoft Share-Point, the appropriate resource will need to locate a web part that will accommodate the integration or have one custom built. Web parts are individual services usually providing a single value-added service. Even when choosing this route, the team could run into some problems.

For example, in one instance of presenting through SharePoint at a military hospital, the nurse informaticist would generate the new data, but would be dependent on the information management department (IMD) to develop the SharePoint web part and make it available to the right audience. Experience showed the IMD web team have their own priorities and don't always get to the SharePoint requirements needed by the nurse. In another situation, information made available via the web may also be "editable." What policies need to be in place to govern what is presented? Will the rules allow users to change content if needed? To further illustrate possible outcomes, is the executive board able to understand what a graph is representing? This too may seem simple enough, but the team cannot assume its stakeholders understand how to read a graph.

There are many great ways to present new information, but before choosing one over another the team needs to understand what it is going to take to support the choice. Specifically, don't always assume the pieces will just come together naturally, especially if data and services are made available across departmental or organizational boundaries. Not everyone's priorities are going to be the same as the teams' priorities.

HOW IS INFORMATION ANALYZED?

This chapter has presented the introduction to how new information is made available by understanding the required and diverse levels of data management. This chapter also introduced and reviewed some of the basics of how to present information. Now that data are shared and presented, how are they going to be analyzed? The team cannot assume that everyone will have the same understanding of how this will be done.

First, the team needs to understand how the data were transcribed into useful information. What business rules were applied? A common communication problem between the military hospitals and headquarters is a disconnect in understanding the data because no one knew how the data were transformed. They didn't understand the business rules being applied. When the rules were presented to each stakeholder, not everyone was in agreement, and therefore required a body of stakeholders to come together to agree on the right type of business rules. This could be one of the most overlooked areas in BI. Do not assume all stakeholders know the business rules applied to the data. Taking this step further, all stakeholders may agree on the business rules, but do they understand the impact caused by "change and effect?"

SUMMARY

Successful BI implementation requires an understanding of an information management culture. This is the multifaceted integration of business processes, enterprise applications, and organizational structures refined through ever-revised and reshaped techniques leading to the creation of a high-performance model for organizational healthcare systems. Success will not simply come from choosing the right applications to support the business intelligence needs or web-enabling the right processes, or forging the right links to legacy systems. Instead, success requires fundamental changes in the organizational systematization, corporate behavior and even the way people think—inside and outside of organizational spheres of influence; getting back to the basics—laying a solid foundation upon which the organization can grow and meet tomorrow's expected and unanticipated demands by focusing on agility, scalability and simplicity. Buying "software solutions" and services are often the easy part. Realigning the organization and culture to recognize the value of information and how to apply it to knowledge is more difficult.

Table 4-2: Chapter 4 Checklist—Assess Your Environment.

Item	Completed (Yes/No)
1. Create a picture of the environment labeled with processes, location of data sources and other resources to facilitate the asset inventory.	
2. Complete inventory of technologies, resources, processes, culture and environment.	
3. Complete inventory of processes and complete analysis—adjust as needed.	
4. Develop and implement a feedback mechanism.	
5. Complete inventory of people resources, outlining skills, knowledge and experience required.	
6. All the required information has been located, and it is understood how the information will be stored and retrieved.	
7. Technologies are in place to allow information to be shareable throughout the organization and available in a variety of formats.	
8. Tools are available along with the resources and skill sets to present the information.	
9. There is a clear understanding by the stakeholders how the business rules will be developed and applied.	

CHAPTER 5

Understanding the Data

By Jonathan Rothman, MBA

Anyone who has ever participated in a mature reporting and analytics project will profess the importance of getting operational, financial and other management goals and objectives organized and documented prior to having the technical staff write their first line of code. Once needs have been established and the source of data has been identified, the next step is determining whether the data are accessible and reliable. Being accessible is defined as the ability to extract the data from the source system in the format and time frame needed, whereas reliable is defined as data that are valid and accurate.

With organizations relying on reporting systems, such as dashboards, it is critical that they can depend on these when making key business decisions. To do this, many leverage the business experts to validate the data prior to the formal use of a dashboard.

But how does a healthcare organization gain an understanding of their data; what data will be needed and how will they be used? What actions can be taken to assist in gaining this information and, in the process, constructing data definitions (referred to in next discussion about Table 5-1)?

This chapter will answer those questions by first explaining why use cases are developed by business experts, as the first step in determining what and how data will be used. To further clarify, the term use case is commonly used in software development and is defined as a "methodology used in system analysis to identify, clarify, and organize system requirements." (Available online at: http://searchsoftwarequality.techtarget.com/definition/use-case)

While the intent of this chapter is to not come across as too technical, it is important to touch on select terms such as extract/transform/load (ETL) or data warehouse, but leave it to other chapters to describe these concepts in detail. As previously mentioned, ETL is the process in which data move from one computer system or database source (E: Extract), get cleaned or changed (T: Transform) and then loaded into another computer system and database source (L: Load). This chapter will illustrate how the context of raw data transforms itself, technically, into information that can be used by executive management and other organization stakeholders.

USE CASES

Technical staff are heavily reliant on business experts to explain and produce scenarios on how, where and when data may be used. What these business experts must do to guide and educate technical staff is to create use cases in a story format describing why information is required, when and what information is required, how often it is required and how that information is best displayed to assist in decision making. Once a use case is developed, the technical staff will use these stories or scenarios to both design and build the system, as well as to complete the ETL design. The risk of omitting the development of use cases can be detrimental to a project and can result in loss of project time (or wasted efforts) and inclusion of the wrong information on reports.

However, many business experts struggle with the creation of use cases in a story or scenario format. In addition, a single business expert may not have the skill set or technical understanding of where data may reside. Therefore, a best practice on where to start would be to construct a bulleted list of questions similar to those in Table 5-1 that can be completed concurrently by the business experts and technical staff. Once complete, the technical staff can turn this list into a use case.

Table 5-1 shows example strategic and tactical questions that may be considered during the development of a use case. The questions should be focused on the goals and objectives pertinent to the use case, and the list should also include questions regarding the source of data and whether it can be extracted and used in reports.

The development of the use cases will provide input into two major tasks:
1. Provides technical staff the information they will need to:
   * Build a more complete use case.
   * Validate the use case prior to build.
   * Use as a foundation for designing and building the system.
2. Provides the foundation of the documentation for the BI system.
   * Understand the business need.
   * Understand the source and frequency of the need data.
   * Understand how the data will be used.

METADATA

Metadata is simply the data about the data. Understanding data is important to knowing the purpose and value behind collecting and reporting data. Answering many of the tactical use-case questions in Table 5-1 actually constructs these data definitions.

Metadata creation is a best-practice exercise users of information construct to remove all questions regarding why and what information is collected, how data should be collected and stored, their attributes, desired behavior and their relationship to other data. Once this is designed, technical staff are well prepared to begin defining the components of the data required to actually build the system. Components of understanding the data include data subject, elements, source, characteristics and entities (further discussed in Chapter 6).

Metadata is created for and used by multi-dimensional data structures. These structures allow an organization to "slice and dice" data in multiple ways to gain the view they need, as well as to report on key performance indicators (KPI) selected for viewing.

Table 5-1: Questions Asked when Constructing the Framework for a Use Case.

Strategic Questions	Tactical Questions
• What is the goal or objective to be achieved? • What actions must be taken after achievement of key performance indicators (KPI) or metric analyses? • What patient or other processes are involved and being measured? • Are these patient processes intra- or interdepartmental? • Are computer systems used during these patient processes?	• What information is available and who is entering this information? • What information/metrics are required in the future? • What metrics can be produced from these computer systems that would support the goals and objectives? • How often must metrics be produced? • What is the frequency of metric data capture? • What is the desired metric behavior (positive/negative, higher/lower)? • What is the desired trend in metric behavior (up or down)? • What are sufficient metric substitutes if that specific metric is not available? • What potential problems may impact data entry and extraction integrity? • Do data required to produce a calculated metric reside in only one computer system? • Are data easily available or extractable in these computer systems? • What alternative metrics (or surrogates) may be produced in the event of deficiencies in primary metric production?

Table 5-2 is a sample that combines information collected as part of both a use case and metadata.

The example in Table 5-2 illustrates all the components necessary to fully understand and build the KPI, including format, frequency, targeted values and surrogate(s). Surrogates are defined as additional measures that may be captured as part of the information collected.

Defining the use case alone does not ensure reliability. There are additional steps that must be performed and/or collected to evaluate reliability. An organization must begin reviewing the details of each data element. There are two ways to accomplish this activity:

- Quality of the data can be reviewed and scrutinized based on the defined criteria (previously stated) to understand the process flow and break down the data elements in a sequential flow.
- Accurate calculations of the data can be performed by conducting manual audits and calculations to validate the data.

For the purposes of this chapter, we will elaborate on the process review approach.

Table 5-2: Sample of Metadata Documentation for the KPI: Patient Arrival to Initial Treatment.

KPI: Patient Arrival to Initial Treatment (Emergency Department)	
Goal:	To decrease the time between when a patient walks through the door and is placed into an ED treatment room.
Objective:	Decreasing this time will positively impact patient walk-out results, as well as satisfaction results.
Desired values:	The lower the result, the better the performance.
What happens when performance drops?	Consider placing a discharge nurse into triage.
What contributes to poor performance?	Patient arrivals increased too fast; beds are full because patients cannot be moved to inpatient units.
Source system used to isolate data:	Emergency Department Information System (EDIS).
Patient definition:	A patient is defined as a unique chart number created by the hospital's EHR or registration system.
Metric definition:	A calculation in minutes between the patient's earliest arrival time stamp and the first room time stamp (after the waiting room) assigned to the patient.
Metric availability:	Available for all patient visits using distinct chart numbers.
Patient exclusions from all metrics:	Exclude all patients who arrive by ambulance or who are directly admitted through the ED because they follow a different patient flow process.
Participants:	Greeter, triage nurse, clinical nurse.
Data are required:	Real-time and on a retrospective basis.
Data are reported in this format:	As a numeric field using the following data format ##.##.
Related metrics:	Arrivals per hour, patient walk-outs, physician to discharge, decision to admit.
Surrogate metrics:	Arrive to physician.
Additional ways metric needs to be reported:	By physician, ED area, nurse name, time of day and day of week, acuity level, ICD-10.
Valid times:	Due to potential human data entry using the EDIS, do not use time-increment values that calculate where the value is either <0 or >600 minutes. However, report these invalid time increments at a clinical nurse level and present results at monthly meetings to improve EDIS compliance.
Target value:	30 minutes.
Threshold value:	60 minutes.

The Patient Process Flow

Let's review how data can be validated using a patient flow process. Using Table 5-2, one of the fields collected was "Valid times." Within this field, the upper and lower data tolerance limits are defined for valid times. In addition, the information also suggests that invalid results are directly influenced by improper use by clinical nurses in the ED of the computer system used to capture this information. Therefore, to improve the use of the computer system (in this case the Emergency Department Information System [EDIS]), results would be reported back to users with the goal of using these statistics to improve data collection. By defining the upper and lower limits of the data in the use case, this is built into the BI system, allowing results to be routinely reported to the business owners.

The patient process flow suggested focuses on assessing the quality of data produced by operational systems, tied to by whom and when data are entered into these systems. As patients move through their clinical and operational processes, information is entered into a computer system.

Expanding on Table 5-1 and Table 5-2, an example of what is meant by a patient process flow in the context of understanding the data is provided in Table 5-3.

Table 5-3: Sample Patient Process Flow

Action	The ED Process	HIS (health information system)/ EDIS Interaction	Data Point
Patient Does Not Arrive by Ambulance			
Patient Arrival	Patient who arrives through the main entrance is greeted by a triage nurse where the basic demographic information is collected from the patient. This is the patient's first point of entry and the first time a patient time stamp will exist in the EDIS. This is called Express Registration.	Demographic and reason for visit data directly entered into HIS where a medical record number is either created from scratch or selected for the patient's prior visit. A patient chart number is also created by the HIS system.	Patient arrival time for non-ambulance arrivals.
Triage	The triage nurse creates a triage note, assigns a triage acuity and collects from the patient clinical information associated with the visit.	When the triage nurse opens the triage form in the EDIS, a time stamp is created. This is the triage start time. Each time the triage nurse saves the triage note, a time stamp is created. The latest save time equals the triage end time.	Patient triage start & triage end times.

Table 5-3: Sample Patient Process Flow (cont.)

Action	The ED Process	HIS (health information system)/ EDIS Interaction	Data Point
Registration Start	A complete patient registration process is performed. This information is transferred from the HIS system into the EDISm where information is merged with the patient record.	The registration start time begins when the registration person clicks the registration start box within the registration screen in their HIS. Sometimes this step gets missed when the ED is overcrowded.	Registration start time
Registration End		The registration process is complete when the admission, diagnosis, triage (ADT), Health Level 7 (HL7) message is sent by the HIS, accepted by the EDIS and the records are merged.	Registration end time
Waiting for a Bed	At the conclusion of registration, the patient is sent back to the waiting room where he will wait for an available bed. This is an indication to clinical nursing that the triage and registration processes are both complete.	Registration clerk changes the patient status on the EDIS patient tracking grid to Waiting for Bed (WFB) and assigns an ED Room value of Waiting Room (WR).	Ignore time stamps where ED Room = "WR" when calculating arrival to room metrics.

Table 5-3: Sample Patient Process Flow (cont.)

Action	The ED Process	HIS (health information system)/ EDIS Interaction	Data Point
ED Room Assignment	When a bed becomes available, the patient is transferred by the clinical nurse from the waiting room to a bed.	Clinical nurse changes the patient status on the EDIS patient tracking grid to "ACT" and assigns an ED room value. This does not always happen as the patient is moved into the bed, and sometimes the value is entered by the physician *even after* the patient has been seen. Therefore, sometimes the Physician Time Stamp is earlier than the ED Room time stamp.	Patient room time.
Physician **Non-Physician**	As the physician or associate practitioner goes to a room to see a patient, he assigns himself to the patient using the EDIS.	On the main EDIS grid are a number of columns where the physician, resident, fellow, nurse, non-phys provider, or other Health Care Professionals (HCP) enter their name when going to see a patient. If this time value needs to be manually changed/updated, another screen is made available to the physician/nurse to enter a new time value.	The earlier of these time stamps is the first provider time.

Table 5-3: Sample Patient Process Flow (cont.)

Action	The ED Process	HIS (health information system)/ EDIS Interaction	Data Point
Patient Arrives by Ambulance:			
Arrival, Triage, Registration Room, Nurse & Physician Times	A patient who arrives by ambulance will go directly to a bed or be placed in a hallway, if an ED room is not available, where triage and/or registration will be performed. As soon as a bed is available, a clinical nurse will log the bed value into the EDIS. Therefore "arrive to room" metrics should not be calculated for these patients.	The patient's arrival, triage, registration, nurse, room and physician times will be extremely close together and may not be sequential. Sometimes the physician time will be before the room time. Sometimes the nurse time will be after the room time. Sometimes the nurse time will not be entered at all.	Arrival to ED room or arrival to nurse or physician will not be valid or meaningful. ED room to physician will not be valid or meaningful.

In this example, the process begins with the patient's arrival to an emergency department and then concludes with the notation that a physician has seen the patient in an ED treatment room. The key fields include the "Action"—what the ED process is at that point; the information system interaction or function; and the resulting data point that can be captured based on the action.

Using this approach will help an organization understand where mistakes in the patient time line or data collection may occur. By describing the patient flow process in the context with how people interact with the HIS and EDIS, this flow can also serve as another reference point as the technical resource (e.g., data architect) completed their data mapping of data models. Finally, this flow identifies why compliance in data capture may be lacking and offers opportunities for improvement.

SUMMARY

Figure 5-1 shows there is significant interrelationship between the process flows, the data, the metadata and how the data will be used.

Throughout this chapter on understanding the data, a common theme of communication between business users and technical staff has resonated. Business users bring the domain expertise to define the business problem and their information requirements. Technical staff work with business users to translate those requirements into data models and architectures that support the acquisition, transformation, storage and presentation of information that business users need to address their functional requirements.

With large amounts of data available, it is easy for business owners to become overwhelmed and produce metrics without taking the time and effort to vet its quality and usefulness by performing the recommended tasks listed in this chapter.

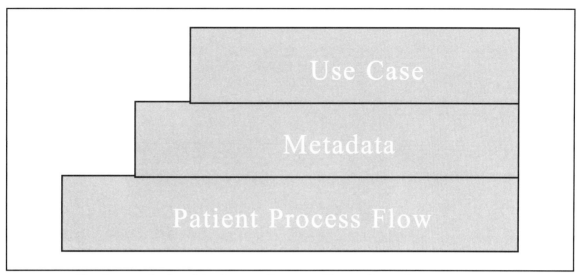

Figure 5-1: The Interrelationship Among Process Flows, Data, Metadata and Data Are Used.

Table 5-4: Chapter 5 Checklist—Understanding the Data.

Item	Completed (Yes/No)
1. Possess strong understanding of business need for business intelligence.	
2. Clearly understand the goals and objectives.	
3. Identify business owners/experts to assist with use cases and metadata.	
4. Identify technical staff to assist with use cases and metadata.	
5. Develop use cases scenarios/stories for each indicator.	
6. Define metadata for each Key Performance Indicator.	
7. Map out process to understand input and outputs.	

CHAPTER 6

Design the Framework

By Eric Adjei Boakye, MA

When an organization opts to build rather than buy their business intelligence (BI) solution, there are many elements that must be considered. BI applications can be very complex. There are many moving pieces to put in place, including software applications, technology, data, processes and sponsorship. This chapter will explore the technical aspects of building a BI application.

Transactional systems process massive quantities of data. Transforming raw transaction data into a consistent and coherent set of information suitable for BI use requires much more than just collecting and storing data. The BI solution must be able to quickly provide users with reliable, accurate information and help them make decisions that vary widely in complexity. It also must make information available through a variety of distribution channels, including traditional reports, *ad-hoc* analysis tools, dashboards and spreadsheets. In addition, there should be processes that relate to how data are acquired, standardized and secured.

An important initial step for any organization planning to build a BI solution is to understand the elements of BI architecture. A BI architecture is a framework for organizing and integrating the data, along with information management and technology components that are used to build BI systems for reporting and data analytics. The BI architecture or strategy should be developed in parallel to—or directly after—an assessment of the organization's environment and data (described in Chapters 4 and 5). There is a tendency to go straight from the assessment of the current BI environment to evaluating software vendors, specific technology approaches and products. As tempting as it is, organizations should take the time to develop the architecture from the ground up.

The components of a BI architecture include the data users' need to meet their business requirements; the information management components (software and hardware) used to convert data into useful information for users; and the technology components (software and hardware) used to present information to business stakeholders to enable them to analyze

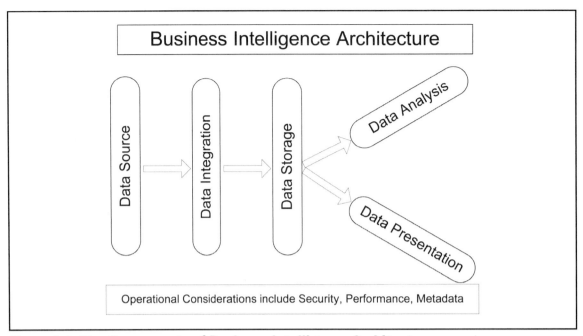

Figure 6-1: The Components of Business Intelligence Architecture.

data. Specifically, the typical conceptual architecture of a BI solution comprises five major areas and a set of operational considerations; these are illustrated in Figure 6-1.

Data source deals with all the source systems that will provide data for the BI solution. Data integration transforms the data from the data source layer into meaningful information. Data storage is the end result of data source and data integration layers and is where the transformed data are stored for use. Data analysis and data presentation will leverage the information stored in the data storage. To gain a better understanding, each component is outlined next.

Data Source

The first component in the BI architecture is the data source, as shown in Figure 6-2. Data source (any device that has data needed for the BI system) will provide the data needed to implement a BI solution and include mainframes, relational databases, flat files, spreadsheets and external sources.

One of the challenges when working with data in a BI system is that they typically originate in many different data storage systems. Thus, the data are inconsistent, fragmented, not standardized and out of context. Extracting data from those different sources and merging the data into a single, consistent dataset is always challenging. However, it is very important to invest the time to understand the source applications and the data in detail before starting any BI solution implementation (Chapter 5). This stage is critical to achieve project success.

The following outlines a few main questions an organization must ask at this stage. Information gathered during the environment assessment along with an understanding of the data, including requirements gathering, should assist in answering some of these questions.

The first question is *what data are needed for the BI solution?* In other words, what data are needed by the users to make useful decisions or analysis? This is a very important question to answer because typically, business and information technology (IT) people fault others when the wrong data are collected or when the right data are not available.

Traditionally, IT leaders believe business leaders do not know what data they need, and business leaders believe IT leaders lack the business insight to make meaningful data available.

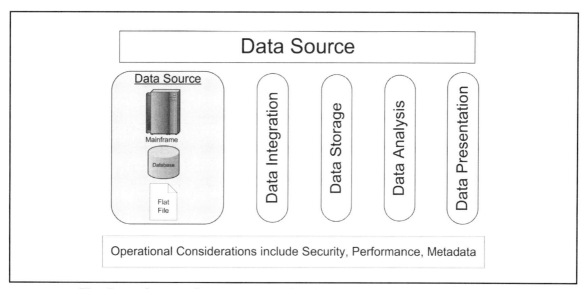

Figure 6-2: The Data Source Component in Business Intelligence Architecture.

While there is no easy solution to this conflict, what can be done to solve or at least minimize it is for business leaders and IT leaders to work together right from the beginning. Organizations should think through this tough dilemma before making full use of BI capabilities. Information gathered through the organization assessment should assist in addressing this conflict.

Once the needed data have been identified, the second question is, *where can the data be obtained?* For example, if the user wants to see patient satisfaction metrics on a dashboard, the team has to decide where it can get patient satisfaction data. The data for the BI system likely originates from several transactional systems (any devices where data are stored in the organization) such as legacy transaction systems, mainframes, relational databases and even spreadsheets. The data will reside in different source environments with different platforms (different databases or storage devices). At this point, the team has to identify all sources that have the information needed. Information described in Chapter 5 should be used to direct the addressing of this requirement.

Once the process determines what data are needed and where to get them, the third question is, *how much data are needed?* In addition to gathering the right data, organizations need to collect the right *amount* of data. This is another difficult question, one that will require IT leaders and business stakeholders to work closely together to answer effectively.

Organizations need a lot of data to produce trends, but collecting large quantities also has costs. The first rule of thumb is to make sure that the cost to collect data does not outweigh the benefit it will provide. The second rule of thumb is to make sure to collect only the data that are meaningful to the BI solution. In other words, do not collect data just because they are available and easy to capture. Business executives must be clear about what drives value in their organization and this will assist collection of data that are meaningful to the business and that prevent the organization from collecting data unnecessarily. The requirements and use cases developed in Chapter 5 should assist in answering this question.

Another question that must be answered is, *how can the organization make the data more valuable?* After deciding on the amount of data needed for the BI solution, the team has to decide how to make all data useful. The details to achieving this will become evident during the design phase, but overall, data must be correct, standardized, non-redundant and cleaned.

The last question is, *what rules and processes are needed to manage the data from its acquisition through its retirement?* Organizations must create policies and procedures to determine when and how data that are no longer needed will be saved, archived or retired. Also policies and processes must be developed to ensure data privacy, security and integrity (this will be further explained in the Operational/Logistical Considerations section later in this chapter).

Data Integration

Data integration, shown in Figure 6-3, is how data is captured, temporarily stored, studied, cleaned, transmitted and loaded into data storage. Once an organization has addressed the source data component, it must determine how to capture, transform and load data into the target database (destination) before the data can become usable for the end users. The process to capture, transform and load data into their destination is known as extract, transform, and load (ETL).

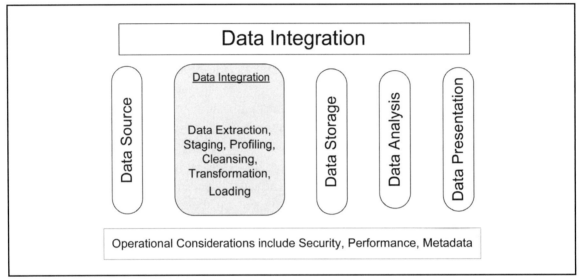

Figure 6-3: The Data Integration Component in Business Intelligence Architecture.

While extracting data from their source and loading them into a database are fairly straightforward tasks, transforming data is not. The transformation process involves studying the source data for data quality issues, coming up with a process to cleanse the data, translating the data into a single format and applying business rules. Transformation also entails standardizing data definitions to make certain that business concepts have consistent, comparable definitions across the organization. Large organizations with multiple health systems should expect to face a difficult task of establishing standards. Therefore, senior executives must consider forming data governance committees to lead the data standardization charge. Both business and IT managers should understand they will have to expend significant effort in order to transform data into usable information.

These are the main decisions that need to be made and documented during the data integration phase in the BI architecture. First, organizations should decide if data profiling will be part of the integration phase. Data profiling is studying the underlying data available in an existing data source and collecting statistics and information about those data. Since the data in source systems are stored in functional silos, it generally tends to be a disorganized mess. It is generally argued that the second challenge organizations face when building a BI system are data quality (only behind budget constraints).

Data profiling usually involves collecting information about descriptions of the relevant table structures (that is, definitions of each field/column and their data types, format, etc.)

and some statistical properties of the data (such as record counts, range of values found in each field). For most organizations, especially large healthcare systems, with several operational data sources, profiling can be a huge and time-consuming job. The team should decide whether or not they want to perform that task.

The number of data quality issues identified when trying to understand the data (Chapter 5) should help make this decision. If a considerable number of issues are identified, then the project team will be better off performing data profiling rather than skipping it. It is recommended that organizations perform some level of profiling; otherwise, they may find they are spending more time later in the validation process dealing with data quality problems. Also information collected during profiling provides guidance to what transformations are needed, what validation rules to implement and what to test for during the design and development phase. This is another factor that should be considered when making the decision to perform data profiling or not.

The second decision that must be made at this phase is whether or not to stage data as part of data integration. Data staging refers to a location where data are temporarily stored before the data are either manipulated or loaded into a destination database. Staging uses storage space and, as a result, there is cost involved, so organizations must decide if they can afford the extra space required to stage data. The following factors are major considerations for staging:

- There is a time lag between when data are captured and when the data are loaded into their destination—if the data capture occurs at 7 p.m. and loading to the destination happens at midnight, then the captured data have to be stored somewhere in the meantime; in this case staging is a reasonable option.
- Restart on failure—if various parts of the ETL process are vulnerable to fail, recovery is easier if a staging database is available as the starting point.
- Auditing requirements—a staging area can provide a level of auditing support and assist with troubleshooting. For example, if it turns out a specific patient visit is missing from the target database, an analyst could examine the staging database to help identify why the visit was lost.
- Multiple source systems—if there is a need to perform complex transformations that involve multiple sources, it will be easier to stage the data and perform the transformations on the staged data.
- If there will be huge overhead on the source systems that could negatively impact performance, then staging is recommended.

If these factors are applicable to the organization, then it is recommended to stage data, even if the organization has to invest more in storage. This decision should be made upfront, as it will affect the design and development phase.

Data extraction is how the process will capture data from the source systems. Data cleansing ensures that inconsistent and invalid data are cleaned before the data are loaded into the target database. During this process, data quality problems, such as absent data values, inconsistent values, duplicate values and violation of business rules are detected and corrected. Data transformation is where business rules/logic is normally applied, data are changed into consistent formats and data are aggregated or summarized. Data loading is populating the target database with data that have been cleansed, transformed and ready for use. These ETL decisions will be dominated by the IT team; however, the business team should still be involved, especially when it comes to deciding what business rules are needed and when there are questions about source systems.

For users to employ analytical and presentation tools to access the data that have been integrated, the data need to be stored in a target database (destination). Where the data are stored is what is being referred to as data storage, shown in Figure 6-4. Normally, the target database is built to store massive amounts of historical data (especially in big organizations) at all levels of summarization and aggregation. Organizations have three main options for organizing and storing the data for their analytical and presentation tools to use. The organization can use any of these options in the BI solution. The team must decide which option to use as this will affect the design and development phase. The three main data storage types are operational data stores, data marts and data warehouses.

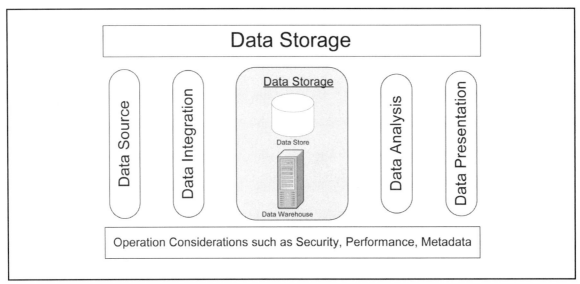

Figure 6-4: The Data Storage Component in Business Intelligence Architecture.

A data warehouse (DW) is a data storage system designed and built to gather historical data (integrated data) from different operational systems for the purpose of creating reports and performing analyses. In other words, DWs support business decisions by collecting, consolidating, and organizing data for reporting and analysis across the whole enterprise. Normally, a DW contains cross-functional data that support the informational needs of the organization as a whole. A DW holds multiple subject areas, detailed information and works to integrate all data sources.

Data mart is a data storage system used to support a single business function or process such as finance, quality and materials management/supply chain management. Data marts support business decisions by collecting, consolidating, and organizing data for reporting and analysis for a single business theme. There can be multiple data marts inside a single organization each one relevant to one business unit or functional area for which it was designed.

A data mart may hold more summarized data (although it could hold full detail). A data mart may derive data from a data warehouse or directly from transactional systems. Reasons for creating a data mart: It is normally cheaper to implement compared to a DW, the response time is faster compared to a DW and implementation is less complex than a full DW.

Operational data store (ODS) is a data storage system that functions like a DW; they both store integrated data from multiple source systems for data delivery purposes (analysis and data presentation). However, unlike a DW, the operational data store is not meant to handle historical data; it is meant to contain current or recent data. An ODS maintains data in near real-time, and the data are usually at the transaction level.

The option the organization uses will largely depend on what kind of problem the BI system is attempting to solve, as well as resource and time availability. If the organization has a need to take snapshots of current operational data that can be made available for real-time or near real-time decision-making purposes, then an operational data store will be a perfect choice. If the intent of the BI solution is to solve a business problem involving multiple functional areas or business units, then it will need to use a DW. However, if the purpose of the BI implementation is to solve a problem that relates to a single business unit/functional area, then a data mart will be a good choice.

In practice, most organizations typically use a combination of these data storage systems. The BI team can use an ODS to store raw data from multiple operational systems (staging the data), DW to store the transformed and integrated data for multiple business units/functional areas and data marts to store data for each business unit/functional area. For example, the organization has decided to develop a dashboard that will have finance metrics (to tell how the organization is performing financially); patient satisfaction metrics (to tell how well they are providing services to the patients); and quality metrics (to tell how well their quality initiatives are working).

Since the data needed to build the dashboard involve multiple functional areas, a DW has to be selected as the storage option to get a cross-functional view of the data. However, they can still use ODS and data marts. An ODS will be designed to integrate data from multiple sources in their unaltered form (raw data from finance systems, quality systems and external data from a patient satisfaction survey vendor).

Then, the data in the ODS will be cleansed, transformed and stored in the DW. At this point, the data can be used to create the dashboards. The BI team can still go further by building data marts for each of the functional areas: one for finance, another for quality and another for patient satisfaction. They can then create detail dashboards for each of these business units. This allows analysts to use the data marts to perform a detailed analysis if a metric has a red indicator and they want to find out why.

An organization's BI solution can start with few data marts before maturing to a full-blown DW. Ideally, the DW is the best place to start, which is then used to spin off and build data marts. It is, in relative terms, easier to create data marts from a DW than to create a DW from several unrelated data marts. As a rule of thumb, always start with a DW even if the project is dealing with a single business unit. This is because the organization is definitely going to have to see a cross-departmental view of data sooner or later. With that said, if the organization does not have adequate resources (budget or time), then it can start with a data mart. As stated earlier, organizations must decide which option their BI solutions will use at this stage, as this will affect how the target database is designed during the design and development phase.

Data analysis components, shown in Figure 6-5, are the technology components (software) that are used to present information to business users to enable them to analyze the data. Once the data are organized and ready, it is time to determine the analytical technologies and applications needed to access the data. These are tools and techniques used for managing, summarizing, querying and analyzing data. There are various BI applications that can be used for analytical technologies, including but not limited to:
- Spreadsheets.
- Online analytical processors (OLAP).
- Statistical or quantitative algorithms tools.
- Data mining tools.
- Text mining tools.
- Simulation tools.

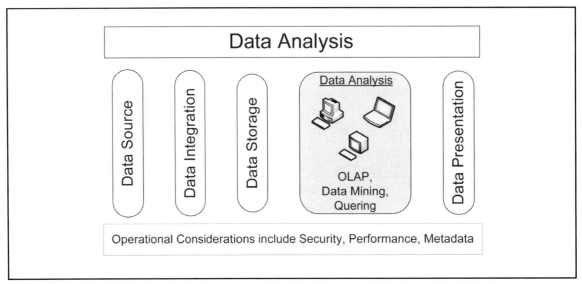

Figure 6-5: The Data Analysis Component in Business Intelligence Architecture.

Predictive Analytical Tools

The required decision relates to whether the organization should use a third-party application or create a custom solution in house. The "build vs. buy" decision hinges upon whether a packaged solution exists or whether the level of skill required to build one exists within the organization. Some tools can accommodate a variety of data types, while others are more limited.

Some tools work very well with slice-and-dice or drill-down abilities, and others may work well predicting patterns. In the past, different vendors had different products that had different capabilities—for instance one for *ad-hoc* queries, simulation and yet another for statistical analysis. Today, however, vendors have begun to offer BI suites, which normally have more integrated capabilities (offer several analytical technologies in one suite). Even with integrated BI tools, most large health systems will likely end up with more than one analytical vendor.

Presenting meaningful and visually appealing information in interesting ways is critical to helping analysts, managers and leaders make informed decisions. In addition to analytical technologies, there are data presentation tools such as reports, dashboards and performance scorecards. Data presentation, shown in Figure 6-6, allows the information to flow outward

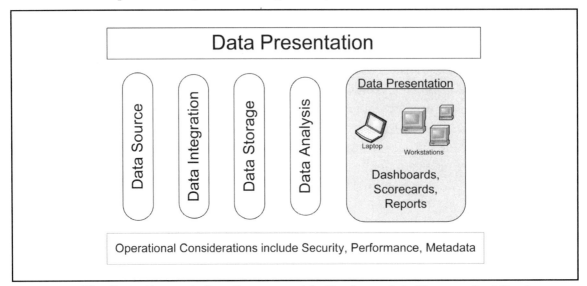

Figure 6-6: The Data Presentation Component in Business Intelligence Architecture.

from the target database (data storage) to all levels of an organization or to employees without the need to have IT programming experience.

For example, reports and dashboards can allow anyone in an organization who is authorized to have a read-only view of the data in a database (DW, data marts and operational data stores) with minimal to no training. Presentation tools also include portals (normally web-based) where users can access reports, scorecards etc. The "build vs. buy" question described in the data analysis section also applies here.

OPERATIONAL/LOGISTICAL CONSIDERATIONS

The operational/general considerations element of the BI architecture (shown in Figure 6-7) answers questions about how the organization creates, manages and maintains data and applications in the BI system. Organizations should detail what standard set of approved tools and technologies are to be used for the BI applications. Standards, policies and processes must also be defined and enforced across the entire organization with regards to security and governance. Policies and processes must also be developed to determine when and how data that are no longer needed will be saved, archived or retired. It is recommended not to wait until the implementation phase to perform this analyses, as it should be done before the design and development begins.

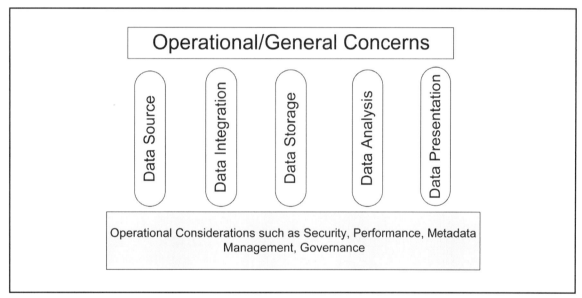

Figure 6-7: The Operational/Logistical Component in Business Intelligence Architecture.

SECURITY

Issues such as privacy and security, as well as the ability to audit the data, are of critical importance to BI. Both the Health Information Technology for Economic and Clinical Health Act (HITECH Act) and the Health Insurance Portability and Accountability Act (HIPAA) require organizations to protect the privacy of patient's information. Organizations should assess their controls and infrastructure against the security standards set forth by HITECH and HIPAA in order to avoid penalties. Defining and implementing an organizational security model for a wide variety of users with different roles and access privileges is always very challenging and difficult. However, organizations should take the time upfront to build their security model to satisfy internal security controls, as well as external requirements (legal and regulatory). Protecting the privacy of patients and providers from unauthorized access is very critical because lapses in privacy and security (for example, when a patient's medical information is accessed by an unauthorized user) can have dire consequences.

Organizations should make sure the data in the BI applications are correct by instituting audit controls (internal controls), especially when they are dealing with financial information. Executives can be found criminally negligent if they fail to establish procedures to document and demonstrate the validity of data used for business decisions.

For example, in the case of for-profit healthcare organizations, the Sarbanes-Oxley Act of 2002 requires executives to demonstrate that their decisions are based on trustworthy, meaningful, authoritative and accurate data. Organizations can establish their own internal audit departments to help them meet external audits. Internal auditors will help organizations evaluate financial and operational information and processes, as well as the IT used within those processes, to ensure that the organization is compliant with federal and state laws.

If the organization cannot afford to have internal auditors, it should still institute processes and policies around how to make changes to the data and how to test and validate data. For instance, using proper change management methodology can help control how changes are made to the data in the BI system. This will help organizations prove compliance with both federal and state laws and satisfy external audit requirements.

SUMMARY

In summary, a good business intelligence architecture document will include information on the following areas:

- As far as the data sources are concerned, the team will want to know what data are needed, whether they have the data, how much of the data are needed and whether the quality of the data in the source systems meet the standards for the reporting and analysis systems (needs). Some of the important criteria in the source selection process include data accuracy, data quality and the level of detail in the data.
- Data integration should contain information about how data are moved to a central storage and made available for queries and reports. It should also cover data cleansing, transformation and business rules.
- Data delivery should describe the functions available to the end users in the form of reports, queries and analytical tools. It includes how users will manipulate the information, drill through capabilities or perform advanced analysis.

Table 6-1: Chapter 6 Checklist—Design the Framework.

Item	Completed (Yes/No)
1. Understand all of the elements of BI architecture.	
2. Determine what data are needed for your BI solution and where they can be obtained.	
3. Determine the framework for evaluating and managing the data throughout the BI process.	
4. Develop a plan for extracting the data from the disparate systems and then integrating them into one usable source.	
5. Establish methodology to store your data.	
6. Determine what tools will be used for data analysis and how each tool will be applied.	
7. Evaluate and understand presentation tools.	
8. Develop/evaluate security, performance, metadata management and governance into the BI plan.	

CHAPTER 7

From Design and Build to Implementation and Validation

By Eric Adjei Boakye, MA

This chapter will explore the process of designing, developing, testing and deploying a business intelligence (BI) system. The assessments and high-level strategy and architecture documents that have been developed will point the way to the technical design, development, testing and deployment of the BI system. The technical design includes creating the source-to-target mapping document, performing data profiling, creating the dimensional data model, designing the data environment—extract, transform and load (ETL) process—and designing the user interface—the front-end tools. BI implementation also includes developing the BI system, testing the system, providing training to the end users and deploying the system—getting the product into the hands of the users.

BI DESIGN PHASE

During the design phase, it is critical to avoid trying to address all the issues at once. It's almost always beneficial to start with a limited solution that grows into a full BI implementation after several subsequent phases. Taking a limited approach ensures that any early failures are small and can be quickly overcome. It also gets something into the hands of end users, which will reduce the pressure on the BI committee to satisfy audience anticipation. However, it should be cautioned that providing end users with a snapshot of progression can also lead to scope creep. This is where a solid governance program can minimize scope creep in a more formal fashion.

Wherever possible, the BI solution should aim to solve a problem that is critical to be solved—one that's really important to the organization or individual department. In other words, the initial phase should be building solutions that add the most value to the organization. If possible, start with solutions where there are requirements available, sources can easily be identified and reports already exist that could be easily replaced for end users. Another important factor to consider is that even though the BI implementation strategy is built to solve an existing problem, think ahead. That means ensure the BI solutions provide the flexibility to adapt to changing environment and requirements (technology, legal and regulatory).

Note that the design and development stages can easily be dominated by IT (such as developers, data architects, data analysts, database administrators [DBAs] and data modelers). However, it is critical that close interaction occurs with the business stakeholders during the design phase. The end result must be a tool they can use. It is highly recommended that check points are built into the schedule where both teams can review the progress and/or output. It is always important to maintain buy-in from the business unit affected by the technical design.

SOURCE-TO-TARGET MAPPING DOCUMENT

Before beginning the design, it is recommended that a source-to-target (S2T) mapping document be created. S2T mapping, also called mapping document or data mapping document, is a living document that captures source data information, target database information, business and data transformation rules and validation rules, among others. It is normally completed in a spreadsheet, but can also be done in an automated mapping tool. An S2T mapping document is normally completed and used by ETL developers and testers, data analysts and modelers (data architects and designers) during the design and development phases.

The following provides more details on the contents of an S2T mapping document:
Source system definition specifies:
- Source system name.
- Source database name in the system specified earlier.
- Column name or field name in the database presented earlier.
- Data type and field length.

Target database definition specifies:
- Target database/table name.
- Business name of field (optional, but helpful to have).
- Database column/field name.
- Data type and field length.
- If nulls are allowed or not for each column.
- The primary and foreign keys for table.

Transform rules specify:
- Mapping transformations or business rules (e.g., if value is 999999999, populate field with 01/31/9999).
- How to standardized data (e.g., if source value='A', then XXX or if source value='B', then XYZ where XXX and XYZ are the standardized values).
- Default value, if nulls are not allowed and source field is null, what default value should be substituted to prevent the record from being rejected. Example default of '0' for fields that have integer and decimal data types.
- If the destination is a derived field, then the logic for derivation is described here.

Validation rules or data quality requirements specify:
- Referential integrity (e.g., key value must exist in key column of tables; do not populate if column is null).
- Valid values list—specifies a valid list of values for the target (e.g., if source data value is not equal to 'A, B or C', then do not populate with source data).

- The process can go further with validation by logging an error whenever one of these rules fails so it can be troubleshot later.

Audit rules specify:

- Checking to make sure all valid records in the source were loaded to the target table.

Test plan and scripts (Optional):

- Tests to be performed for the table could be annotated in the document as well; this is optional.

A comments/questions section is used during data mapping to record and address. Also, document other information about the source or target that has not already been documented e.g., what is the frequency of refreshing the target table (will the data be refreshed daily, weekly etc.); does this table have to be populated after another table finishes populating, etc.

Figure 7-1 shows an example of an S2T mapping document completed with some information (for demonstration only). From the example, information about the source system is documented—such as who to contact and the restrictions that data could not be extracted until 7p.m. each day. Information about the target table is also documented such as the frequency of refresh, process sequence (this table has to be populated before other tables) and load type.

Looking at the table, the first four columns represent the source—source system name, table name being used, column being used and their data types and length. Columns five through 12 represent the target table. The fifth, sixth, seventh and eighth columns show the target table name, business name of the field, the database name of field and the data types and length of the fields, respectively. The ninth column states whether the field can be null or not (e.g., medical record number [MRN] cannot be null, but gender can be). The tenth column is where the transformation needed for the table is documented.

In the example, MRN is being standardized to 10 digits to account for an increase in patients in the future. If the record contains an MRN that is fewer than 10 characters (e.g., 123456), during the ETL transaction will add preceding zeros to make it 10 characters

---

Source to Target Mapping Example

Source Information (Patient Registration):
IT Contact: John Smith (999) 123 - 4567
Business Contact: Jane Smith, (999) 123 - 9876
Notes: Data will only be available for extraction after 7 PM daily

Target Table Information
Frequency of Refresh: Daily
Process Sequence: This should be loaded before Visit table is populated
Dimension or Fact: Dimension
Load Type: Incremental
Forward population: Not Required
Historical Requirement: Need History
Notes: Any special note about the target goes here.

Source System Name	Source Table Name	Source Column Name	Source Table Data Type	Target Table Name	Business Name	Database Name	Target Table Data Type	Nullability	Transformation Rule	Validation Rule	Audit Rule	Notes/Comments/Questions
Patient Registration	Patients	PatientID	varchar (6)	PATIENT	Patient Medical Record Number	PT_MRN	varchar (10)	Not Null	Left pad source patientID with zeros to make them 10 characters and remove all special characters like dashes and spaces	Cannot be Null or blank. If Null do not load record but log an error.	Counts of Patients in source should match target	
Patient Registration	Patients	Gender	char(1)	PATIENT	Patient Gender	PT_GEND_CD	char (1)	Can be Null				
Patient Registration	Patients	Date of Birth	date	PATIENT	Patient Birth Date	PT_BRTH_DT	datetime	Not Null	If source is NULL, then convert to "01-01-9999"			

Figure 7-1: An Example of S2T Mapping Document with Some Information.

(0000123456). The validation rule column checks to make sure only valid or standardized data are loaded (e.g., checking to make sure there will always be an MRN with every patient). The audit column is checking to make sure every record in the source was loaded into the target table. The last column is not populated in the example, but it is where any question on a field or comment is further documented.

DATA PROFILING

Normally the first step in designing the BI system is data profiling. Data profiling involves a description of the relevant table structures, definitions of each field and data types of fields, as well as some statistical information such as record counts and range of values. Some organizations opt not to perform data profiling (Chapter 6), and therefore this section will not be relevant. The impact of not performing data profiling is the potential of having to deal with an increased number of quality issues when they arise during the development and testing stages.

Assuming data profiling will be performed, here is where it should occur at this stage of the process. When trying to understand the data (see Chapter 5), it is easy to gain an idea or a list of source systems and data needed to be profiled. At this stage, data profiling actually occurs rather than identifying what needs to be profiled. There are several things to look for while profiling, such as:

- Checking for data consistency or data quality problems.
- Checking for redundancy in the source systems (e.g., patient medical record number should be unique).
- Checking the source for enforced integrity constraints properly (e.g., patient cannot have a visit if the patient is not in the patient table).
- Checking for NULLs on key columns—for example, patient medical record numbers in the source should be profiled to make sure there are no nulls.

Document all applicable information about each source system in the S2T document during the profiling phase.

DIMENSIONAL DATA MODEL

After the source has been analyzed and profiled, the next step in designing and developing the target database is creating the data model. A dimensional data model is the set of rules and constraints for how information will be organized and stored in a database. In other words, a dimensional data model defines data elements and the relationships between them. Dimensional data models provide a method for making databases simple and understandable. The data models are normally created by the data architectures and designers, BI infrastructure architects, ETL developers, database administrators (DBAs) and data analysts. The BI committee and subject-matter experts (SMEs) are also involved when standardization issues arise or when questions arise about source data.

There are three main types of data models:

The conceptual data model includes high-level entities (tables) and the relationships among them. No attributes (data fields) and primary and foreign keys are specified in a conceptual model.

The logical data model describes the data in as much detail as possible in business terms, without regard to how they will be physically implemented in the database. A logical data model includes the entities and relationships among them, attributes/data fields for each entity specified, and primary and foreign keys for each entity specified.

The physical data model represents how the model will be built in the database. A physical database model includes all table structures in database terms—column name, column data type, column constraints (whether a column could be null or not), primary key, foreign key and relationships between the tables. It also includes other fields that are useful to the tables, such as the date field to show when a table is populated.

Figure 7-2 shows an example of a conceptual, logical and physical data model for the same data. As illustrated, the logical model is at a very high level, just listing the entities: provider and patient. The logical model is more detailed, specifying the data elements (e.g., provider name, revenue) and primary and foreign keys (data elements underlined such as ProvideID and patient number) for each entity. The physical model is similar to the logical model specifying data elements and keys, except they are in database names (e.g., COST, PROV_SPEC, PT_DOB). There are additional fields such as TBL_DT, that are not in the logical models.

It is very tempting to go straight to creating the physical data model, but organizations are advised to create all three data model groups, starting with conceptual to logical to physical. Conceptual data models are useful when explaining the project to sponsors and high-level executives and physicians. Details are not required when trying to show the concept of what an organization is trying to do. Logical data models are very helpful, especially if there will be an *ad-hoc* environment. It will help users understand the data more easily than using the physical data model. For the physical data model, be aware that it will be different for different database management systems (DBMS). For example, data type for a column may be different between two DBMS.

A data model is represented by what is called dimensions and facts (in IT terms). A dimension table is a business entity of the source system, and a fact table is a central table in a data model that contains numerical measures and keys relating facts to dimension tables. The dimensions need to be identified and what facts are needed as part of creating the data model.

Using Figure 7-2 as an example, patient and provider are dimension tables. There are several types of dimensions, which will not be discussed in this book, but three commonly used

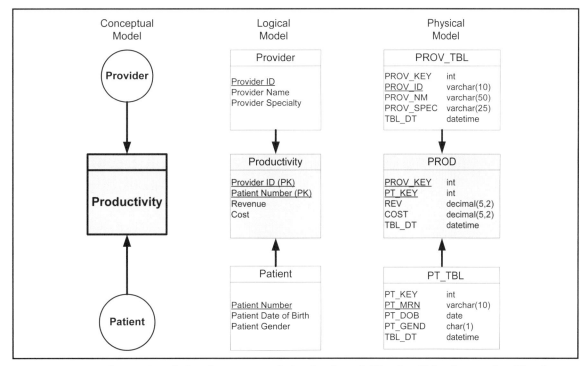

Figure 7-2: An Example of the Conceptual, Logical and Physical Versions of a Single Data Model.

dimensions are slow changing, rapidly changing and static dimensions. For slowly changing dimensions, attributes of a dimension undergo changes infrequently over time. It depends on the business requirement of whether a particular attribute history of changes should be preserved or not in the warehouse. For instance, a patient's address attribute may undergo changes over time but not frequently. There are three ways of logically dealing with a slowly changing attribute:

- Type I: The existing record is updated with change.
- Type II: History is preserved; a new record is added to the dimension and old record is marked as inactive.
- Type III: Preserves a version of the history by adding it to the dimension record in a different attribute.

For rapidly changing dimensions, attributes of a dimension change frequently. For example, an OrderNum attribute for an orders dimension may change very frequently since ordering happens frequently. Static dimensions are not extracted from the original data source, but are created as part of the BI implementation. An example is a date dimension.

As just noted, a fact table is a central table in a data model that contains numerical measures and keys relating facts to dimension tables. From Figure 7-2, productivity is an example of a fact table. A measure is a numeric attribute that would typically be derived from transactions; examples are revenue and costs in the productivity fact table. Fact measures are normally additive in nature but are not a requirement for fact tables to have numeric measures; they could be semi-additive or non-additive.

The functional requirements and existing reports will help with identifying the dimensions and facts. In identifying dimensions, look for attributes that are business descriptors that users believe are important to understanding the measures in the fact table. The words "by," "for," "of" and "in" often flag a dimension.

For example, the requirement or question "How many patients does a physician see in a day, week, and month?" represents the use of three dimensions (patients, provider and date) to specify the information to be summarized. In identifying measures, look for the measurable results of a business event and keywords, such as "how." For example, from the question "How many patients does a physician see in a day, week and month?" patient counts as a measure. There are basically two types of structures that are popularly used when designing the physical data modeling; they are Star Schema and Snow Flake Schema. These will not be explained in detail; however there are several theories that explain when to use one or the other. Organizations should research these further, if needed.

DESIGNING THE DATA ENVIRONMENT (BACK-END)

One of the most important steps in the BI implementation is building the target data environment that deals with how the data need to be moved from the various source systems and stored into a target database. The state of the data sources will have an effect on how the ETL process harvests the data, cleanses them and transforms them into a single format that the front-end systems can use. Users' needs/requirements will also influence the design of the data environment, as well as the ETL technology being used.

Figure 7-3 shows how a typical back-end in a BI environment will look. It assumes the following is being used: operational data stores (ODS) for staging, data warehouse (DW) to store integrated data and data marts to store data for specific functional areas, such as patient care and supply chain. Note that if a decision is made to use only data marts or a DW at the conceptual architecture stage, the same principle still applies. For instance, the diagram

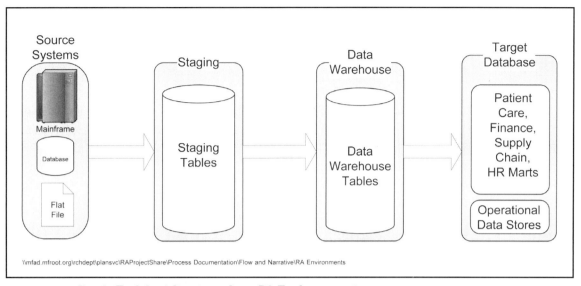

Figure 7-3: Back-End Architecture in a BI Environment.

could look like source systems ➔ staging ➔ data marts or source systems ➔ staging ➔ data warehouse or staging may be omitted all together. Designing the back-end data environment involves designing staging tables and the ETL.

ETL DESIGN

Once the data have been profiled and the data models have been designed, it is time to design the ETL process. ETL processes are the steps that the system takes to move information from source data systems to the target databases. This is another important step (if not the most important) in making the BI environment function successfully. If the data get loaded into the target database in an unrecognized format or if the values are inaccurate, the data become worthless to users. Extracting and loading are simply moving the data; however the transformation is where the complexity lies. The transformation part is what makes the data usable—where a single, standardized, useful data to be used by the BI front-end applications is created.

Figure 7-4 shows a simplified rendition of what an ETL process might do. In the example, patients' medical record numbers (MRN) in both systems (Source 1 and Source 2) do not have a standard format (some have dashes, whiles others do not, some have preceding zeros while

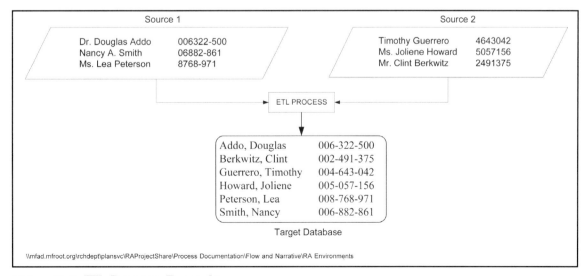

Figure 7-4: ETL Process Example.

others do not among other inconsistencies). In order to combine the lists into one, the data have to be cleansed, standardized and stored as one common format. In this case, the names were stored as "Last Name, First Name" and the MRNs were saved as a nine-digit number with zero preceding each number to make it nine digits. Also, dashes are added in a consistent format.

There are several theories on how to design the ETL processes (that is, how and when to extract data, how data are loaded, among others). Detailed explanations of each of the steps in ETL process are described next.

ETL—Data Extraction

No matter what tools are being used, consider answering these main questions during the design phase of the data extraction step:

- What data extract model should be used? Should a Push Model be used—in which the source system initiates the data extraction process, or a Pull Model—in which the staging database initiates the data extraction process, or a Hybrid Model—in which the source system extracts data to keep in an intermediate store from which the staging system picks it up at regular intervals?
- How frequently will data be extracted? Real-time extraction or at a set time extraction?
- Will only changed records be captured in the source from the last capture, or will all records be captured and replace the destination data each time?
- How are failures during data extraction handled—if for some reason extraction failed, what is the resolution process?

Note that there may be other questions, but these are the most common questions that must be considered/answered. Most choices will depend on functional requirements and security access to source systems.

Data Staging

Data extracted, transformed and loaded from the source to destination may require temporary staging for various reasons such as addressing failures, reducing load on the source system, data cleansing and auditing purposes, etc. Data staging is creating tables to store data from the source systems, so work will be performed on the data at a later time or to store transformed data before the data are loaded into the target database at a later time. Whether or not data are staged as part of the ETL process is a common design decision that will need to be made (during the conceptual architecture process). If the organization decides not to have staging, then this section is not relevant. If on the other hand staging is required, decisions are required on how to stage the data. There are various types of staging that can be used either independently or combined. These are the most commonly used data staging types:

- Multiple sources staging: Used when the data arriving from different source systems has to be temporarily stored in a staging location before the transformation and loading processes take place.
- Staggered staging: Used to create multiple staging databases for different stages of the ETL process. This approach is appropriate if the transformation and loading processes are very expensive to repeat and are also vulnerable to failure, since it allows multiple levels of restart capability, without having to restart the whole process.
- Persisted staging: Used to allow an archive copy of the staging database to be created routinely. This allows auditing of the extract and transformation processes for more than the current cycle.

- Chunked accumulated staging: Used when there is a need to extract or load huge volume of data, but you want to spread the extract and/or load process across a period of time.

ETL—Data Transformation

Data transformation is the key process in the ETL cycle. Transformation is the phase in which the raw data from the source systems (staging tables) is transformed into a more meaningful form for meeting business analysis and objectives. The first step is to decide whether a transformation is needed. Some data will be pulled straight from the source without any modification. The following factors are major reasons for creating transformations:

- Data quality problems: If data extracted from source systems have data quality issues such as repeated primary key values (unique identifiers), incorrect date formats, inaccurate data and data values that are inconsistent and redundant between multiple tables, then the data have to be transformed.
- Business rules: If there are business rules, then it should be handled as part of the transformation process.
- Heterogeneous data stores: If the data is extracted from heterogeneous data stores, the source systems may have different data types, different column names, different column orders and different data formats. These inconsistencies can be resolved (standardized) during the transformation process.
- Custom calculations: If custom calculations have to be performed for some fields or columns, they are done during the transform stage.
- Summarization: If the source extracted data has to be summarized or aggregated to a predetermined level, then this is done as part of the transformation process.
- Conversion: If values from the source have to be changed to make them easier for end users to understand in a report or to fit to the schema of target, e.g., if the incoming data have first name and last name as one column (first name + last name), but the target has this column as two different columns, then the incoming data will be split into two to fit the target schema.
- Count check: If a check is required to ensure the records are extracted as expected, that will happen during the transformation phase.

Once the need for transformation is determined, the next question is where to perform the transformation. There are four places where transformations are normally carried out: as part of the extraction process; as a separate layer; as part of the loading process; and in memory. Factors, such as the complexity of the transformations and hardware and software processing speeds, will contribute to the chosen option. It should be noted both business and IT managers must expend significant effort in order to transform data into usable information. While there are some automated tools on the market that can ease this process, considerable manual effort is still required.

ETL—Data Loading

Data loading is the process of loading processed data to the target database. The first time the BI system is deployed to production, a historical load will be required. Historical loads typically happen only once; unless a major redesign occurs in which the data need to be loaded again. Data are normally loaded to the time period decided during the conceptual framework design. This normally takes a long period of time to load, especially if a larger BI solution is needed. After historical loads, two options should be considered:

1. Will an incremental load (changed data only) or trunk and reload (empty table and populate again) be used?

2. What is the periodicity of loading the tables—daily, monthly, etc.?

Also consider the process for collecting and troubleshooting the failed records that will occur and how to create appropriate indexes on target tables to make queries run faster.

DESIGNING THE FRONT-END TOOLS ENVIRONMENT (FRONT-END)

Once the back-end design is complete (i.e., the ETL process ensures the source data flow into the target environment), how the users will access the stored data will need to be designed. In most BI environments, the front-end includes, but is not limited to, reporting, dashboards, querying (*ad-hoc*) and other custom analysis packages. Figure 7-5 shows what a typical front-end looks like in a BI system. The selected front-end BI tools should have a portal (normally a browser-based interface) that end users can use.

There is a new object between the target table and presentation tools called semantic layer in Figure 7-5 that has not yet been mentioned. Organizations may choose to create a semantic layer between the database and reporting environments instead of accessing the database tables directly. A semantic layer is a business representation of data that helps end users access data autonomously using common business terms instead of database names (which are normally cryptic). The semantic layer relieves business users from underlying data complexity, while ensuring the business is accessing the correct data and using terminology with which they are familiar. By using common business terms, rather than database language, to access, manipulate, and organize information, the complexity of business data is simplified. A semantic layer normally mirrors the logical model in terms of the business names used. Reports, online analytical processors (OLAP), and dashboards can all use the semantic layer and not the database name. It is also helpful to developers; instead of using the database names and translating them to business terms on reports, they just use the names in the semantic layer.

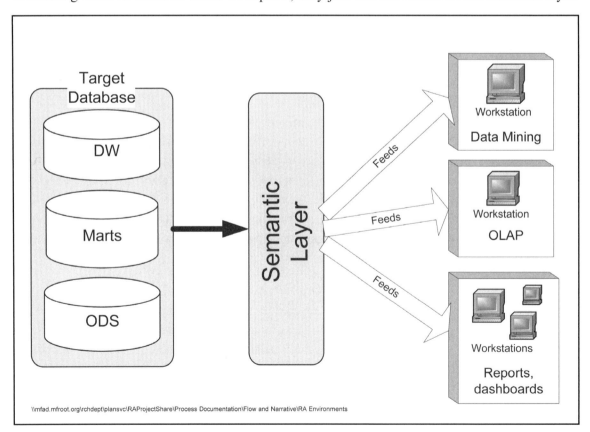

Figure 7-5: Front-End Architecture in the BI Environment.

Calculated values could also be added to the semantic layer that are not in the database. A typical example is age (where an employee's date of birth and today's date to get their age may be used).

An example of how data will look in the database versus the semantic layer is illustrated in Figure 7-6. As the example shows, end users and developers will have an easier time understanding what is displayed in the semantic layer (Provider Credential) than target table (PROV_CRED). Some BI tools come with a semantic layer designer. If your organization does not have a semantic layer designer, the front end can still go against the target tables directly.

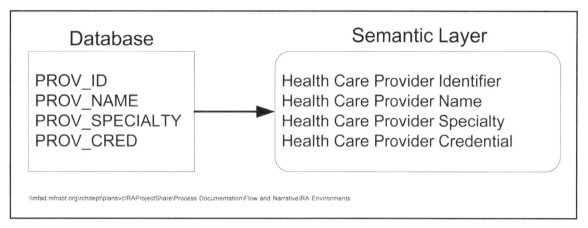

Figure 7-6: Semantic Layer Example.

REPORTS

For any BI solution, the core of the front end is the reporting environment, which includes dashboards as the vehicle to show results. The main aim is to make sure the reports are user-friendly and provide the information users need in a timely fashion. The development team will use the functional requirements gathered by the business analysts to design standard, canned and *ad-hoc* reports for users.

In the design phase for reports, it is advisable to create templates that all reports will use to ensure standardization and consistent appearance throughout the organization. A template will normally include report number, reference source (help desk contact information), organization's logo and legal disclaimers. There may also be standard features that every report could use, such as totals, date, font type and size for headings/main title and main fields, number formatting for currency, negative numbers and justification for columns. In all likelihood, the organization currently produces reports (may be different across functional areas) that can be leveraged at a starting point and standardized across the organization. Chapter 10 will explain in detail how to develop a reporting strategy that will have most of this information.

Ad Hoc

There is likely going to be the need to go beyond simple standard reports for the BI solution. One main request is normally an *ad-hoc* reporting environment. *Ad-hoc* reports (like OLAP) allow for customized reporting. The logical data model should help the end users understand the data, since the data will have the business names and will also show how tables are related. There are several *ad-hoc* tools on the market, and the chosen product will have an effect on how the *ad-hoc* reporting environment is designed. For example, some allow users to access data at a detailed level, whereas others allow users to access data at a summarized (aggregated) level. Whichever *ad-hoc* tool is chosen, make sure the design will return accurate data to the users in a timely fashion. Some BI tools come with both reporting, as well as *ad-hoc* querying tools.

OTHER ANALYTICAL TOOLS

Other analytical tools include data mining, statistical analysis, text mining and simulation. In terms of the design, the approach should be the same as the one used for *ad-hoc* tools. Even though these tools tend to be more complex than *ad-hoc* tools, they almost do the same thing—allow users to analyze data beyond using standard reports. Some BI tools may not be included, so there is likely a need to buy one or more. Whatever analytical tools the organization decides to use, two key features will be the backbone of the design, both the *ad-hoc* and other analytical tools.

DEVELOPMENT AND TESTING

The development phase encompasses creating a work plan, developing the component, performing a walk-through review and testing the BI applications. It is essential that a testing strategy be developed in advance for the BI application. This is because mistakes caught early are easier and quicker to fix than when the system is in production. In addition, it is beneficial if the implementation team finds the errors in advance of the users to enhance confidence in the system. Remember that users will always compare the new tools to what they already have and know. If they are not satisfied, they will return to the old inconsistent way of doing things. Testing includes making sure the ETL process loads the data correctly, as well as ensuring that the presentation tools are displaying the data correctly. These are the main tests that are normally performed:

- Unit testing: Conducted by developers, for example, to determine if the ETL code loaded the target table correctly or if the report is scheduled correctly.
- Integration testing: Tests for the combined parts of an application to determine if they function together correctly (e.g., if the ETL tool is communicating with the source systems correctly.
- Functional testing: Tests the functional requirements of an application and normally performed by a Quality Assurance (QA) team (testers). (Does the report conform to the report standards the organization has developed?)
- Performance testing: Tests to see whether the applications meet performance requirements. (e.g., does the ETL extract, transform and load data in an agreed time or does a report return data in a specified time limit?)
- Security testing: Determines how well the system protects against unauthorized internal or external access and also tests to ensure authorized security groups allow access to functionality documented in the specifications.
- System testing: Involves performing a complete application test that mimics real-world use (from start to finish). For example, from data extraction to testing a report; normally performed just prior to deployment.
- Usability testing: Determines how user-friendly the application is. It depends on the end user or customer (ideally, people who have not seen the system before). Usability testing can include user interviews, surveys, video recording of user sessions and other techniques. Usability testing is carried out very early in the development phase.
- User acceptance testing: Testing to see if system meets customer-specified requirements. Normally performed by end users (who are also frequently referred to as SMEs). Until

users sign off on the tools, do not deploy; doing so will run the risk of the users not using the application.

Testing will most likely be divided into two distinct types: back-end testing and front-end testing.

Back-End Testing

ETL testing is one of the most critical QA efforts of the entire testing activities, as mistakes with the ETL will affect the whole BI system. The ETL is tested to ensure the validation rules, transformation rules and summarizations, etc., are working correctly. Unlike front-end testing, end users are normally not involved with ETL testing—mostly carried out by a technical team but still rely on SMEs when questions arise with business rules and validation rules. Testing performed includes unit, integration and performance.

Front-End Testing

The front-end testing follows ETL testing when data are ready to be used. Front-end testing checks that queries are populating reports as expected, the calculations (data) on the report are accurate, and the analysis tools are being fed the correct data. Testing should also include functionality (e.g., do the reports appear correct, and do they match what the users requested?) Functionality tests are appropriate when conducting usability tests and also the user acceptance tests. Security tests should also occur during this time to make sure users are seeing only what they are authorized to see. Take caution to maintain close control over the original requirements and expectations during user testing. During this phase, many organizations may experience scope creep. It is common for users to change their minds about the requirements once they actually see it. A method to reduce this is to conduct routine check points with the users, so they are aware of the build throughout the process.

Thoroughly document the testing strategy and results. Evaluate all requirements of the business system, and develop test plans and scripts according to needs. Have the QA team (testers) create a test plan and test cases (for each of the tests previously described) while developers are building the system. Document the outcome of every test, and record results for future reference and audit purposes. There are tools on the market that allow testers to save test scripts, run the tests, save results and create defects if tests failed among others. They are very helpful as the BI team can comply with internal and external security controls (such as audits, which could prove to auditors how testing with test scripts, test results, etc., is conducted).

DEPLOYMENT

When the new BI application is ready for use (development phase is complete), it must be deployed to a production environment. The deployment phase includes preparations for implementation, conducting a system test, preparing the operational environment for a new application, creating the user documentation, training the end users, and sun setting (decommissioning) old legacy systems. It requires all stakeholders to prepare the system for assembly and transfer to the end users.

TRAINING

A training strategy deserves as much attention as other parts of the design, as training can make or break successful deployment of the BI tool. Develop a comprehensive training strategy and program, including developing training materials, running a pilot, maintaining the documentation and ensuring thorough distribution of materials. Some factors to consider with regards to training include:

- Who will conduct the training?
- What approach will be used? Train all individuals or use a train-the-trainer approach?
- What training vehicles will be used? Classroom, computer-based training, workshops?
- What type of materials will be developed? Will the materials be customized for each user group?
- Will there be ongoing education as the system evolves?

Start developing the training strategy early in the design and development phase. Involve and leverage the organization's training department if available. The BI solution does not end with deployment; the next step is the post-implementation/maintenance phase, such as questioning whether the BI system is meeting the users' needs, if the users are using the BI tools, etc.

SUMMARY

Implementing a BI solution involves a robust design phase that includes creating the S2T mapping document, performing data profiling, creating the dimensional data model and designing the ETL process and the presentation tools (reports, dashboards, scorecards and *ad-hoc*). It also includes developing the BI system, testing the system, providing training to the end users, getting the tools into the hands of the users and retiring the old systems. A successful BI implementation will be able to quickly provide users with reliable, accurate information and help them make decisions of widely varying complexity.

Table 7-1: Chapter 7 Checklist—From Design and Build to Implementation and Validation

Item	Completed (Yes/No)
1. Determine appropriate scope for the first BI release.	
2. Create source-to-target mapping document.	
3. Possess working knowledge of data profiling.	
4. Complete data profiling process.	
5. Develop working design for your target database.	
6. Develop and document the ETL process.	
7. Document issues that can plague ETL and evaluate the risk.	
8. Create and approve the front-end design.	
9. Develop the testing plan.	
10. Create the training strategy.	

CHAPTER **8**

Post-Implementation

By Michael Whitecar, MIS, LCDR (ret.), MSC, USN

"On Jan. 1, 2011, the oldest baby boomers turned 65. Every day for the next 19 years, about 10,000 more will cross that threshold."[1] A hypothetical scenario to address this surprising information may be where the executive management team of a large healthcare facility will choose to dedicate 5 percent of emergency room services to seniors this year and increase it by 5 percent over the next five years. Let's say their mission is to serve their local community by providing the best healthcare for an aging population. Monthly safety metrics would begin to report the number of falls, the percentage of patients that were seniors serviced in the emergency room and time to triage. The emergency room has been helping 20 percent of seniors, which was only 5 percent five years ago. Many will find a slight change in work efforts as the New Year begins turning their focus on services that provide care for the elderly in their emergency.

This scenario reflects a perfect day when using a fully functional business intelligence (BI) infrastructure. This is the type of goal a BI implementation is trying to achieve. Not only are results produced whereby sound business decisions are made, but also a successful BI implementation is the outcome. This does not happen overnight, and it does not happen through the implementation itself. Performing post-implementation tasks with continuous monitoring produces results like these.

This chapter will review the scenario the quote describes, and working our way backwards, ensure that the project answered the questions and completed all the necessary steps prior to executing the BI plan. Additionally, we will revisit the models presented in Chapter 4 with the expectation that the team has addressed the findings, whether through organizational change or simple modifications to processes and resources. Following this assessment of the environment, we will examine some important tasks to ensure the BI implementation is sustainable. Sustainability means the presence of the BI results will be continuous, supporting current and future measurable requirements.

A few of these post-implementation tasks include a feedback loop, implementing by a governance structure, establishing policies, procedures and standards, and ensuring the resources designated are available.

Table 8-1 shows the quantitative details the Detroit team requires for the BI project to reach its expected targets.

Table 8-1: Requirements Necessary for the Detroit Team to Meet Expected Targets for BI Project.

Quantifiable Metrics (Anticipated Benefits)	Baseline (Current State)	Target (Future State)
Number of incidents reported will increase, thereby providing more information; management has to nimbly and quickly make process changes.	96 total incidents on average are reported each day on the current paper process.	123 incidents per day. Expect an increase of 33%-50% when moving from a home-grown system.
Increase number of near-miss incidents reported, so risk management activities can focus on prevention.	The 40% of current data that constitutes severity are either 'no severity score' (18%), 'event has the capacity to cause error '(18%) or 'event did not reach patient' (5%).	Increase 5% per day. Which is (96 X 0.5) 5 additional 'near misses' per day reported.
Reduction in time entering events into the system, so clinical staff spends more time on patient care.	Five to 30 minutes is the current timespan experienced using paper.	Decrease to 2 minutes. This results in labor redeployment of 12 minutes per incident. This will result in 19.2 hours per day redeployment.
Decrease number of days to close the incident/grievance investigation.	Largest hospital system takes one week to close an incident.	Decrease by one day. Due to sending incident reports immediately to the incident floor manager.
Decrease the number of touch points to close an incident investigation while decreasing the alarm delivery time.	Current process forces managers to review all incidents during regular business hours (8 a.m. - 5 p.m. Monday-Friday) and 'assign by e-mail' next-steps to hospital staff.	Decrease by one step. Remove 'assign next steps via e-mail' as system business rules will process work assignments. Remove time lag as system immediately sends notification to staff when incident reported.

REVISITING THE BEGINNING

The idea of developing a BI infrastructure addressed the need to assess the environment. Thus, a complete asset inventory was required. The inventory of assets included not only IT resources but also governance, existing policies, culture, people and most critical, business processes.

Recall that the inventory dictates how the organization is going to use the new information. It started with some basic questions to stimulate new thought about the initiative: What impact will the new information have on the original owners of the data? If there is change in the data, what are the communication processes in place to ensure the calculation will either be or not be affected by the change? What is the process to share the results? If someone has a question about the results, who do they contact? Who is going to be in charge of keeping track of the requests? Many of the answers lie in establishing a feedback loop.

Feedback Loop

A feedback mechanism is essential so the responsible presenter or representative can ensure they are retrieving, calculating and displaying the metrics correctly. If the presenter does not have an answer, he or she must know where to turn for assistance. This way the stakeholders will gain a better understanding of the organization, its processes and the positions required to have the knowledge to make the metrics and calculations work.

Using the Results from the 360-Degree Organizational Look

In Chapter 4, a framework was presented for improving the access, flow and value of organizational information. The outcome of the framework provided an in-depth view by looking at how information is created, stored, shared, presented and analyzed. From this informational view, the BI strategy and execution plan was developed. It is this strategy and plan that needs to be followed during the BI implementation and compared with the post-live environment.

Starting with processes, use the flow charts created in Chapter 4 and label accordingly; review each to determine if attention is needed for high-risk steps. Many business processes are required to support the BI implementation either directly or indirectly. What does the list of processes look like? Did the team determine that some processes are effective as was their original intent? Did they have to tailor or delete any processes? Most importantly, did they have to create new processes? Tracing the processes through the diagrams can assist with this post-evaluation.

Further, recall that each system diagram contained boxes with the actual work step—or action. Processes were created to provide clarity to anyone performing or managing the work. Each process was further dissected into smaller sub-processes and expanded to include a system diagram, findings, accountable positions, resource requirements and system standards. Knowing when each sub-process needs to be performed is a key element to obtain the desired results. Each process required a certain level of resources. Have they been checked? Are the processes identified by position, not by person? Who is accountable for the system as a whole, and who will be accountable for each of the sub-processes? The positions that should have been identified are those with overall accountability, those that will participate, in-house or contractual staff and the technical staff. Is there a commitment from all of these stakeholders in order to sustain the accomplishments?

Revisit the Cultural Assessment

How is executive management reacting to their first bit of new information? Have any changes been noticed within the board as far as attitude, willingness to work together or excitement about their new awareness? As discussed earlier, culture is hard to change. Is there a need to implement a change management program? Does the team have access to a change manager who is assisting with any needed changes? From a post-implementation view, culture may react differently than expected. Culture is one of those areas that will need to be continuously monitored, even long after the implementation. There may be a need to modify the BI strategy to either adopt more to the culture or support the change.

What Do Stakeholders Think?

Since organizational information will be valued differently among various stakeholders, have the differences been identified? Are the expected BI results aligned with the organization's strategic goals and objectives? Are the initial key performance indicators (KPIs) meeting their targets? Do employees value their new transactional data, and does the data help them perform their duties and make better decisions in serving their customers?

Responsibilities

The case study in Chapter 13 presents a step-by-step way to run a project, initiative or collaboration, ensuring each role represents its perspective and completes its responsibilities.

Responsibility is an influential aspect of governance. Establishing clearly defined roles and responsibilities helps ensure data continuity and reliability. Responsibility provides clear ownership of tasks so individuals have a solid understanding of the scope of the metrics they are assigned and how to create, summarize, build and present the metric, resulting in a trustful relationship with the data and the corporate members involved.

Establishing Policies, Procedures and Standards

Corporate scorecards can provide key BI activity measures to ensure business activities are compliant with corporate policies. The presentation of the dashboard, the frequency of reviewing the KPIs, and the buy-in from the executive leadership team to assign responsibilities to each of them, requires policy and process. For example, policy is important because even though company participants may agree, the goals should be presented monthly, not everyone may make their milestones on time. Additionally, it is crucial the stakeholders agree on how the goals are going to be presented.

Procedures guarantee a consistent process for metric computation. Procedures should be well-documented to allow for repeatability and consistency. Be cautioned that although procedures support structure, there also needs to be methods to allow individuals to try various paths or ways of doing things differently. In other words, carefully allow responsible individuals to color outside of the lines if it adds additional value to the overall results. Decisions to consider when finalizing metrics policy and procedures:

- Unit of measure
- Frequency of measurement
- Quantitative target
- Frequency of reporting
- Data sources
- Accountable ownership
- Accountable provider
- The definition for each metric with limits
- Realistic and challenged assumptions
- Risk assessment
- Estimated cost of measurement

Ironically, post-metrics may be used to measure the development of the metrics expected from the BI initiative. To ensure everyone complies with policy and procedures, utilize a standard toolkit to measure the knowledge of the responsible individual, to provide the organization with a better understanding of the data sources, corporate processes and to offer insight into stakeholder expectations.

Standards provide controls over policies, decision-making algorithms and presentation style of information. For example, consider the development of a standard form or "toolkit" for consistency of the look and feel of the scorecard. A toolkit can generate standards for those who design processes for the creation of metrics.

Through universal adoption of a standard form for dashboard creation, everyone in the organization speaks a common language; they understand information sources, and they agree on the algorithm used to compute the metrics for the dashboard. As an example of standards, see Table 8-2.

Table 8-2: A Standard Form for Dashboard Creation.

Item	Standard Conversion
Fields	Data entry fields are highlighted in yellow and underlined and are the only editable cells in the scorecard. Be sure to include zeros where the correct answer is in numeric fields, rather than leaving those fields blank.
Navigating the Scorecard	• Use the tab key to move between data-entry fields. • Move the mouse over red corner triangles to view on-screen help. • Create a carriage return within any text box by selecting Alt-Enter.
Date Formats	Dates will be displayed in the DD-MMM-YY format (for example, 15-Oct-05), irrespective of how they are entered.
Currency	Cells that require currency input are formatted in thousands ($000s). For example, to input $250,200, enter 250.2 into the cell. Currency values are expressed in U.S. dollars.
File Naming Convention	Save the project scorecard using the following format: <#_project name_YYYY-MM.xls>, where the month reflects the data included within the scorecard, not the month during which the scorecard was prepared (if those months are different). For example: 1234-Customer Info System-2012-10.xls.
Worksheet Scoring	Scores are based on the absolute value of the data. Any variances (+/-) could indicate successful completion may be jeopardized; use the scorecard to spur conversations. Blank entries that are part of a section's score are scored at the highest risk value.

GOVERNANCE STRUCTURE

Governance addresses the need for a process or set of processes to ensure the rules, policies, standards and procedures are followed. Governance should be charged with providing oversight to the BI project to see the initiative is accomplished in a manner that satisfies principles and policies to successfully sustain the environment. It is recommended the governance structure exhibit the following three key characteristics:

- Simplicity. Mechanisms unambiguously define the responsibility or objective for a specific person or group.
- Transparency. Effective mechanisms rely on formal processes. How the mechanism works is clear to those who are affected by or want to challenge a governance decision.
- Appropriateness. Mechanisms engage individuals in the best position to make given decisions.

Governance is about specifying the decision rights and accountability framework to encourage desirable behavior in the use of the BI system. Good governance harmonizes decisions about the management and use of the new tools with desired behaviors and business objectives. The behavioral side of governance defines the formal and informal relationships and assigns decision rights to specific individuals or groups. The normative side defines mechanisms formalizing the relationships and providing rules and operating procedures to ensure objectives are met. Therefore, the approach to implementing effective governance will begin with addressing three simple questions:

- What decisions must be made to ensure effective management and use of the BI infrastructure?
- Who should make these decisions?
- How will these decisions be made and monitored?

The governance structure specifies the distribution of rights and responsibilities among different participants on a project or initiative. This may include project members such as the executive board, managers, clinicians and other stakeholders. It should spell out the rules and procedures for making project decisions. By doing this, it also provides the structure through which the project objectives are set and the means of attaining those objectives and monitoring performance. Why?

- To *define* the major BI infrastructure required.
- To *determine* organizational change.
- To *organize* the BI functions to build and leverage these services.
- To *develop* metrics, sharing, and BI service reusability.
- To *ensure* success is measured and full benefit is achieved.

Increasing emphasis on cross-functional business processes will lead BI initiation to focus on process governance mechanisms. The marriage of process and IT is natural because cross-functional business processes depend on information flows that cross organizational boundaries and are supported by the BI infrastructure. During the preliminary work, the team needs to address the following key questions:

- What is the core governing business processes required by the BI infrastructure? How are they related?
- What information drives these core processes? How must the data be integrated?
- What technical capabilities should be standardized enterprise-wide to support IT efficiencies and facilitate process standardization and integration?
- What activities must be standardized enterprise-wide to support data integration?
- What technology choices will guide the organization's approach to effective governance?

Figure 8-1 represents a "system of governance process" showing the sequence of events and how they relate to each other.

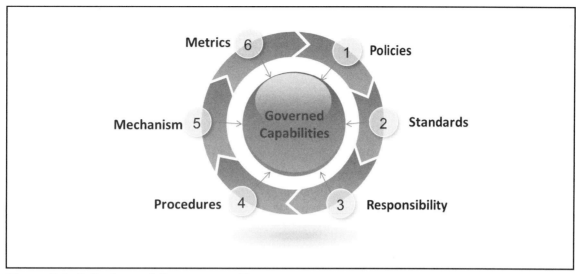

Figure 8-1: A System of Governance Process.

Each entity in the system diagram is actually a work step—or action. When each action is identified in a sequence, sub-processes are created that make the process clear and unmistakable to anyone who will perform or manage the work.

An ultimate goal of this approach is to ensure the systems and processes that support each of the program governance boards operate predictably, reliably and independently from individual personalities and preferences. Therefore, it is recommended the assignment of accountability by position, not by person. This position is accountable for the system as a whole and for each of the benchmarks. Knowing when each benchmark needs to be performed is a key element of getting the desired results. Therefore, decide to establish appropriate timing for the steps and for the system as a whole.

Every system requires these resources: staffing, work space, facilities, equipment, supplies and information. List the specific resources and quantities of each resource required to operate the system. Identify the resources to develop descriptions of the types of skills needed for experienced facilitators (designated key personnel who will serve in this capacity). Lastly, health IT content expertise can enable meaningful discussion during each of the individual governance board processes.

Next, set the standards for performance of the system and behavior of the staff operating the system. Standards are most easily stated in terms of quantity, quality and behavior. Assure the results needed from the system are being accomplished through quantification, which will provide an objective view. This step will help develop an evaluation method to assess the extent to which the governance assistance provided was helpful.

Communication is critical for managers in the governance process. A good approach to communication throughout the organization is to use mechanisms intended to "spread the word" about the BI governance decisions and processes and related desirable behaviors. Experience has shown that effective communication results in stronger outcomes.

Engage, engage, engage is a significant requirement to ensure effective communication. Top governance performers will achieve a higher percentage of senior management knowledge about governance simply by engaging more often and more effectively. The more senior managers are directly involved in the BI governance, the better the governance performance.

Rarely do all affected managers enthusiastically embrace governance decisions. When managers engage in behaviors that undermine the BI process, disregard investment guidelines, duplicate shared infrastructure or ignore project-tracking standards; they are demonstrating lack of awareness of governance decisions or an unwillingness to adopt approved practices. Working with managers who stray from desirable behaviors is a necessary part of generating the potential value of governance processes.

IMPLEMENTING DASHBOARD REVIEW PROCESSES

Effective governance ensures the BI initiatives are managed from an organizational perspective, and they contribute to the mission, strategic goals and objectives. The BI governance model should include adequate controls to ensure thorough accountability and effective monitoring of the dashboard lifecycle. The controls should provide structured processes and feedback loops to ensure all metrics are configured and created through appropriate identification of information sources and locations. This may often be performed by the BI committee or through the establishment of Dashboard Review Board (DRB). It really depends on the size and complexity of the BI requirements.

Review boards should be established to conduct pre-implementation, implementation and post-implementation reviews of the development and on-going operations of metrics. Some suggested goals of a review board or BI committee include:

- First and foremost, catch errors in the project early, and thereby reduce the cost and risk of changes required later in the lifecycle. This, in turn, means the overall project time is shortened, and the business gets the bottom-line benefit of the architecture development faster.
- Ensure the application of best practices to dashboard implementation and operations.
- Provide an overview of the compliance of architecture to enterprise standards.
- Identify where the standards themselves may require modification.
- Document strategies for collaboration, resource sharing and other synergies across project teams.
- Take advantage of advances in technology.
- Communicate to management the status of technical readiness of the project.

Checklists should be developed to use for reviews, which require descriptions of how the project and metrics meet the governance policies, standards and procedures. Some example checklist items include:

- Describe the major data structures passed between major system components.
- Describe how data are summarized to create metrics.
- Describe the purpose of the metric.
- Describe actions to take based on values of metrics.
- Describe the business/clinical and technical review process used to build the system.
- Describe the unit testing used to test the system components.
- Describe the pre- and post-condition testing included in various metrics.

SUMMARY

Effective governance ensures the business intelligence initiatives are managed from an organizational perspective and that they contribute to the mission, strategic goals and objectives. To understand the post-implementation process, we have worked backward through the scenario presented earlier to review the necessary parts and work to ensure the project answered the questions and completed all the necessary steps prior to executing the BI plan. Additionally, the models presented in Chapter 4: Assess Your Environment were revisited with anticipation that the team has addressed the findings, whether through organizational change or simple modifications to processes and resources. Important tasks were addressed in order to ensure the BI implementation is sustainable. Sustainability means the presence of the BI results will be continuous, supporting current and future measurable requirements. Sustainability is achieved through an effective governance program.

Table 8-3: Chapter 8 Checklist—Post Implementation.

Item	Completed (Yes/No)
1. Establish a feedback loop to receive and respond to communication from the recipients of the BI information.	
2. Tailor the necessary processes to optimize use of BI.	
3. Tailor the BI strategy if needed due to unexpected cultural reaction.	
4. Define post-implementation responsibilities.	
5. Document procedures to allow for repeatability and consistency.	
6. Develop a toolkit to communicate the standards of the BI framework, how results are measured and how the metrics are calculated.	
7. Evaluate the governance structure to maximize support of BI.	
8. Implement a Dashboard Review Board (DRB) to ensure post-implementation compliance.	

REFERENCE

1. Cohn D, Taylor P. Pew Research Center. Baby Boomers Approach Age 65 – Glumly, December 20, 2010. http://pewresearch.org/pubs/1834/baby-boomers-old-age-downbeat-pessimism.

CHAPTER 9

Change Management and Adoption

By Robert Jablonski and Rich Temple

This book has covered the need for business intelligence (BI) and how organizations can start the BI process. However, just as important is the change management and adoption process. Change management is all about assisting an organization through the change process. Change may be a new process, new people, or new technology. Any type of change in an organization needs to be delicately crafted to meet the needs of the specific organization. It must consider the organization's culture, the speed of change they are willing to adopt and the tools needed to help them through the process. This chapter will focus on the various elements of change specific to BI and how to gain organization adoption.

WHY BI HAS NOT CAUGHT ON IN THE ORGANIZATION

In most healthcare organizations, understanding of the concepts and potential of BI lies hidden within the organizational structure. A few individuals within the IT organization, finance department or health information management (HIM) department, formerly known as medical records department, may know the power of the data maintained in organizations' databases and applications. In general, however, they are few and far between and are usually not in frequent contact with each other. This condition results in pockets of knowledge in which a few interested end users pursue their own specific solutions, sometimes using either arcane tool methodologies to meet their narrow requirements or off-the-shelf solutions that can impose limits on their ability to realize the benefits of their knowledge. Neither solution is optimal. Why is the promise of BI hidden in these pockets of expertise?

The answer lies primarily in the history of technology deployment in the healthcare enterprise. Applications were acquired and installed for a multitude of reasons, promising numerous benefits, but all too often, failing to deliver completely on the promises. Over many implementations, technology and its proponents installed applications that met a limited number of requirements, but which came to be seen as an information sponge, soaking up vast amounts of data but failing to meet the needs of either end users or management.

What information came out of "the system" was in the form of standard reports designed by programmers to meet what *they* thought might be useful. Anything else required either a special project costing time and money or the use of a reporting package that was difficult to use or seemed to require a graduate degree in computer science to leverage effectively. Over time, end users and management simply gave up trying to get what they wanted or needed out of the systems. Those who persevered either badgered IT departments to get the data they wanted or learned to use data extraction tools on their own, leading to these islands of expertise.

Interestingly, when more computer-savvy individuals enter the organization, they activate expectations of instantaneous access to information due to the proliferation of the Internet and personal communication devices. When these expectations bump against the difficulty of accessing pertinent, real-time data, frustration and discontent with the system mount, causing additional problems for the caretakers of the data and the applications that capture and store it. The gap in understanding between the IT organization and the rest of the enterprise widens with each unsuccessful attempt to access information, frequently leading end users to give up and blame the system.

How to Overcome this History and Reintroduce the Concepts

As has been shown elsewhere in this book, there are numerous instances and examples in which the use of BI tools and techniques can provide a diverse range of benefits to end users of all stripes. It is this rainbow's end of benefits on which skilled practitioners of the BI discipline can focus to overcome the organization's history, touting the enhanced access and usability of the tools. As in any sales effort, BI professionals should concentrate on the desired solution and show how the technology has changed, enabling far better access and analysis than past efforts have accomplished.

So these technologically gifted individuals are finding their way into healthcare organizations and the expectations they must now fulfill make them the prime audience for a BI approach. It is to these "heat seekers" who will be drawn to and more likely to adopt BI solutions that we direct the next sections that discuss the steps involved. An example of where to start the process, speaking directly to these heat seekers, is to provide the technologists with quick wins and assist them in sharing their experience with their peers and the rest of the organization. Choose a few pilot projects, execute them to success, demonstrate the willingness and ability to deploy new technologies and approaches in a variety of settings, and the project will be on its way.

Factors that Will Sell BI to Skeptical Audiences

The factors that will overcome skepticism are the same ones formed by the initial promise of IT in healthcare: access to up-to-the-minute information, ease of use and the transformation of data into information, information into knowledge and knowledge into wisdom.

While more elegant data extraction and manipulation tools are available than ever before, the bottom line for end users will always be near-instant gratification: the ability to easily pull information from diverse applications to support a business case or identify issues before they morph into problems and devise appropriate solutions in a timely fashion. The tools and techniques are important, but they are not the solution—detecting and improving processes leading to superior outcomes are the goal.

Drivers and Enablers

The primary drivers in healthcare are cost and quality. BI professionals need to demonstrate that their solutions are cost-effective and have a direct and positive relationship on the quality of patient care. End users will value applications and tools that can be quickly and easily deployed by non-IT professionals over those requiring routine and frequent interaction with IT staff to use. Similarly, BI gurus who can show the linkage between efficient data capture, storage, access and manipulation and improvements to patient care in the form of reduced errors, improved outcomes and an increase in informed clinical decision making will be more successful than those who cannot or do not. BI professionals should initially sell their skills as the ounce of prevention and later, as the pound of cure.

SETTING TRANSFORMATIONAL GOALS FOR THE ORGANIZATION

As mentioned previously, cost and quality remain the drivers in healthcare. Evidence-based medicine, pay-for-performance, meaningful use and accountable care organizations (ACO) are all primarily buzzwords for approaches to improving the quality of care while reducing cost. This has been the case for two decades. The difference in today's environment is that health IT has made significant improvements to the methods and tools available to IT professionals and clinicians who support organizational initiatives in the cost and quality arenas.

The focus of these overarching imperatives is on squeezing inefficiency out of the healthcare delivery system by capturing clinical information, maintaining it and automating information handoffs between clinicians. The objective is to reduce errors at the point of care, capture the outcomes and results produced by clinical decisions and retrospectively examine the clinical data to determine the relationship between the clinical decisions and outcomes. The requirement is for clinical choices and decisions to be informed by best practices rather than subjective judgments on the part of providers based on past experience.

BI techniques support the quality improvement process by making both concurrent and retrospective data analysis quicker, easier and less costly. Clinical decisions based on more (and more recent) information lead to better outcomes, fewer mistakes and reduced cost of care.

How Is Culture Likely to Change as a Result of Executing these Initiatives?

Because of the impact of the American Recovery and Reinvestment Act (ARRA) on care providers, the organizational culture is likely to shift even more in the direction of the technology enabled healthcare provider. The reporting and documentation requirements that comprise meaningful use are driving healthcare organizations and their IT vendors to develop and deploy technologies that support the documentation of care and the near-instantaneous access to the clinical information contained therein at all points of care.

Provider organizations are likely to be more and more data-driven. While physicians' preferences and practice patterns will always be important, their employers will require proof (evidence) those preferences and practice patterns yield appropriate outcomes and warrant their cost. This can only be done using IT to record the type of care provided and the outcomes and results attributable to it. BI's role is to aggregate this information to enable contrasts and comparisons to be made among diagnoses, procedures and treatments to identify those most effective, efficient and practicable. BI tools will also be used to differentiate among practitioners for pay-for-performance purposes and to allocate financial and other resources in ACOs. All these trends point to an increasing reliance on the ability to aggregate, maintain and manipulate large amounts of data for management and clinical reporting purposes and the continuing evolution of the data-driven healthcare enterprise.

What Is BI's Role in Facilitating the Development of the Organizational Culture?

Business intelligence can and should be used to support the shift in the culture to a more knowledge-driven model. BI professionals can strive to assist the organization in acquiring, maintaining, protecting and disseminating data, information and knowledge across the enterprise. This means identifying the data, information and knowledge needs of the organization, acquiring the best technologies available to meet those needs, capturing and safeguarding the information resources and facilitating use of these tools by end users to meet the changing needs of caregivers, managers and executives.

As mentioned previously, BI should be the ounce of prevention, but it can also provide several pounds of cure. BI practitioners can present themselves and their skills as solutions to problems, as well as purveyors of cutting-edge technologies. Technological proficiency is a wonderful skill to have, but the bottom line to the organization will always be identifying and avoiding problems when possible and resolving them quickly and cost-effectively.

MEETING OPERATIONAL NEEDS USING BI TOOLS

What Do Operations Managers and Line Staff Really Need?

Much of the current dissatisfaction with health IT among managers and staff has more to do with timing than with content. To be sure, content and formatting are issues with these individuals as well, but a great deal of their frustration lies in the retrospective nature of the information provided. It is particularly irksome for nurse managers to receive reports showing they were overstaffed on their units three weeks ago or for supply chain management to discover supplies were outdated the previous week. Information has value primarily when it is provided with sufficient lead-time to take action. Finding out there was a problem that could have been averted but was not, is managerially worthless. By the time "the system" spews such reports, managers and staff have already heard of the problem from their peers and superiors.

What BI Characteristics Lend Themselves to Meeting Operational Needs?

One of BI's virtues lies in the ability to scan current data and present real-time warnings of conditions that can lead to problems if not addressed quickly. BI practitioners can use IF-THEN-ELSE logic to specify conditions that precede problem occurrence and route that information to the appropriate resource to take action. In our previous example, supply chain management can specify expiration dates be scanned weekly to identify supplies that are approaching becoming outdated and take action to either use them or return them for credit. Likewise, a report detailing movement on an hourly basis measured against thresholds to assure that patient movement is optimal would be useful. Also called throughput, organizations can detect if they are on track with their discharges so the admissions will have beds. Detection can also ensure that patients in the emergency department are moving through and have been transferred to the beds that have been assigned to them. This is the near real-time report that helps an organization stay on track.

These may seem simple or trivial examples, but the underlying situations occur on a daily basis in hospitals across the country. Managers and supervisors want proactive data scanning, dashboards, trend analysis and period-to-period data comparisons that are quickly and routinely generated. While many are using spreadsheets and graphic packages on an *ad-hoc* basis to meet their needs, they need BI tools that enable prospective data analysis.

BI Investments Operations Staff Need to Make

First of all, operating managers and staff need to invest their time and talent. This means they may have to learn to use new applications other than Excel and PowerPoint. They will also have to learn where the information they need resides, how and when it was acquired and what the data really mean. They will also have to work with BI practitioners to develop an understanding of the methods by which data can be extracted, when and how often data should be refreshed, how data should be presented and to whom. Healthcare organizations need common nomenclature and data definitions as a requirement for BI to flourish. The required investment of non-IT management time and talent is critical.

WORKFLOW ISSUES

Where Can BI Tools and Techniques Be Deployed at the Point of Need?

BI capabilities are not limited to generating data extracts for retroactive analysis and reporting. Capabilities also allow managers and supervisors to examine operational data to identify opportunities for improvement in day-to-day workflow when they have access to appropriate tools and data.

Frequently, it is the staff at the point of patient care or contacts that has the best ideas for eliminating waste, improving cycle and process times and reducing cost. They have the subjective and anecdotal background that leads them to believe improvements are possible but lack the data to make a business case for change. BI can fill the gap by identifying where to look for the data and determining how best to aggregate data to make the case for change.

Operational Example: Supply Chain Decision Making

Too often supply chain managers lack sufficient data to assess their purchasing effectiveness or efficiency and rely on their suppliers or group purchasing organizations for purchasing data. This can cause issues in determining levels of compliance with group purchasing agreements, tracking high-value items from requisitioning through payment and determining the cost of performing some procedures.

Use of BI techniques to revamp the supply chain to enable tracking of items from requisitioning through purchase, issuance and reimbursement can assist providers in determining the cost of patient care. Using surgical procedures as an example, the cost of each case can be determined by drilling down to determine how long the case took, what items were supplied in the case cart, which items were used, which were returned and the cost of individual disposable items used in the case. Cost per case can be compared among surgeons and combined with outcome data, such as length of stay, recovery time, post-operative infection rates, subsequent problems and other information to make a determination as to whether specific supplies, prosthetics, implants and other devices have a measurable effect on results.

Such an effort would require identification of data elements contained in the materials management/purchasing, patient record, billing, accounts receivable and quality management applications. Data for each type of case would have to be identified and standardized for comparison purposes. Data extraction programs would aggregate the data and reporting software used to format them for analysis and presentation. This is challenging to accomplish ex post facto, but with appropriate front-end design and build, the applications and data used to supply the information for this type of analysis can be further configured to facilitate efficient collection.

LEADING THE WAY

Who's in Charge of Setting Expectations?

Leadership always starts at the top. Those who set the strategies and priorities for the organization are the ones who establish the expectations. Getting a BI initiative started and changing the culture require a commitment from management at all levels to make it work. BI is not about technology. It uses technology, it requires technological skill and ingenuity to implement, and it drives technology deeper into the organization than it might have been previously. However, BI is primarily a transformative process. IT provides the technological wherewithal to provide people the means to accomplish their tasks—it helps them in *how* to do things. BI takes it a step further and provides the technological capability that enables people to know *what* to do, by providing them with access to data, which are transformed into information, and thence to knowledge. IT provides information; BI provides the capability to discriminate among bits of information, aggregate the right ones and react in a manner that benefits the organization and its customers.

Senior leadership of healthcare organizations grappling with meaningful use and ACO development must understand the adjectives "meaningful" and "accountable" as applied to the two major imperatives driving healthcare: differentiating between simply using data and information to operate efficiently and using data to effect change in a positive way. They must therefore set the expectation that the enterprise information assets—data, information and knowledge—be used to move the enterprise forward toward "meaningful" change in outcomes and results, thereby allowing an "accountable" organization can quantify, monitor and document its contributions to its community.

Once established, expectations should cascade through the organization, each level establishing expectations and demanding performance from the bottom to the top. Leadership at all levels needs to embrace the concepts of evidence-based, data-driven decision making and demand the tools and technology to support it.

Eyes on the Prize

If leadership were the sole requirement, very few projects would fail. Most large-scale, culture-changing initiatives do not lack for leadership, but they tend to flounder not on the technological problems or workflow redesigns but on the change management approach—the "people" problems. Conceptually, BI is a no-brainer—very few people can argue about having more and better knowledge applied to solving problems, particularly clinical. As the old saying goes, "Everyone wants progress, very few want to change," and it applies particularly in healthcare.

Cultural change in healthcare is slow and can be painful. The bumps in the road are magnified in an environment where people will get sick, and even die, if poor decisions are made. The challenge for leadership is to focus on the end result—the destination—not the potholes in the road. The road to the BI-enabled healthcare organization will be bumpy, there will be failures as well as successes, and leadership is required to learn from the failures, replicate the successes and keep the organization moving toward the destination. The best way to accomplish this is to monitor and report progress, celebrate and recognize success, learn from mistakes and keep moving forward.

Recognition and Reward

The old business maxim "what gets measured gets managed," has a corollary, namely, "what gets acknowledged gets accomplished." Recognition among peers is a strong motivator and helps meet people's needs for esteem. One of the most effective ways to celebrate success is to recognize and reward those who contribute to it. Simply adding a BI component or requirement to job descriptions will not motivate staff to succeed. Establishing awards and prizes for the most innovative use of BI tools and featuring web site or newsletter items about individuals who use BI to realize improvements can go a long way toward getting others on board, as well as motivating others to emulate these successes.

External recognition and achievement work equally well in getting employees and leadership working in the same direction. Achieving "Most Wired Hospital" status or winning the Malcolm Baldrige Award is a source of pride for organizations that have established achieving such recognition as an organizational objective. Moving healthcare organizations up the levels of HIMSS' (Healthcare Information and Management Systems Society) EMR Adoption Model^{SM} is another example of using technology innovation and enhancement to drive the healthcare organization forward. Again, it is leadership that determines the objectives and provides the impetus and resources to achieve them. There is no substitute for it.

WEAVING BI INTO ALL ASPECTS OF THE ORGANIZATION'S CULTURE

Why this Has Been an Ongoing Struggle

As noted in a previous chapter, a compelling case needs to be made for the adoption of BI from the very top of the organization. While leadership is an essential component of success with BI initiatives, merely championing the concept isn't going to make BI effective. The organization has to make it clear that measuring key metrics from all parts of the organization is going to become front-and-center to the organization's quest for clinical and financial excellence, and that individuals are going to be held accountable for managing and reporting on those metrics. People will have their evaluations in large part predicated on how they meet certain measurements and whether they are taking the initiative to use the stores of data available in a meaningful way to manage their respective areas and provide best-of-class service.

This is not intended, though, to wield BI as a blunt instrument that says "do it or else" to the leaders and managers within the organization. That is not going to create the momentum for change desired; it will make the use of reports perfunctory and people will likely do just enough to give the impression they are using reports.

Mandates do have to be "real" for BI to succeed, but mandates also have to be coupled with true recognition of how profound the changes will be in so many aspects of many people's day-to-day lives. Individual people's managers will have to work closely with their teams to work out what the changes will be in the new BI culture and lay out new work processes to accommodate these changes. IT staff with particular business savvy will need to be heavily involved in these discussions, as success will be in large part predicated on how easy it is to access the information provided through BI, how the data are displayed (for ease-of-use and easy access) and how valuable the metrics provided are for fulfilling business goals.

These collaborations need to be taking place *at all points during the BI development process* and not just at the end when people are being trained on how to use the new BI tools. There will be times when the process may seem frustrating to all involved; if done right, there will be numerous iterations, back-and-forth of design changes, testing and one-on-one sessions with users and IT. But, that needs to be understood as an inevitable component of the process and accepted. The payoff at the end of the road for this type of rigor will be great and will last years.

Make extensive use of BI as the norm within the organization and be confident the BI paradigm will not be disruptive to key players within the organization.

ADOPTION

Getting People to Embrace the Change–What's in it for Me?

There is the old adage we often hear in business that "change is good." Many people buy into that—as long as change is happening to somebody else! Most people tend to embrace change in principle but push back and even fear it (after all, it does introduce uncertainty) in practice. So, in order to get people to change—*really* change, not just give the cosmetic impression of changing—an organization needs to clearly articulate the benefits of the change with a targeted communications approach that clearly speaks to the "what's in it for me" to all different types of stakeholders.

Again, saying it is one thing—being able to produce some demonstrable use cases that show people they can easily relate to can really help build the necessary buy-in for effective adoption of BI. From a leadership perspective, as the BI team blazes forward with its planning for BI transformation, they will undoubtedly be peppered with many different potential use cases for BI in many different settings.

Encourage thought process—it represents a big step forward for the organization—but do not try to immediately bite off everything that is requested. Identifying a handful of compelling use cases that are technologically doable and have the potential to incur a significant business impact could be readily understood and appreciated by the broadest possible group of stakeholders.

Being able to share these very successful pilot use cases in many different settings (departmental meetings, director's meetings, board meetings) will get people excited about the prospect of converting data to actionable information and will allow them to manage their responsibilities in ways they never had been able to before. Demonstrate *before BI* and *after BI* states. Explain the business drivers that catalyzed the use case being discussed. And finally, have sharp-looking graphics, drill-down capabilities and trending functions ready to be displayed. These demonstrations will likely generate a lot of excitement on the part of the audience and, armed with excitement, people will be more willing to go out on a limb and alter their day-to-day activities to realize the benefits of robust BI.

SUMMARY

Change management is all about assisting an organization through a necessary change process and driven by executive management. Change may be a new process, new people or new technology. Any type of change in an organization needs to be delicately crafted to meet the needs of the specific organization. It must consider the organization's culture, the speed of change they are willing to adopt and the tools that are needed to help them through the process.

Table 9-1: Chapter 9 Checklist—Change Management and Adoption.

Item	Completed (Yes/No)
1. Ensure senior management is onboard and supports the change required throughout the organization.	
2. Develop a change management plan.	
3. Monitor activities that have been implemented to support the change to determine its effectiveness and its shortfalls.	
4. Establish a reward and recognition program to identify those individuals who are successfully contributing to the need for change.	
5. Develop a communication plan to clearly articulate the reason for change, the benefits of change and what's in it for "me."	
6. Create policies that ensure that BI processes that get built continue to get utilized for ongoing management reporting.	

Basic Components of Business Intelligence

CHAPTER 10

Presenting Results through Dashboards

By Cynthia McKinney, MBA, FHIMSS, PMP

Based on the overwhelming literature written about dashboards, it is clear there is a dashboard for just about every purpose that may be needed. While this chapter will cover the different types of dashboards, its purpose will primarily focus on understanding what dashboards can and cannot do for your organization, and how dashboards support the use of advanced business intelligence (BI).

Dashboards come in all shapes and sizes. They serve many purposes and audiences and use various infrastructures as their foundations. A dashboard can be created with a simple spreadsheet, a clinical or financial health information system (HIS) or a stand-alone dashboard application. Dashboards can be a very simple tool, providing a snapshot view of results and trending or "basic" business intelligence such as trending and alerts.

So what was meant when it was stated earlier that dashboards can support the use of advanced BI? To start, dashboards provide the ability to quickly see the performance of key performance indicators (KPIs), helping organizations identify and act on meaningful trends, using charts, graphs and alerts for the identified indicators. The functions of trending and alerts, often considered to be basic BI functions, are commonly part of a dashboard. However the more advanced BI functions, such as data mining, simulation and predictive analysis, are usually not part of a dashboard due to their complexity. So how do dashboards and advanced BI fit together? An organization using a dashboard can rapidly identify an indicator they need to learn more about and determine whether additional advanced techniques are needed, such as predictive analysis, simulation and further data mining.

THE BACKGROUND ON DASHBOARDS

Due to variability, it is not uncommon for an organization to quickly become overwhelmed with dashboards and get caught up in the "glitz and glamour" of their sophistication. But what is the real purpose of a dashboard and why have one? To set the stage, here are some simple terms:

Metric. A metric is a measurement of a specific indicator developed specifically to quantify the established goal or objective. An organization may monitor many metrics on a routine basis, but not all of these metrics are part of their developed dashboards.

KPI. Key performance indicators are the selected metrics used to help an organization measure progress toward critical organizational goals. The terms *metric* and *KPI* are often used interchangeably. The slight difference is that an organization may have many metrics, but may only include a few of them for continuous review on a dashboard. Those few are often referred to as KPIs.

Dashboard. A dashboard is a visual display which allows an organization to quickly grasp the performance of key indicators.

Executive dashboard. The term *executive* refers to the audience for the dashboard. These tools usually show the highest level metrics and indicators.

Recognizing that dashboards meet many needs, have multiple audiences and come in a variety of shapes and sizes, one can find figuring out what a dashboard is to be very confusing. Table 10-1 is a simple comparison of what a dashboard is and what it is not.

Table 10-1: What a Dashboard Is and Is Not.

Dashboards Are...	Dashboards Are Not...
Comprised of a variety of indicators based on their intent.	One size fits all. Customization is highly recommended.
Supportive of the goals and objectives of the organization or project.	Intended to provide answers, but rather to help provide insight and target areas for drill-down.
Also referred to as an executive dashboard (normally includes C-suite indicators).	Standardized for all users and with the flexibility to meet the needs of the intended audience.
Used for clinical, financial and operational measures.	Just a summary of metrics. The indicators must be thoroughly vetted prior to implementation.
Constantly changing with the flexibility to support changing KPIs, views and drill-down information.	Static views that can be set up and forgotten.

DASHBOARD CONSIDERATIONS

Although there is a critical need for dashboards, not all healthcare providers have them. In a study performed in 2010 by International Business Machines (IBM), more than 50 percent of respondents indicated they still produce their operational metrics manually.[1] While the intent of this chapter is not to explore why this is the case, it is safe to say the following challenges contribute to the continuing use of manual methods:

- Lack of standardized data.
- Lack of a single system across facilities in multi-hospital systems.
- Inability to obtain needed data from system.
- Inconsistent extract/transform/load (ETL) or data-cleansing processes for all data used in the dashboard.

While critical gaps, these challenges are just some of the considerations. A BI project team needs to work through a full list of items during the development stage. The resulting list will provide clarity on what the project team wants to include in its dashboard, how it should look and what they hope to achieve from the dashboard. It is strongly recommended that each of the following items be reviewed and agreed to when designing the dashboard. Considerations for each item are provided in Table 10-2.

Table 10-2: Considerations for Development Stage.

Item	Considerations
Purpose	• Clearly define the purpose of the dashboard. • Do not try to make one dashboard meet all needs.
Ownership	• Identify the key stakeholders. • Identify who will "own" the dashboard and be accountable for the results.
Audience	• Define who is accountable for reviewing the dashboard results. • Involve the accountable stakeholders.
Staffing	• Identify how the dashboard will be developed (internal or external). • Identify the staffing to support the dashboard.
Use	• Define how the results will be used: tracking, monitoring or alerting. • Make the indicators and dashboard actionable.
Drivers	• Understand the internal or external drivers. • Potential drivers may include regulatory, patient safety and financial performance.
Priorities	• Agree on how dashboards will be prioritized. • Priorities are highly contingent on the identified drivers.
Frequency	• Understand the frequency of the dashboard and associated indicators. • Frequency will drive the type of dashboard that will be developed.
Data Source	• Identify the source of the data. • Clearly document the data source, data definitions and proposed KPI. • Understand the ETL process for the proposed data.
Data Integrity	• Evaluate the integrity and reliability of the data. • Fully define and document how data integrity will be validated and at what frequencies. • Engage the stakeholders evaluating data integrity.
Targets	• Establish targets for each indicator to include on the dashboard.

Table 10-2: Considerations for Development Stage. (cont.)

Item	Considerations
Display	• Define how the information will appear on the dashboard. • Potential displays include trend reports, analog gauge, digital readout, stop-go traffic lights.
Functionality	• Define each function to be included on the dashboard. • Potential functionality may include summary, trends, drill-down and/or alerts and triggers.

TYPES AND USES OF DASHBOARDS

Once an organization decides it's ready for a dashboard, it begins working through the list of considerations just noted. While the exciting part of the process is designing the dashboard, all items must be worked through to reach effective results. Developing a dashboard is a lot of work and requires organizational commitment for time and resources. While organizations have benefited from using dashboards, additional resources often need to be committed to the project.

Dashboards can be quite diverse and vary greatly based on what is needed to be shown and/or achieved. Dashboards incorporated on an effective BI platform should enable an organization to include and present actionable items (e.g., drill-downs, real-time trends or alerts). Most organizations use a combination of dashboard functionality.

Purpose of Dashboards

Aside from the project start up referred to in Chapter 3, the dashboard process begins with determining the intended purpose. The majority of dashboard elements fall into three categories: operational, financial or clinical/quality. An organization may focus on one or more of these categories; specific needs will determine the optimal starting point. The purpose of a dashboard can be:

- **Operational:** The dashboard should include key operational indicators managed to improve operational effectiveness or efficiency. Example measures include staff productivity and bed turn-around time.
- **Financial:** The dashboard should convey fundamentals about the business, pinpoint areas of growth as well as areas of concern, and most importantly, aid decision making. Example measures include average daily census, days in accounts receivable and cost per discharge.
- **Clinical/quality:** The use of clinical dashboards has expanded significantly over the past 10 years due to the increasing need to manage and report the multitude of compliance regulations. A clinical dashboard should provide quick, relevant information such as CMS core measures, meaningful use indicators or other information that the organization would need to monitor clinical effectiveness.

Functionality

Determining the functionality of the dashboard will help the organization determine what type of dashboard to implement. If basic functionality is required, a simple spreadsheet may be adequate. However, if there is the need to drill-down or receive alerts, a more sophisticated system would be necessary, as depicted in Table 10-3.

Table 10-3: Dashboard Functionality.

Functionality	Brief Description
Summary	Provides a snapshot of KPI performance. The summary functionality may or may not be real-time.
Trends	Show how the KPIs have performed over time.
Stop Lights	Provide an assessment of the actual to targeted results by showing a red, yellow, green button next to the results.
Drill-down	Provides the ability to go from summary information to detailed information—normally by selecting a variable in question.
Alerts/Triggers	Enable an organization to set a threshold and then notify the user if the value drops below the threshold.

Table 10-4 provides a summary of advanced BI functions an organization may have or need to have. While these are not part of a dashboard, it is helpful to be aware of these functions while identifying the functionality the organization may need.

Table 10-4: Advanced Business Intelligence Functionality.

Data Mining	Allows ability to analyze data from multiple perspectives.
Modeling	Creates representations of situations and scenarios to determine a future state of an activity or action.
Simulation	Shows how processes react under different circumstances, by using data on existing processes and then defining scenarios to measure the impact of changes on process results.
Forecasting	Leverages the current environment, in relationship to historical trends, to make statements about the future.

Each of the mentioned dashboards may possess varying degrees of functionality as just discussed. Table 10-5 contrasts the types of dashboards and possible functionality:

Table 10-5: Types of Dashboards.

Functionality	Simple Tool (e.g., spreadsheet)	Integrated with Health Information System
Summary	•	•
Trends	•	•
Stop Lights	•	•
Drill-down		•
Alerts/Triggers		•

Leveraging multiple functionalities and views on a single dashboard is often the best mechanism to meet the needs of the organization. Dashboards built on a consolidated source of data or single platform are the best mechanisms to ensure all stakeholders are focused on the same target or end result.

The use of dashboards can be cyclical—meaning that each dashboard may tell a different story. Figure 10-1 shows how the functionality of different dashboards can be applied to better understand the organization or item under review. No single dashboard is the *right* answer. The question to ask to arrive at the right answer is: "What are you hoping to achieve and what information do you need to help answer key questions?" To better understand the types of dashboards, Figure 10-1 highlights some of the key features of each:

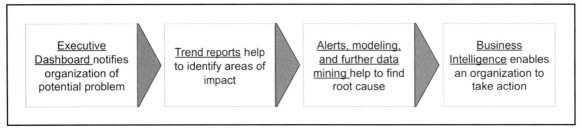

Figure 10-1: How Functionality of Different Dashboards Can Be Applied.

CASE STUDY 10-1

The following case study presents an overview of how one organization identified a need for further analysis and tracking, how it developed a dashboard to monitor the problem and the outcome.

IMPROVING PROGRAM RESULTS FOR PATIENTS

Including its inpatient rehab facility, Brooks Rehabilitation (Brooks) has 25 outpatient centers that provide several specialized therapy programs, including Balance, Women's Health, Pediatrics, Sports and programs for neurological conditions such as stroke, brain injury, spinal cord injury and orthopedics. Brooks implemented a BI solution in 2008 and began aggregating data from disparate HIS systems into a single data repository to provide dashboards for scrutinizing operational data by staff, as well as front line managers.

Business Need

With an increase in patient co-pays, the slower economy and overall patient non-compliance, Brooks had been seeing a decrease in the number of patients completing outpatient therapy programs. Patients were getting physician orders for 12 visits of therapy, but many were dropping out by the eighth or ninth visit. Brooks had limited insight as to why this was occurring, as the patient would just stop participating. While routine metrics provided the average visits per case, they did not provide answers. The impetus to change occurred when Brooks saw a decrease in average visits from 10.7 to 9.1 over a three-year period. While the root cause was uncertain, the assumption was that economic factors like the price of gas or co-pays were becoming an increased burden. Operations managers felt they needed to up the value of that "last mile of care" to the patient, but they were not clear on where they needed to focus the value proposition.

Business Solution

Brooks implemented a BI initiative with dashboards to track the percent of total patients completing their program and reasons for not completing. They began tracking this in 2008 and were shocked to learn that 51 percent of patients did not complete their program. (The financial impact of this was soon explained when Brooks determined that, with over 21,000 new patients a year, having just 50 percent of these patients come to one more visit could result in almost a million dollars added to their bottom line.) Staff and front-line managers monitored the underlying factors for the decrease over time and began to see trends. By far, the primary reason for patient dropout was patient "self-discharges," indicating they were not finding enough value in continuing their programs. This insight helped clinicians to identify specific factors affecting the patient's decision, from financial reasons to lack of transportation and work constraints. They concluded that, overall, patients needed a better understanding of the clinical and quality impact of not completing a program and how they could benefit from receiving the full plan of visits regardless of constraints.

Benefits\Results

As a result of the data analysis, outpatient clinics developed education to help patients understand the goals and benefits of personalized programs of care. The therapist now reinforces program value when the patient begins the program and during visits and relates it to their progress along the way. The more information shared with the patient, the more the patients bought into the value of the care plan. In addition, care was coordinated between the front desk and the clinical staff. Administrative staff was coached to identify patients who needed to spread out the visits and the financial burden of co-pays, and provide payment options that helped manage the full scope of their visits. This worked not only on the front end but has resulted in higher collections on the back end, with payment plans being paid versus bothering the patient with collection calls. The percentage of patients completing their clinical therapy program has gone from 50 percent when tracking began to as high as 88 percent. Overall clinical outcomes for these patients have also improved as a result of program completion. This metric is tracked with a clinical quality dashboard and has been incorporated into the therapist's annual performance evaluations. An effort is underway to correlate satisfaction by visit to each patient's completion rate. This area continues to be monitored and improved by the front-line staff, who now depend on dashboards to help them take the patient through the last mile of care.

DASHBOARD EXAMPLES

To better understand the types of dashboards, the following section provides several dashboard examples. Specific functionality has been highlighted, including summaries of how they were used. While these are real-life dashboards, the intent is to provide examples and ideas on what may be helpful to include when developing a dashboard.

Summary Dashboards

Summary or executive dashboards provide a view of key indicators at a snapshot. They allow an organization to manage performance by measuring actual results toward the organization's established targets. Dashboard refers to the synopsis view of indicators and can be used for any department, not just executives. Executive dashboards may include a multitude of functionality such as status bars, trends, pie charts and stop lights. An example of a summary dashboard is depicted in Figures 10-2 and 10-3.

Trends

Trending provides an organization with the ability to view activity over a period of time.

Through this view organizations can track cyclical trends that may impact the organization. Trending is effective for different types of monitoring including financial, operational, and clinical/quality. However, trending is most commonly used in operational reviews for measuring productivity and financial analyses (Figure 10-4). Trending is most effective when coupled with the ability to drill-down to perform further analysis.

Drill-Down

Drill-down functionality provides the ability to perform further analysis by creating flexible tables and pivot analyses to answer specific questions. This functionality is invaluable when attempting to determine the root cause of a potential problem. Report views can be quickly created by a non-technical business user. Drill-down functionality is most commonly used with patient level information (Figure 10-5).

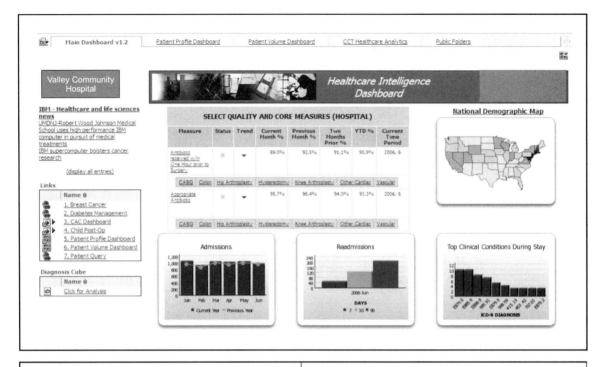

Functionality: Executive and Trend	Key Features
Purpose: Clinical/quality	• Bar graph with trend
Source: IBM	• Historical view for month and year

Figure 10-2: Example of a Summary Dashboard (From IBM, used with permission.)

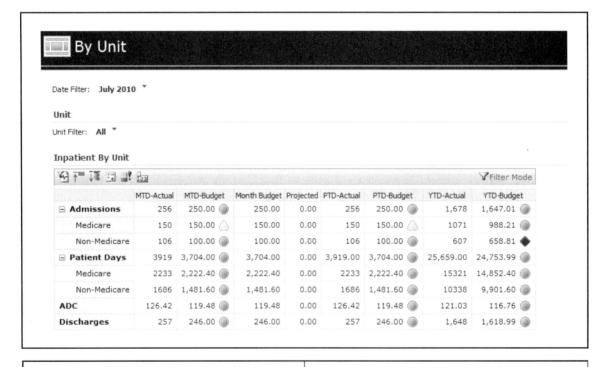

Type: Executive/Score Card	Key Features
Purpose: Operations	• Stop Light – Actual to budget
Source: Brooks Rehabilitation	• Filter based on unit

Figure 10-3: An Example of a Summary Operations Dashboard. (From Brooks Rehabilitation, used with permission.)

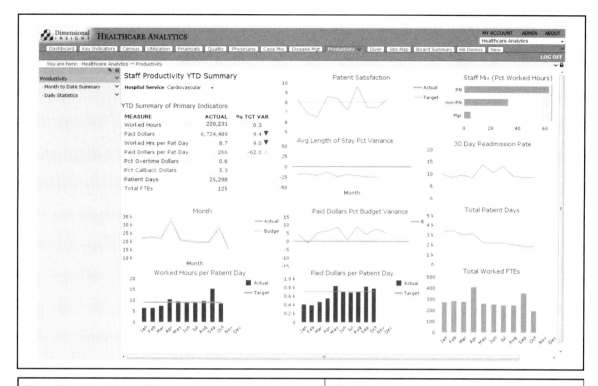

Type: Trending/executive	Key Features
Purpose: Operations/Financial	• Trends, actuals and budgets
Source: Dimensional Insight	• Various trends to meet needs

Figure 10-4: Trend Operations/Financial. (From Dimensional Insight, used with permission.)

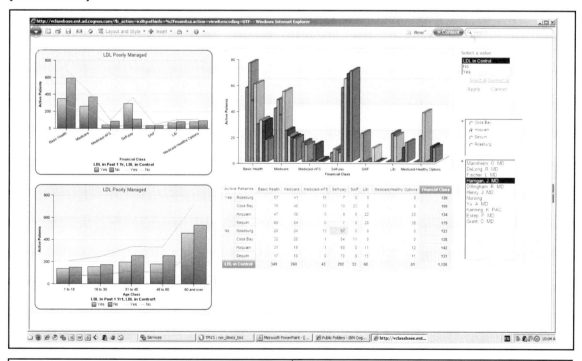

Type: Drill-Down/Trend	Key Features
Purpose: Clinical	• Sort and filter function to support enhanced
Source: IBM	drill-down

Figure 10-5: Drill-Down Clinical Functionality. (From IBM, used with permission.)

Alerts and Triggers

Proactive notification is critical to addressing performance issues. A critical dashboard function is to quickly make the audience aware of issues. This is most commonly done through alerts and triggers. The dashboard should be able to alert users to progress (or lack of progress) against targets, whether or not users are currently examining the detailed data. Proactive alerts and reminders can be set to automatically push updates to key stakeholders via e-mail based on business rules and thresholds. An effective performance management application would have hundreds of these alerts set on key metrics, ensuring that nothing slips through the cracks. This function is an example of what is seen throughout this book, that BI is much more than alerts and triggers. It is the ability to provide the right information to the right person as soon as possible. Alerts and triggers are two of the more common functionalities used within dashboards. However, as seen in the next examples, the role of BI within dashboards continues to expand (Figures 10-6 and 10-7).

SUMMARY

Dashboards can be extremely beneficial tools for managing operations and providing patient care. However, organizations must be thoughtful about what they want to obtain from dashboards before creating them. The list of considerations provided in this chapter can help an organization walk through the process. Organizations that do not carefully consider the essential elements risk wasting time and resources for rework.

Finally, to get the most out of dashboards, consider the status of business intelligence in the organization and how its role will evolve. Do opportunities exist to further leverage its capabilities? Be creative in mixing functionality as seen in the examples. Do not clutter the dashboard. Make the dashboard a useful tool that can be embedded at multiple levels across the organization to bring relevant insights to inform decisions.

Table 10-6: Chapter 10 Checklist—Presenting Results Through Dashboards.

Item	Completed (Yes/No)
1. Define the purpose of the dashboard.	
2. Identify the key stakeholders and ownership of each KPI.	
3. Outline the look and feel of each dashboard (e.g., trends, alerts).	
4. Outline the frequency of update.	
5. Develop prioritization criteria to develop each dashboard.	
6. Identify the source of data and complete validation.	
7. Establish targets for each indicator.	
8. Develop dashboard appearance: analog, gauge, digital readout.	

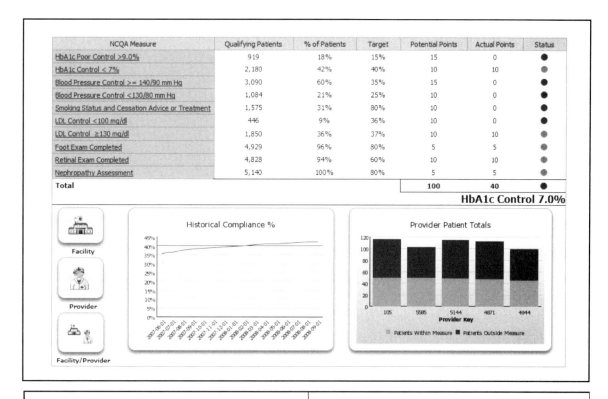

Type: Alert/trend	Key Features
Purpose: Clinical	• Alert created when status falls below target
Source: IBM	range

Figure 10-6: Alerts and Triggers—Clinical. (From IBM, used with permission.)

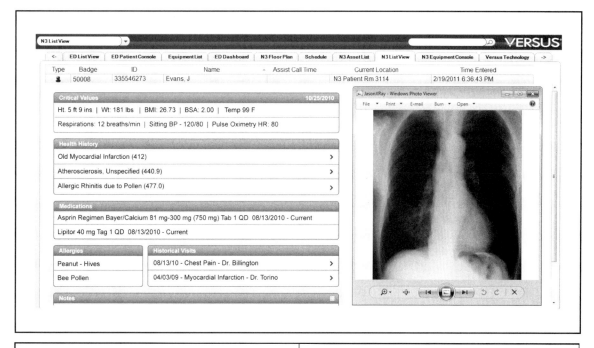

Type: Alerts/clinical intelligence	Key Features
Purpose: Clinical	• Incorporation of clinical results and current
Source: Versus	and historical information

Figure 10-7: Alerts and Triggers—Clinical (From Versus, used with permission.)

REFERENCE

1. IBM Global CFO Study, March 2010.

CHAPTER 11

Communicating through Robust Reporting

By Prashant Natarajan

Reporting is a crucial ability for most, if not all, healthcare organizations—and the ability to provide robust reporting may be effectively used to communicate to multiple levels of healthcare providers and regulatory institutions across the continuum of healthcare. Robust reporting provides the opportunity to communicate the results of an effective business intelligence (BI) program. Additionally, robust reporting may even provide *ad-hoc* opportunities to discover new useful data or trends. An effective reporting program can validate the quality of a healthcare organization's BI program, validate the technologies used to implement the program and validate the expected outcomes extending into the hands of front-line operations.

This chapter discusses key aspects of a robust reporting system, including examining four levels of BI reporting capabilities that may currently exist or need to be developed in the healthcare enterprise. Each level will be presented with its characteristics, advantages and disadvantages. This chapter will also present a rationale for why an organization ought to consider a comprehensive Level 4 enterprise reporting strategy along with recommendations for best practices. Additionally, the chapter will focus on how the BI project team can develop and leverage existing resources and skill sets to implement the desired highest Level 4 reporting capability that encompasses strategic, tactical, operational reporting requirements, as opposed to the more limited efforts that are usually sufficient to achieve capability in Levels 1, 2 and 3. Case studies provided will observe organizations that have successfully implemented a robust BI reporting system.

One of the key components of a robust reporting system are the tools and interfaces recipients use to access their data and monitor trends. These tools and interfaces include business and clinical query and reporting, production reporting, online analytical processing (OLAP), dashboards and scorecards, and Microsoft Excel. These tools typically have distinct operational capabilities and may vary based on the intended user's needs. For example, executive management may have a requirement for reports that provide a higher-level organizational view than a clinical nurse. Thus, each type of user requirement will dictate how to select the appropriate reporting system.

A key visual component of any information management, analytics or data warehousing effort is how the data are presented. This component provides the front-end entry into the outcomes of the BI system and processes. As a result, the visual component remains one of the most salient and discussed topics in healthcare BI. A visual presentation may consist of:

- Documents that present healthcare clinical, administrative and financial data (electronic or printed reports).
- Software applications that allow human users to access and interact with data (i.e., *ad-hoc* query tools, report writers or Excel).
- Analytical tools that facilitate the conversion of data into actionable healthcare BI (i.e., statistical reports, hierarchical report drill-downs, filters and charts).

In a KLAS survey of health system executives in 2010, "[Sixty-nine percent] of respondents said BI solutions would play an important or critical role in meaningful use. One provider told KLAS, 'Never before have we been so carefully scrutinized, and the BI system helps us provide the information and reports needed to be successful.'"[1]

While the choice of a visually appealing front-end reporting solution is a frequently discussed topic, a review of current literature on healthcare BI and analytics also indicates an inordinate emphasis on "eye candy"—dashboards, scorecards or other graphical tools. The topic of reports, pre-packaged; *ad-hoc* or advanced, is less frequently discussed, despite the fact that report creation, production and delivery are, and will continue to be, at the very heart of every successful healthcare BI effort.

REPORTS—A PRIMER

At its core, the basic definition of a report has remained unchanged since the advent of Gutenberg's printing press. A report is simply a document or medium presenting text, numbers and charts in a coherent and structured manner that facilitates analysis and action. Reports can be developed and accessed using many different media methods, including the use of the Internet, online portals, pre-packaged reports or *ad-hoc* query tools. These methods emphasize self-service information retrieval and allows non-information technology (IT) users to ask spontaneous, *ad-hoc* questions and receive structured reports in near real-time or on demand.

Understanding the organization's needs to produce information, reporting capabilities become a prominent component of BI success. The use of visual reports is the primary method by which results of retrospective and prospective analysis are communicated within the healthcare organization. The reasons for their popularity and reach are easy to understand given:

- The basic structure of a report is easy-to-understand and use—humans have been creating and using structured reports to present information prior to the advent of the information age in the mid-20th century.
- The result of advances in IT is that today's visual reporting tools are capable of producing *ad-hoc* reports on demand in a variety of online and print media.
- Reports are easier to learn, create and use compared to other BI visual tools.
- Reports are versatile—there is little healthcare data that cannot be presented effectively in a report.

For these reasons, reports can be expected to remain the preferred visual tool for the delivery of information to diverse audiences that make up the healthcare organization. A reporting strategy that uses a combination of standard pre-packaged reports, *ad-hoc* reports and statistical reports based on common form and structure can improve communication and collaboration among users that span multiple facilities, specialties, departments and positional roles.

It is not an accident that most healthcare organizations and related stakeholders, such as Centers for Medicare & Medicaid Services (CMS) and state governments, require or rely on standard reports that are built upon key metrics or measures to demonstrate efficiencies and potential for improvements in cost and quality. William Fera, MD, Vice President of Medical Technologies, University of Pittsburg Medical Center, underscores this reality when he says moving forward, "hospitals will have to create more reports for such things as [CMS' core measures], making automated reporting mandatory."[2]

While healthcare organizations must evaluate important information and performance management topics such as source system profiling, key performance indicators (KPI) selection, data quality, data warehouse (DW)-BI architectures and data governance among other important topics, it is equally critical to define and implement a unified reporting strategy across the healthcare enterprise. Given the key role reporting plays in BI delivery, having such a strategy in place ensures reports are:

- Topical—The reports contain information that is meaningful and relevant for the target audience.
- Timely—Reports are published based on a reliable schedule or on-demand based on the type of report being requested.
- Temporal—Reports support prospective and retrospective analyses by allowing for the versioning of the final reports and/or the "point-in-time" *ad-hoc* query/dynamic filters.
- Template-driven—Content and visual styles used for specific reports/report types are based on a unified template that reflects the organization's goals and priorities.
- Transparent—Reports contain metadata to describe the purpose and intended uses of the report; contain formulae, definitions and additional documentation/references; and provide clear and traceable data lineage to the original data source (e.g., EMR, LIS, RIS, PACS, pharmacy, CPOE, ADT, billing, ERP or other operational source system).

The use of a reporting strategy assures that intended recipients receive reports appropriate for their specific roles. Physicians, nurses, department managers, patient accounting analysts and hospital executives need reports that are user friendly and reliable for their specific roles. Not all reporting strategies are alike—there is no "one size fits all" approach.

REPORT CAPABILITY LEVELS: 1-4

The four capability levels for healthcare organization reporting are:
1. Level 1: Stand-alone spreadsheets.
2. Level 2: Operational reporting.
3. Level 3: Tactical reporting.
4. Level 4: Enterprise reporting.

As the name of each level indicates, the data sources, business drivers, processes and deliverables constitute each capability level. These levels vary considerably as one moves from lower to higher levels of reporting capability. What's acceptable in terms of Level 1 reporting capabilities may not be sufficient to achieve Levels 2, 3 or 4.

The focus on getting the most appropriate reporting capabilities in place is critical, not just from an information management perspective but also for very real reasons that involve the changes in healthcare today: "Achieving the government's definition of meaningful EHR use is only half the battle. It's the reporting requirements and how they will be done that is the real challenge."[3]

LEVEL 1: STAND-ALONE SPREADSHEETS

Characteristics

A stand-alone spreadsheet is a visual media approach to provide a single source of information in a grid format independent of any other application to external data sources. Spreadsheets are usually designed and maintained by a "guru" who understands how to manipulate imported data and present useful information. Additionally, stand-alone spreadsheet reporting would provide better service if the results could be exported to other applications or devices for further analysis.

Advantages

Spreadsheets are flexible, inexpensive and easy to use and are available with most commercial (may be expensive) and open source office packages. Spreadsheets are a good fit when there is a need to create one-off, "on the fly" reports or in making impromptu data calculations. Most spreadsheet packages provide support for analytical and mathematical functions and provide options for simple to complex graphical charting. For these reasons, spreadsheets continue to be popular as a reporting solution in healthcare organizations, and in some cases, have found use as a basic, multi-purpose, desktop-based solution for BI analytical reporting.

Despite their popularity and features, spreadsheet-based reports may require more experienced skill sets to integrate disparate data elements from multiple sources into a single report. This is a common requirement today in healthcare; examples include reports for CMS Core Measures, Healthcare Effectiveness Data and Information Set (HEDIS) and Meaningful Use Measures. Oftentimes sourcing and managing data to meet this Level 1 capability involves the approach of "exporting data into a spreadsheet and the ensuing data chaos."[4]

Disadvantages

Level 1 spreadsheet reporting has the following process and technical disadvantages over the higher reporting capability levels:

- Due to the nature of their primary desktop-based usage and lack of sophisticated validation rule frameworks, spreadsheets are particularly susceptible to inadvertent human errors such as copy/paste errors, incorrect data input, wrong calculations or improper reference range or benchmark selection. This risk can be mitigated by the use of locking cells and using automated means to populate the data instead of manual copy/paste.
- Spreadsheets may impose a security risk due to the lack of server-side access and authentication; spreadsheet reports can present challenges to secure storage and use of protected health information.
- It is not uncommon for organizations that rely only on spreadsheets for reporting to overlook the important aspects of appropriate security, version control and back-up/recovery, without which can create many uncontrolled spreadsheet reports and introduce patient security risks.
- Level 1 spreadsheet reporting is prone to inconsistent organization-wide reporting—this often happens when a summary or an aggregate report for an organization is fed data by different departments that use their own individual spreadsheets. Even if most of the data in these spreadsheets were exported from a single healthcare source system, erroneous linking and a lack of semantic and metric conformance can lead to inconsistent and contradictory reports.

- Analysis of complex clinical, financial and quality indicators in healthcare using spreadsheet reporting will be risky, complex, non-integrated and may lack both detail and report-level metadata and documentation.
- Level 1 spreadsheet reporting brings with it the inability to scale or foster collaboration and shared healthcare insights—spreadsheets are susceptible to subjective analyses. They do not support advanced querying and lack the features and functions that support the ability of healthcare organizations to obtain reliable and actionable BI—analysis of data and sharing of insights across regions, facilities and departments are much more difficult to implement using Level 1 reporting capabilities.
- Finally, despite their report presentation and charting capabilities, "PC-based graphical rendering of tabular [report] data are usually inappropriate for all but small, department level KPI reporting projects."[5]

In conclusion, Level 1 capabilities have little potential to meet the dynamic and diverse needs of BI in today's healthcare organization. Level 1 requires little more than the collection of data of uncertain lineage and quality, and the resultant querying, analysis, security and presentation are based on relatively rudimentary desktop-based functions—a sure-fire recipe for disaster given the prevalence of sensitive patient data and confidential employee and business data in the enterprise.

(Note: In recent years, most BI tool vendors have started providing for greater integration between popular spreadsheet software and an underlying and dedicated BI front-end tool–in line with the capabilities described later in Level 3. In such scenarios, when the disconnected nature of stand-alone spreadsheets and their other disadvantages are buttressed by Level 3 capabilities, a spreadsheet-based report interface may be considered for a specific report consumer segment, such as healthcare finance teams.)

LEVEL 2: OPERATIONAL REPORTING

Operational reporting refers to reports that are typically generated and published within any single transaction source system—usually through a client-server or hosted environment. Operational reports present data that are generated in the transaction source systems used to run the business operations such as EHRs, billing, contract management, patient registration/admission or other source systems. Operational reports are generally available for distribution as pre-packaged reports from the transaction source system in question and are flexible enough to answer most questions on operational intelligence, such as "How many patients were admitted at the facility today?" or "How many vials of Epogen are in stock currently?"

A focus on operational reporting of the BI implementation is perfectly acceptable if the business requirements for BI are met initially by Level 2 capabilities. In some healthcare organizations that might indeed be the case. For example, if a practice can address its analytics capabilities based on operational reports and does not have the need for Level 3 or Level 4 reporting, so be it. Therefore, the desire for an organization to operate at Level 2 capability is not determined by so-called "maturity," but its decision to focus on measuring and optimizing operational processes.

Disadvantages

- Due to their origins in transaction source systems and given their very nature, operational reports may be limited to focusing on current data, with little or no support for historical data. The lack of historical information in operational reports makes their use limited for answering questions that deal with past performance, trending or "point-in-time" analysis.

- Given their antecedents in a single source system and their primary focus on narrow business processes measurement, most operational reports affect a relatively small percentage of users in the entire organization as a whole.

- Additionally, due to the silo nature of many transaction source systems, operational reports may well be duplicated across your facility or enterprise and may even lead to unclear insights if the organization is forced to rely on many operational reports from a number of different source systems.

- Analysis across business processes, business units or source systems is not possible with just operational reporting.

- Transaction source systems don't often contain support for report hierarchies that are essential to perform drill-down/up/across dimensional data. Even when such hierarchies exist, they are rudimentary and not flexible enough to meet reporting needs.

- By their very nature, transaction source systems are optimized for insert and update data operations (where the focus is on writing data into the database). Detailed reports, on the other hand, rely on queries that may need to run across silo source systems, aggregate (by period, region, etc.) or dimensions. Consistently fast and reliable reporting is required for meaningful use, for example, and may not be served by limiting capabilities to Level 2. By doing so, this approach may very well be consigning the organization to making changes to the EHR each time a meaningful use or other reporting rule is extended or modified.

Table 11-1: Differences Between Level 2 and Level 3 and 4 Reporting.

Difference	Level 2 Reporting	Level 3 and Level 4 Reporting
Purpose	Analysis of business operations usually based on data from a single transaction source system.	Supports tactical and historical reporting across more than one source system and typically uses an underlying data mart or DW.
History	Current information with little history.	Historical data that supports trend analysis, comparative analysis across dimension, "slowly-changing" dimensional analysis.
Timeliness	Real-time or near real-time.	Batch or near real-time.
Level of Atomic Detail	Atomic data only.	Atomic and aggregate/summary data with varying levels of granularity.
Query Response Time	Not optimized for complex queries; optimized for write/ update inputs.	Optimized for complex queries that can support pre-packaged/*ad-hoc*/ advanced reports.
Hierarchies	Limited or not available.	Can be defined with a great amount of detail and optimized for analysis.
Report Detail	Pre-packaged reports that are fixed in terms of facts and dimensions.	Fixed or *ad-hoc* reporting and analysis by multiple drill paths and across different healthcare business functions.

In conclusion, Level 2 capabilities have the potential to meet the dynamic and diverse needs of BI in the healthcare organization if the focus is limited to measuring operational processes and efficiencies. Level 2 reporting capabilities do not require the use of standard reporting processes, a dedicated BI tool, or the definition of facility- or enterprise-wide Meta Data Model (MDM) or business rules—the absence of these characteristics doesn't prevent Level 2 as a way to begin BI efforts. If the organization's BI requirements change, the current Level 2 capabilities can be used as a stepping-stone to Level 3 or 4, as depicted in Table 11-1.

LEVEL 3: TACTICAL REPORTING

Characteristics and Advantages

Level 3 reporting is characterized by:

- Use of a distinct and common BI reporting tool across the organization.
- Creation of underlying reporting databases or data marts that are distinct from transaction source systems.
- Definition of common templates for content and look and feel across individual departments or smaller facilities.
- Support for pre-packaged, online and *ad-hoc* reporting (based on the selected tools).
- Support for atomic and aggregate data.
- Support for historical data, versions and slowly changing dimensions (based on the selected DW-BI architecture).
- Varying levels of support for a standard reporting strategy across the entire organization (to be discussed in detail in Level 4 in the next section) mean that Level 3 can serve as a good starting point in an organization with varying degrees of comfort with a culture of healthcare data analysis and performance management.
- Support for standardization of select hierarchies and master data across reports for one or more departments and business units.

Level 3 capabilities provide a common presentation front-end at the very least and may additionally provide a common information architecture that can be expanded upon if the organization's BI requirements require a more enterprise-wide Level 4 approach.

Tactical reporting refers to the set of capabilities that must be developed to support reports and BI across multiple transaction source systems, departments, business processes and roles. Level 3 capabilities are midway between Level 2's operational reporting and Level 4's integrated enterprise reporting.

Disadvantages

- As the focus in Level 3 is mostly on a common front-end reporting tool and standard report templates, there is a strong possibility the underlying data might still be sourced from silo transaction systems, albeit with organization of those data for complex report querying and analysis. As a result, Level 3 reporting tends to be adequate only if the numbers of source systems are relatively fewer in number or the current BI requirements (for example, for meaningful use) can be met entirely by a set of common reports.
- The lack of an enterprise reporting strategy may result in perpetuating the silo nature of transactional source system data except for the fact that the results are now presented within a common reporting tool. The absence of dimensional conformance, standard report metadata and standardized master data may still result in reports that don't serve the requirements for cross-functional comparisons.
- Reliance on a common reporting tool and little else in terms of reporting strategy may result in a situation where reports are duplicates of each other across departments or facilities even if they convey the same information to similar audiences.

- Typically, Level 3 capabilities involve a heavy reliance on IT and report developers to deliver infrequent and unplanned reports; as a result, it may end with a set of pre-packaged reports limited to what IT can deliver in their window. This over-reliance on IT, by its very nature, reduces self-service and *ad-hoc* reporting and restricts users from asking questions beyond the limited ones they have been given access to and beyond ones obvious to a limited set of users.

In conclusion, BI requirements should drive the adoption of Level 3 capabilities or beyond. In a smaller hospital setting (such as community hospitals), a Level 3 reporting capability might get the required reports that answer operational, tactical and limited strategic BI questions.

LEVEL 4: ENTERPRISE REPORTING

In the previous sections, Levels 1, 2 and 3 reporting capabilities were discussed and characterized by differing advantages and disadvantages. In order to achieve the full potential of the BI front-end, maximize investments in data warehousing and management and meet the varied information needs of diverse users across the healthcare organization, the BI project team must consider establishing comprehensive reporting capabilities that are reliable, scalable, timely and usable serving as a driver for analysis-based action.

A Level 4 enterprise reporting capability is more than just meeting the immediate reporting needs of the next government regulation. Developing and maintaining this capability allows a healthcare organization to define reports that can help their readers better understand not just the trends, say in enterprise-wide quality and patient safety, but also understand the reasons behind outliers and abnormal patterns. More importantly, an enterprise reporting capability accounts for and addresses the different reporting regimes–at federal, state and accreditation organization levels–and their changing requirements.

Finally, integrated reports supported by the ability to query conformed data from multiple source systems can help providers get a view into integrated financial and clinical outcomes, thus leading to healthier patients, improved operational and financial efficiencies and more informed users.

An important point to note here is that achieving Level 4—enterprise reporting capabilities is not the same as implementing an enterprise data warehouse (EDW)-based on its requirements, an organization could well create a comprehensive EDW of the conformed/fully-integrated/hybrid variety and still be found lacking at presenting data effectively to the broadest audience by failing to come up with the needed Level 4 approach.

Understandably, coming up with the required Level 4 capabilities is not easy for any organization in the absence of a clear definition of what constitutes BI reporting success in an enterprise approach. As a result, the next section will introduce nine factors that define BI reporting success and will list some best practices that can be deployed to achieve success on each of these factors.

1. Determine Scope and Purpose of Reports across the Enterprise

- Identify the operational, tactical and strategic reports required for the organization, based on its current and anticipated BI needs.
- Start with a limited and manageable set of reports at first. While it is tempting to define a large ecosystem of diverse reports using a "Big Bang" approach, consider starting small with a limited scope of measurements and reports and expanding that number incrementally while keeping the larger picture in mind. What is the reason for starting small? Well,

creating reports is only one part of the equation—the team must still define the queries, organize appropriate data sources and cleanse/integrate data in order to create reports trusted by their consumers.

- Define a "living" report inventory and report business owners/stakeholders/consumers; doing so avoids the problems of duplicate reports and efforts and provides a shared road-map of future report scope and focus.

2. Audience Analysis and Report Types

- A report is effective when its intended audience understands what to do with the infor-mation. Therefore, it is essential to understand the job roles, responsibilities and expecta-tions of the intended audience for each report. After all, there is little use in publishing or enabling access to a report containing detailed tables and pretty charts if it does not meet the needs of the intended consumer. For example, the head of surgery in the hospital might require a set of reports around turnaround times and same-day cancellation rates, while the director of supply chain might require reports on inventory—each with their specific requirements on report frequency and granularity.

- Choose and use the right medium—reports can be developed for print or online media with multiple options for each. The choice of the medium must be based on the audience for the report, as well as the intended action expected of the report recipient. Reports that need to be shared collaboratively and accessed by multiple users are better off being delivered in one of many online formats—PDF, native BI report formats, and web-based interfaces among others. Reports being submitted as a part of a documented request for proposal (RFP) or a printed grant application might be better off optimized and deliv-ered via print.

- When required, consider delivering the same report across multiple media—say, via the web, as a PDF and on paper. Choose a BI front-end tool that provides such a publishing feature.

- Based on analysis of users across the organization, the BI project team might want to consider providing access to all three types of BI reports discussed earlier in this chapter:
  a. Pre-packaged reports: these reports are canned and are published via a fixed format and with static summary or aggregated data that are organized typically along a single dimension.
  b. *Ad-hoc* reports: these reports are dynamic—while the presentation can be based on a standard template, an *ad-hoc* report is created dynamically based on a spontaneous (or *ad-hoc*) query that is generated by the report user using either a graphical user inter-face (GUI) or using a querying language such as Structured Query Language (SQL). *Ad-hoc* reports can serve as a foundation for self-service where business users across your organization—and not just IT—have the ability to create, save and manage their own report queries and results within a well-defined framework of templates, data conformance and standardized master data.
  c. The BI front-end tool and its reporting capabilities must allow for the ability to con-vert and publish *ad-hoc* reports into pre-packaged reports.
  d. Advanced reports: these reports are also dynamic and offer a set of advanced report features such as multiple drill-paths, multi-dimensional filtering, user-defined sub-select query criteria, and statistical tools—in addition to the option of creating both pre-packaged and *ad-hoc* reports.

3. Report Scheduling and Frequency

- Report scheduling refers to the published schedule that accompanies each report. The report schedule must be included or referenced from the report inventory and must account for the entire gamut of data management activities that will be required to make sure the report is available to its audience on the date it is supposed to be available. For *ad-hoc* reports, scheduling must take into account query response times for reference data sets.
- Report frequency, on the other hand, refers to the published and pre-defined interval at which each report is refreshed with updated data and published or made accessible to business users. Some reports, such as Quarterly Cash Flow, will be required to be refreshed and republished at lower frequency than a report on ED Waiting Time. Specific reports designed for a particular department or service head tend to be required at greater frequencies than a summary report on combined departmental data.[6]

4. Presenting Text, Tables and Charts

This sub-section is not intended to be the definitive reference on report design, charting or the visual display of quantitative information. Authors like Fry, Tufte, and Cunningham have written entire books on these topics, while The Joint Commission's *Tools for Performance Management in Healthcare* remains an excellent reference.

There are a few important guidelines that must be followed at the very minimum to ensure the best possible presentation of the available data to the intended report user:

- There is no single best representation of quantitative data; some reports are best expressed in tables while others might also require the appropriate accompanying charts. Users also have personal preferences and creating both text and graphical representations of a single report may sometimes be helpful in making sure the report stays effective across varying media and user preferences.
- Keep in mind that while colorful reports and BI front-end "eye candy" make for pretty pictures and "may even have a place in presenting medical KPI information to decision makers, graphics do not obviate the need for traditional tabular reports."[7]
- Remember report design is a four-step process. The scope/purpose of the report and a thorough understanding of the intended audience is both critical for the remaining two steps of report creation: defining the report data and metadata and arranging them on the page or screen.
- Keep it short and simple; based on the information it contains, the ideal report should be one page long. If the report has to be longer than a page, it must be paginated accordingly so only one page of information is presented to the user at a given time. Report usability requires the content of the tables/text or charts to convey a unified message and to be easily understood by the intended user.
- Use color, shading or graphics like call-outs to highlight key findings, alerts, discrepancies or major indicators such as targets and goals.
- Provide report metadata in the report header, body or footer; such metadata must include at the very least, the objective of the report, name of the report, report and data definitions, important background information or dependencies, and limitations on the data including the confidence factor. Also be sure to provide the necessary date and times of report creation and validity period. Finally, include documentation on the intended audience for the report including any limitations on report distribution.

- Graphs and charts must be used judiciously and when the purpose of the report or its audience demands it. When graphs and charts accompany a report, make sure the type chosen meets the appropriate analytics needs.

Table 11-2: Chart Type and Type of Analysis Supported.

Chart Type	Supported Analysis	Example
Line graph	Identify trends and corresponding values.	Inpatient Medical Diagnosis-related Groups (DRG) Trend Report. Case Mix Index
Bar graph	Displays multiple instances, as opposed to a single instance, of one or more measures; useful to emphasize distribution of individual values as opposed to a trend.	Q1 2011 Total of Inpatient Admissions by Facility. *Few 130*
Bullet graph	Displays a critical measure, qualitative ranges, and current status/progress/ adherence to pre-defined goals or targets.	2011 YTD Patient Satisfaction Report in relation to a target. *Few 125*
Pareto chart	Displays individual values as bars and cumulative total of these values along a categorical scale.	*Few 138*
Sparklines	Tufte's "data intensive, design simple, word-sized graphic that provides a highly condensed form of data display;" do not provide the quantitative precision or detail that exists in a line graph.	Lab result report that includes a concise summary trend of the lab values for a single patient across a defined time period.
Scatter plot	Displays correlation between two sets of comparative or cause/effect quantitative values.	Correlation between patient education and patient outcomes for a population. *Few 146*
Treemaps	Displays large sets of hierarchical or categorized data by making most efficient use of limited report "real estate."	Reimbursement (revenue and % of total revenue) by payer. *Few 148*

Readers may recognize some common chart types like the ubiquitous pie chart or the increasingly discussed radar graph are not included in Table 11-2. The reason for not including these chart types is straightforward—the chart types listed in the preceding table do a better job of presenting quantitative information and require less human cognitive processing to absorb the information than other options available in the wide world of BI reporting tools.

As reiterated earlier, a report is primarily a technical communication deliverable that is optimized for the delivery, display and usage of information; hence, it is entirely appropriate to choose the right chart type for the purpose as opposed to experimenting with the latest report/ chart visualization option just because the option is now available in the newest version of the chosen reporting tool.

5. Managing Report Hierarchies and Drill Paths

Managing report hierarchies is critical to BI success; a hierarchy is a type of a parent-child relationship where the child represents a lower level of detail, or granularity, of the parent. Hierarchies are one of the foundational components of BI and reporting. The following describe uses and provide further description of their role:

- Define the chain of command, i.e., delineate the aggregation of responsibilities from lower level staff members to senior management.
- Differentiate and aggregate business entities like organization nodes and types and groups of codes, products, staff members and clinical/financial dimensions.
- Traverse between aggregate data and summarize data and details via drill up and drill-down paths and perform comparative dimensional analysis using drill across.
- Reports may require support for both balanced and ragged hierarchies.
- Balanced hierarchies are full through all levels of the hierarchy. By full, it is meant all leaves exist at the lowest level in the hierarchy, and every parent node is one level removed from the child node.
- Ragged hierarchies are hierarchies of varying depth and are characterized by missing hierarchy levels across hierarchies within a single hierarchy type.
- As there might be multiple hierarchy types and multiple hierarchies within a hierarchy type within an enterprise, the MDM processes, report templates and BI tool must provide the ability for a user to pick and choose a single hierarchy type and a constituent hierarchy among multiple choices for a specific report.

6. Creating Bi-Directional Reports

A report must not only be the vehicle for delivering pre-packaged intelligence or responding to *ad-hoc* queries, but must also enable user action by providing alerts and triggering source system workflows from within reports.

7. Track Report Usage Patterns and Make the Necessary Changes

- Track report usage patterns to find out what works/does not work in a report or across a larger report category. Solicit feedback (preferably via the ability of the reader to score the usability and appropriateness of information within a report and at its point of use or via stand-alone survey tools) on a regular basis.
- Be prepared to retire reports that don't meet the needs of the audience; conversely, be prepared to create new reports or modify existing reports based on audience demand.
- Use the information from report usage patterns and audience feedback to modify and optimize the organization's report definition/inventory processes.

8. Select the Tool at the End

- Most reporting tools are focused on general business requirements and may not contain all the features, which are required to get the desired level of reporting capability. Choosing a reporting tool before deciding on more important success factors might result in the possibility that the tool in question might not meet the organization's needs.
- Establish business need and value each report will provide. The rationale for a report should be better than "don't we all need better data?" or "our current reporting tool does not have the latest bells and whistles." Determine the value of each report in terms of its cost, impact on quality of care, regulatory requirements and its impact on the humans who will interact and be affected by the report in question.

- Define the processes and communication mechanisms required for data analysis, change management and Level 4 report governance next.
- Then, select KPIs, identify data sources, and define reports with the help of the intended audience.
- When the project is ready to select a tool, make sure it not only meets current reporting levels but is also scalable to meet future requirements around mergers and acquisitions, increasing numbers of report users, report delivery options including automated submission, auditing, and archiving and variety of operational or transactional data.

9. Other Best Practices

- Agility is not just for athletes—in today's healthcare organization, there is a relatively short time frame between a request for a report and the time available to deliver it to accomplish critical business needs. Plan on rapid design and development practices that focus on shorter business requirements to report deployment durations.
- Create report prototypes— creating and testing report prototypes before deployment to their intended audience is always a good idea. Prototyping allows both report developers and users to identify potential issues and address them proactively, as opposed to reacting to problems after they occur.
- Separate development/testing/production environments—exposing reports that are not fully developed or tested to users in an actual production environment is always a bad idea. The production environment, by its very definition, assumes the reports being delivered are appropriate, validated for data quality, and connected to reliable data sources. Using one environment for all three purposes listed here is always a recipe for confusion, uncertainty or worse.

STAFFING APPROPRIATELY: THE ROLE OF THE REPORT ANALYST AS A BRIDGE TO BUSINESS AND IT

The preceding sections in this chapter discuss the whys, whats and hows of best practices that will help the organization obtain repeatable success with a reporting strategy. However, this chapter will be incomplete without a discussion of the people and skill sets required to achieve and maintain Level 4 capabilities.

Healthcare organizations should create a culture of analytics based on reporting. In order to do so, the first step will likely involve the creation of a separate BI reporting team comprising cross-functional roles such as the report analyst, business user representatives, and IT. Getting to Level 4 requires vision, strategy and collaboration; a team consisting of people who are well-versed in these distinct roles will pay off in the long run.

The report analyst fills one of the most critical roles on this team. The person playing this role should ideally have a background that includes prior experience in at least one of the following areas:

- Clinical
- Hospital administration
- Healthcare revenue cycle/supply chain management
- Healthcare informatics, specifically data warehousing and BI

This prior expertise is important for one simple reason—having a background in any of these areas ensures domain expertise and reduces any learning curve that would otherwise be steep for somebody who is trying to fill this role for the first time. The report analyst should also have prior expertise in developing reports and other technical communication deliverables and should be able to understand both the sources of data across the organization, as well as the information demands being placed on the reporting front by multiple and varied audiences. While it is not always essential given the presence of IT representatives on the team, having a report analyst who understands different reporting options and capabilities from both the domain and the technical perspectives will ensure this person truly becomes a bridge between the various cross-functional team members and also to the rest of the organization.

It is also important the report analyst have access to the different business users who will utilize the reports. Such access on an ongoing basis is critical not only for successful requirements elicitation sessions but also for instituting feedback mechanisms and for managing user feedback.

Finally, it is expected the report analyst, while not being an IT expert, knows enough about the selected reporting architecture, technology and information display best practices to be able to create basic, effective reports on their own, while collaborating with the IT team in order to explore and develop more complex reports and advanced functionality.

CASE STUDY 11-1

LEVERAGING HEALTH ANALYTICS FOR EMERGING HEALTH ISSUES

Interview with Dr Jeffrey M. Ferranti, MD, Associate Chief Information Officer, Enterprise Analytics and Patient Safety, Duke University Health System, Durham, NC

Business Scope/Need

"In the wake of a declaration of a pandemic of H1N1 influenza ('swine flu') by the [World Health Organization] WHO in the spring of 2009, the DUHS [Duke University Health System] faced the problem of estimating the amount of vaccine it would need to request in order to meet the needs of the communities it serves."

Business Solution

DUHS used its data warehouse to provide a highly refined estimate of patients likely to need H1N1 vaccine. A query based on CDC [Centers for Disease Control] vaccination priority eligibility criteria was applied to create a report of all patients with a status of 'alive' in the data warehouse. Patients were further grouped according to inpatient status and whether they were noted as having a chronic disease as defined by specific ICD-9 codes.

Benefits

- The use of data from the DUHS data warehouse and the generation of reports based on pre-defined criteria using an appropriate BI front-end reporting tool allowed this organization to refine its estimate of vaccine need and prioritize vaccine administration to high-risk patients (pregnant women and children) across the entire health system.
- The results of the reporting on the underlying data led to almost immediate action; within 24 hours, DUHS created reports that contained generated contacts lists for high-risk patients, coupled with details about their next scheduled appointment in the health system.
- This reporting approach enabled the targeted delivery of vaccine to high-volume clinics and prompted a focused education and marketing campaign aimed at getting the highest-risk patients to a clinic for early immunization.

Key Point

This case study demonstrates how BI tools equip clinical leaders with data that allow them to make the most informed decisions for their patients, as well as helping them adapt quickly to changing circumstances.

SUMMARY

At its core, the basic definition of a report has remained unchanged—a report is simply a document or medium that presents text, numbers and charts in a coherent and structured manner that facilitates analysis and action. Reports can be delivered across multiple media—hardcopy or print, through the web, via online portals, pre-packaged templates or *ad-hoc* query tools, which emphasize self-service information retrieval and allow non-IT users to ask spontaneous (or *ad-hoc*) questions and receive structured reports in near real-time and on demand.

Understanding the organization's reporting capabilities and developing a robust reporting strategy are foundational to BI success. Reports are the most popular visual tool in healthcare BI and remain the primary method by which results of retrospective and prospective analysis are communicated within the healthcare organization.

The four levels of BI reporting capabilities may currently exist or may be developed for the healthcare organization. Rationale was presented whether an organization ought to consider a comprehensive Level 4 enterprise reporting strategy aligned with recommendations for best practices based on research and experience. It has also been discussed how the BI project team can develop and leverage upon existing resources and skill sets. Implementing a Level 4 reporting capability should encompass strategic, tactical and operational reporting requirements, as opposed to the more limited efforts that are usually sufficient to achieve capability Levels 1, 2 and 3.

Table 11-3: Chapter 11 Checklist—Communicating Through Robust Reporting.

Item	Completed (Yes/No)
1. Define the BI reporting requirements unique to your organizational characteristics, staffing and strategic needs.	
2. Evaluate staffing. Starting incrementally, the healthcare organization begins with any appropriate level of maturity and moves on to the next level. Even if there are short-term pressures, avoid the temptation to go back to the previous level (i.e., Level 2) after achieving a higher level (i.e., Level 3).	
3. Determine the scope and purpose of reports across the healthcare organization; the journey becomes easier if the project team has determined these requirements.	
4. Choose and use the appropriate report type, frequency and media to communicate the BI results.	
5. Present text and charts in the most effective way possible for the intended audience; do not allow the reporting tool to determine the choices.	
6. Decide on a reporting tool only after completing at least the vast majority, if not all, of the analyses described earlier in Level 4.	
7. Create bi-directional reports; use reports to institute and drive a culture of data consumption and analysis.	
8. Track report usage patterns, and make the necessary changes in order to drive user acceptance and buy-in.	

Table 11-3: Chapter 11 Checklist—Communicating Through Robust Reporting. (cont.)

Item	Completed (Yes/No)
9. Don't forget about hierarchies and drill paths—the most visually pleasing report is useless if it does not provide support for hierarchies. Hierarchies are critical for organizing data and serve as a foundation for drill-up/down behaviors.	
10. Create a cross-functional reporting team, and identify who will fill the critical role of report analyst.	

REFERENCES

1. Raths D. Business intelligence efforts get a boost. *Healthc Inform*. 2011;(1):18, 20, 22-3.
2. Page D. Data mining is vital as meaningful use looms. *Hosp Health Netw*. 2010;84(2):10.
3. Goedert J. What meaningful use means now. *Health Data Manag*. 2010; 18(9):18, 20, 22.
4. Howson C. *Successful Business Intelligence: Secrets to Making BI a Killer App*. New York: McGraw-Hill Osborne Media; 2007:179.
5. Bergeron BP. *Performance Management in Healthcare: From Key Performance Indicators to Balanced Scorecard*. Chicago: HIMSS; 2006:110.
6. Bergeron BP. *Performance Management in Healthcare: From Key Performance Indicators to Balanced Scorecard*. Chicago: HIMSS; 2006:104.
7. Bergeron BP. *Performance Management in Healthcare: From Key Performance Indicators to Balanced Scorecard*. Chicago: HIMSS; 2006:106.

CHAPTER 12

Further Diagnosing with Drill-Down Capabilities

By Michael Whitecar, MIS, LCDR (ret.), MSC, USN

Drilling is a technique that enables a business intelligence (BI) user to quickly navigate through various levels of data, finding the answers to the questions facing the healthcare organization. Depending on one's needs, drilling can be used to view the data in deeper detail or, in contrast, drill it up to a higher summary level. The drilling to detail technique enables an analyst to look at the values making up a particular summary value. Also, the analyst can drill to related items, adding related information that is not currently included in the initial dashboard display. Drilling down on the data is an important process that looks at trends, variations and helps in figuring out where a root cause may lie.

To drill-down through a series of folders, for example, on a desktop means to go through the hierarchy of folders to find a specific file or to click through drop-down menus. To drill-down through a database is to access information by starting with a general category and moving through the hierarchy of file to record to field.

Drill-down will give stakeholders a deeper awareness of the data by letting them see what makes up the figures they are analyzing. For example, using Figure 12-1 as a measurement of a healthcare organization's departmental profitability, we see that there was a huge drop toward the end of 2010. What happened? Why did this occur?

By providing the ability to drill-down to the specific numbers, the user might be able to gain a better understanding of the cause. The number can be drilled down into the billable units to see what tests or procedures were off. Once a specific procedure is identified, the analyst can drill-down to the physicians involved and see who might be ordering fewer tests or performing fewer procedures. From that data, the determination can be made. It might be as simple as a two-week vacation taken by a high-volume clinician or it could be that a competi-

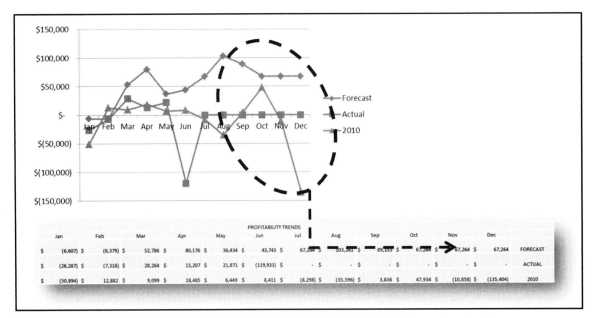

Figure 12-1: An Example of a Measurement of a Healthcare Organization's Departmental Profitability.

tor has lured key physicians to their facility and away from yours. Drilling is the technique that allows users to determine the causes of summary variations.

Drill-down also provides a mechanism to analyze the same data through different reports or using different features and even display it through different visualization methods. This greatly enhances understanding of the data and of the reasons behind the figures. Using the same data from our drill-down example, we can display profitability (net profit margin) a different way—by comparing it to operational margin, as seen in Figure 12-2.

By only presenting one layer of data at a time, features like drill-down lighten the load on the technologies that support the dashboard. This will be important to address so that stakeholders will be able to quickly retrieve the information they are seeking. This is where the feedback loop discussed in Chapter 8 will become very important to ensure that such a loop provides key stakeholders with a way to further communicate findings.

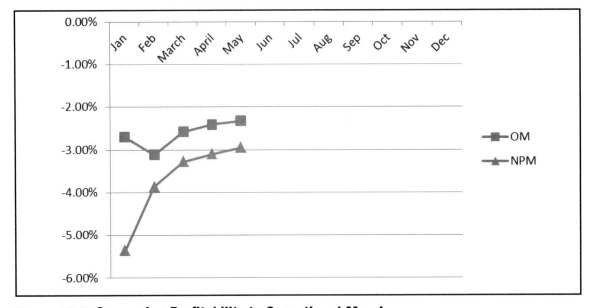

Figure 12-2: Comparing Profitability to Operational Margin.

TECHNIQUES

Drilling down into increasingly specific data is a common task that stakeholders may be interested in. When developing dashboards, developers will need to be on hand to regularly create user interfaces for the users to get to the data they need. While circumstances sometimes require custom user interfaces and tools, an Office application such as Microsoft® Office Excel can often suffice. A user can use smart tags to create a user interface that lets users drill into data progressively. A popular and widely used technique is to use Pivot Tables or Pivot Queries. This technique allows multiple representations of data according to different dimensions. Pivot Queries is similar to a tabular query, except it also allows data to be represented in summary format, according to a flexible user-selected hierarchy. This class of data drilling operation is formally (and loosely) known by different names, including cross tab query, pivot table, data pilot, or selective hierarchy. Analysts may often use a Pivot Table report when they want to analyze related totals, especially when there is a long list of figures to sum and comparison of several facts about each figure is desired.

To illustrate the basics of pivot query operations, consider Figure 12-3, depicting a summary of sales totals for medical devices.

Using a PivotTable report, each column or field in the source data becomes a PivotTable field (field: In a PivotTable or PivotChart report, a category of data that's derived from a field in the source data. PivotTable reports have row, column, page, and data fields. PivotChart reports have series, category, page, and data fields.) that summarizes multiple rows of information. In the example in Figure 12-3, the Medical Device column becomes the Medical Device field, and each record (a collection of information about a field) for Blood Glucose Monitor-

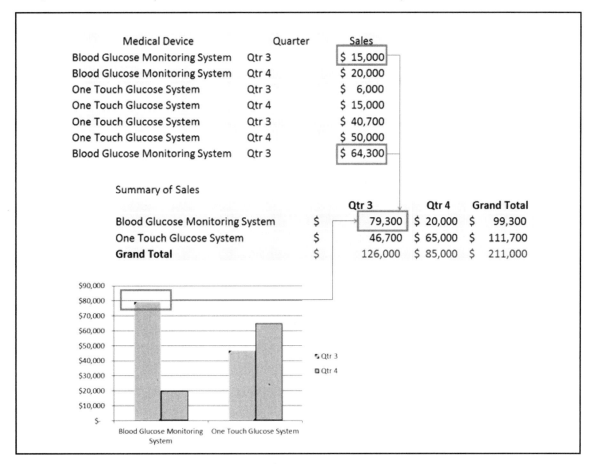

Figure 12-3: A Summary of Sales Totals for Medical Devices.

ing System is summarized in a single Blood Glucose Monitoring System item (item: A subcategory of a field in PivotTable and PivotChart reports. For instance, the field "Month" could have items such as "January," "February," and so on.). This is a simple example of drilling up to a summary level to more easily see the big picture. The power of the pivot is the end-user's ability to easily change perspectives as they work with the data.

A value field, such as Summary of Sales, contains the values to be summarized. In the previous report, the Qtr3 Blood Glucose Monitoring System summary contains the sum of the Sales value from every row in the source data for which the Medical Device column contains Blood Glucose Monitoring System and the Quarter column contains Qtr 3.

The chart in our example is a PivotChart. This report provides a graphical representation of the data represented in the PivotTable report, which in this case is called the associated PivotTable report (associated PivotTable report: The PivotTable report that supplies the source data to the PivotChart report. It is created automatically when you create a new PivotChart report. When you change the layout of either report, the other also changes.). A PivotChart report is interactive, which means that you can sort and filter it to show subsets of the PivotTable data. When creating a PivotChart report, PivotChart report filters are displayed in the chart area (chart area: The entire chart and all its elements.) so the user can sort and filter the underlying data of the PivotChart report. Changes that are made to the field layout and data in the associated PivotTable report are immediately reflected in the PivotChart report.

A PivotChart report displays data series (data series: Related data points that are plotted in a chart and originate from datasheet rows or columns. Each data series in a chart has a unique color or pattern. You can plot one or more data series in a chart. Pie charts have only one data series.), categories, data markers (data marker: A bar, area, dot, slice or other symbol in a chart that represents a single data point or value that originates from a worksheet cell. Related data markers in a chart constitute a data series.) and axes (axis: A line bordering the chart plot area used as a frame of reference for measurement. The y axis is usually the vertical axis and contains data. The x-axis is usually the horizontal axis and contains categories.) just as standard charts do. Users can also change the chart type and other options such as the titles (titles in charts: Descriptive text that is automatically aligned to an axis or centered at the top of a chart.), the legend (legend: A box that identifies the patterns or colors that are assigned to the data series or categories in a chart.) placement, the data labels (data label: A label that provides additional information about a data marker, which represents a single data point or value that originates from a worksheet cell.) and the chart location.

PivotTables should be designed to build summarized reports so that stakeholders can easily and quickly analyze large quantities of data. Features like filtering, top value display, hierarchical value arrangement on the axes, grand and group totals give you a wide range of tools to control the data's level of detail.

Many commercial dashboard systems have basic drill-down capabilities. It is the responsibility of the BI project team to set up this functionality. An admissions indicator might give the drill-down options by diagnosis-related group (DRG), physician, payer and source (ED, ambulatory care, etc.). Each of these elements gives a view into what factors are driving the admissions. Good systems will often have both data and trends at the drill-down level. Some will allow second- and third-level drill-downs. The BI project team needs to work with the key stakeholders to determine the most appropriate drill-down views.

When establishing drill-downs, the budgeted values need to be carefully considered. Often there are global numbers such as admissions per month, but there isn't a detailed budget by a physician or payer. It will therefore be the responsibility of the project team to figure out the most appropriate way to distribute the budgeted numbers across the drill-down values. The team must also be aware of the danger of drill-down values losing statistical significance. A metric like flu vaccine compliance may be below standard, and so the executive drills down by physician to see who isn't ordering the vaccine. As Dr. Smith is showing at 50 percent, the executive calls him into the office to discuss this non-compliant behavior. However, further evaluation may show that Dr. Smith only had two patients in the reporting period and the one who missed the vaccine had unique circumstances. Furthermore, Dr. Smith has a trend record of positive numbers. This is an example of how drilling down can cause erroneous interpretations if the user is not properly trained.

General users should find the previously mentioned systemic drill-down to be adequate for their purposes. More detailed drill-down and analysis requires greater understanding of the data and should be reserved for the power analyst. That analyst will use the pivot tables mentioned earlier or pre-aggregated dimensions, which are discussed next. Make sure that the proper tools and capabilities are available to the proper levels of BI users. Conversely, protect the integrity of the process by not giving access of the wrong tools to the wrong users.

TREND ANALYSIS

The term *trend analysis* or *benefit analysis* refers to the concept of collecting information and attempting to spot a pattern, or trend, in the information. In some fields of study, the term *trend analysis* has more formally-defined meanings.

Although trend analysis is often used to predict future events, it could be used to evaluate uncertain events in the past, such as how many medical devices contributed to high quarterly sales or in our earlier example questioning a low profitability?

Analysis is the step that will let key stakeholders understand their data, turning them into information; without analysis, data lose their context and much of their meaning. Using incorporated feedback loops, analysis will empower the organization to ask questions of their data; this is the main way in which users are said to "interact" with their data. In this sense, the more the analysis interface allows users to obtain meaningful answers to the questions raised by their data, the more the data are interactive. With these answers, the BI analyst is providing a guide for key stakeholders to help them make the correct decisions and take appropriate actions. Again referring to our earlier examples, analysis highlights the critical factors and points the users toward them. By doing so, it facilitates prioritization and makes the overall business process more efficient.

When developing utilities to provide trend or benefit analysis, leverage the power and user's familiarity of the web to make features easy and intuitive to navigate. Empower as many of your stakeholders as possible to analyze the relevant portions of the organization's data. If the institution is using a commercial BI product, try to choose a web-based solution that is licensed to be distributed to unlimited end users without additional cost, as is the case with server-based licensing.

ANALYZING DATA FROM DIFFERENT DIMENSIONS

Multidimensional databases are usually quite complex architectures. In these databases, intersections of relevant data become more apparent, so that the data are easier to group, summarize and analyze. What this means, in simple terms, is prioritizing the way data are shown by a given category or grouping. For example, if there is a table of data about medical devices, it can be analyzed by product type (a dimension), by demographic (another dimension), by geographic region (another dimension), etc. The data that are seen can always be the same, but they are prioritized by whatever column is placed first, which is called a dimension. In practice, this requires the data dimensions to be pre-calculated. Figure 12-4 shows how data are laid out within a cube.

To facilitate drill-down capabilities with multidimensional databases, a common best practice is to use online analytical processing or OLAP; simply a fancy term for multidimensional analysis. OLAP is the process of analyzing data from different dimensions, which is why the data sets to be analyzed are called OLAP cubes. For example, OLAP will allow a clinician to answer questions like "how many prescriptions of such and such type drug did I prescribe last year?" and "of those prescribed for headaches, how many were prescribed to people over 65?"

There are many benefits to using a web-based OLAP analytical service. First, it's very powerful, often providing complete analysis that answers "why" and "how" questions. Multidimensional analysis allows for a great degree of understanding of the reasons behind the data. This is what is called "slicing and dicing" of data—namely looking at data at different levels of detail, as well as from different perspectives to understand them better. To slice and dice cube data on the fly, various dimensions, measures and filters all within a web browser can be achieved by using "interactive access" to OLAP data. With web-based access, the IT department should be able to set up a connection to OLAP cubes in minutes. This is a very nice benefit which gives zero-footprint access to OLAP analysis. When users access the OLAP reporting interface, no client software has to be installed. They easily perform on-demand analysis in the web-browser.

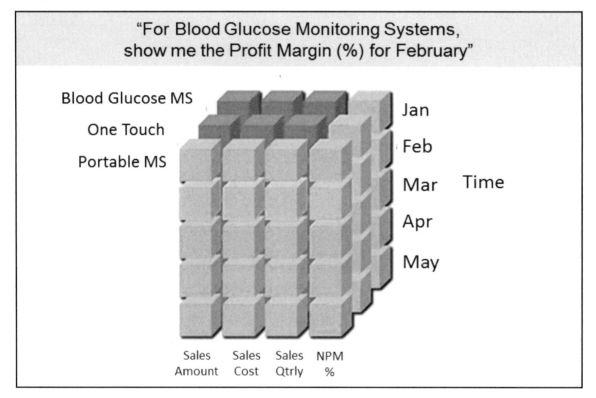

Figure 12-4: How Data Are Laid Out within a Cube.

SUMMARY

Use technology smartly. Identify when it is appropriate to drill-down into data to be able to perform further analysis. It is key to remember that the technology and the features derived from it are only tools. Ask what goal the tools are meant to achieve, and design the analysis interface to attain those goals. Set up reporting and analysis solutions to point the stakeholders to the most critical items, using features like dashboards, key performance indicators, automated business alerts, etc. And finally, make analysis actionable, so that the cycle "see, understand and act" is rendered as efficient as possible.

Table 12-1: Chapter 12 Checklist—Further Diagnosing with Drill-down Capabilities

Item	Completed (Yes/No)
1. Research the drilling capabilities of the chosen BI solution.	
2. Determine which tools will be used.	
3. Set up drilling functionality.	
4. Establish budgeted numbers distribution plan across drilled views.	
5. Set up trending analysis tools.	
6. Create multi-dimensional models.	

CHAPTER 13

Leveraging Benchmarking and External Collaboration

By Joyce Zerkich, MBA, MSBIT, PMP, CPHIMS

Healthcare organizations need a commitment to excellence and a means of measuring that commitment and its results. Benchmarking provides one method for doing this, as it has the potential to significantly improve the efficiency, cost-effectiveness and quality of healthcare services. Benchmarking is defined as the practice of identifying, understanding and adapting the successful business practices and processes used by other healthcare organizations (or even other departments within the same organization) and peer groups to increase business performance. Benchmarking should be used when:

1. Analyzing strategies to improve a process.
2. Calibrating an organization's performance against well-respected organizations.
3. Obtaining information on the best practices of other organizations.
4. Setting priorities and allocating resources by learning from what others are doing well.

Requirements for public overview of healthcare facilities demand that performance data be collected, analyzed and monitored for reimbursement, federal and state record keeping and accreditation purposes. As a result, most healthcare facilities already track key productivity indicators. As state and federal regulations require the reporting of more data, healthcare facilities will be in an even better position to assess their performance and share comparative information about performance and operations with other facilities for mutual benefit.

One of the mistakes organizations make when beginning their benchmarking endeavor is only looking to benchmark another healthcare organization within their own industry. Although this doesn't hurt, enough is probably already known about the healthcare industry to know what works and what does not. Instead, benchmark an organization that is well-known for being a good model, a model that is sometimes referred to either as best practices, exemplary practices or business excellence.

The greatest benefit to be gained from all of the performance data that healthcare facilities are gathering may well emerge from the process of comparing those data. Healthcare facilities often are similar in the complexity of their organizational structures, operational and clinical services and missions. That similarity will benefit healthcare facilities as they begin benchmarking efforts.

The main objective of most benchmarking initiatives is the desire to learn from and overcome the competition. Benchmarking is about comparing, learning from the outcomes of such comparison and consequently learning how to perform the task better. Its purpose is to help a healthcare organization by initiating changes in performance. Its goals are to make advances in performance. The process is relatively simple. It consists of setting goals through an evaluation of past performance and current need and then going after those goals.

The extensive measuring and comparing involved in the benchmarking process focuses on finding and closing performance gaps to prevent a loss of business to competitors. The potential for that loss is in itself a prime motivator for change, and healthcare facilities cannot remain immune to that fact. As the industry faces healthcare reform, the urgency to find solutions that speed delivery, increase access, decrease costs and satisfy customers has grown.

It should be noted too that learning strategies are often used in combination with one another or may be closely linked to one another. For example:

- Association scorecard: A corporate scorecard is an internal tracking and measurement system designed to help achieve long-term goals. Benchmarking is a method for comparing an organization's activities against other organizations for the purpose of improving functions and performance.
- Strategic planning: A strategic planning process may involve using the results of benchmarking to help analyze and make changes to its strategic direction.

THE BENCHMARKING PROCESS[1]

Information about the exact steps involved in the benchmarking process varies in its degree of detail depending on its source. However, the degree of detail in the individual steps will not, in itself, add to the success of the benchmarking effort. Success rests with the basics, and those basics are identified in the steps listed next.

Planning

The planning phase of a benchmarking effort involves three steps.

1. Identifying exactly what will be benchmarked.
2. Identifying the best competitors as potential benchmarking partners.
3. Determining what method will be used to collect data for comparison.

Success in benchmarking is primarily a function of these steps in the process, which relate to obtaining and using the right comparative data.

When healthcare organizations study and use internal data to determine benchmark topics first, the whole process initially begins with defining, measuring and tracking specific internal indicators. The healthcare facility can draw internal information from its own quality assurance studies, financial management systems, budget reports, productivity reports, payroll reports or any other internal information sources that maintain reliable records of performance such as the business intelligence (BI) framework. Most healthcare organizations have already defined and currently track financial and productivity indicators. They are now beginning to define and track clinical, quality and functional indicators. Internal information provides an understanding of an organization's performance more completely, which then makes possible a comparison with the performance of other organizations.

Alternatively, external data can be obtained to determine benchmark goals and then select benchmark partners. Begin by compiling external information primarily developed from comparative databases and, secondarily, from studies, reports, publications, research and other published sources. The value of this approach is in the fact that those who select their partners before studying comparative information may discover they have not selected the best performers for their benchmarking. Determining benchmarking goals ahead of the data collection and sharing process will garner better results, but those relying on a clearinghouse approach of comparative information sometimes find it easier to pinpoint the greatest opportunity and best partners.

A good place to begin benchmarking using external data is with medical industry professional groups such as the American Medical Association (AMA) or other standard-setting groups such as the Agency for Healthcare Research and Quality (AHRQ). These associations provide professionals with target outcomes, as well as the opportunity to provide lessons learned and clinical findings, which help in determining cause and effect relationships.

Analysis

The steps in the analysis phase of a benchmarking effort are:

1. Analyzing collected data to identify competitive gaps.
2. Projecting future performance levels and changes in the competitive gap based on those performance levels.

Reviewing internal and external information for comparative differences and practices will allow healthcare organizations to identify performance gaps and drivers; thus it may be discovered the best opportunities for improvement. The desirable process or function used by the best performer may not be transferable, however. Only through a thorough understanding of their organization will the BI team know what changes are appropriate or feasible. After the appropriate goals and changes are identified, the process of change can begin.

Integration

Once the BI team has identified the needed parameters of change for their organizations, they must integrate their findings into the organization. They do this by:

1. Communicating their benchmarking findings back to their organizations.
2. Writing a set of objectives to establish functional goals for the organization.
3. Developing an action plan to reach the objectives and goals.

Once common objectives, goals and action plans are in place, an organization can initiate the active process of change.

Action

The last phase of the benchmarking process involves initiating the desired changes themselves. The steps include:

1. Implementing the action plans and monitoring their progress.
2. Recalibrating benchmarking measurements.

Successful healthcare organizations say establishing accountability and a specific time frame for completion of the change process ensures success. Without them, change and its benefits can lag. If an organization can obtain and use reliable internal and external information to develop their analysis and choose improvements, then the change process has a sound basis and can move forward with less resistance and greater chance for success. Further monitoring will ensure all of the integrated change will bring anticipated improvements.

In recalibrating benchmarking efforts, organizations review their benchmarking partners to verify they remain the best competitor. Alternatively, organizations can seek other partners and set new goals. There are thousands of healthcare delivery enterprises in the United States. Each of them represents a unique potential benchmarking partner. Defining the scope of service and measuring elements inherent in performing that service is achievable in healthcare. It is easy to find benchmarking partners who are not competitors, but who face similar challenges and problems.

Table 13-1: A Chart to Determine if a Benchmarking Exercise is Worth the Investment.

#	Criteria	Weight (%)	Question	Yes (10) Maybe (5) No (1)
1	Sponsor	15	Does the benchmarking project have a Business Management or benchmark sponsor?	
2	Business Partner Commitment	10	Does the benchmarking project have Business Partner's commitment to providing resources?	
3	Project Scope	15	Is the benchmarking project scope manageable enough to be completed within a time frame not to exceed three months?	
4	Alignment	5	Is the benchmarking project aligned to a business-supported strategy?	
5	Change Potential	5	Could the results of the benchmarking project lead to process and/or systems change, i.e., a change that can realistically be achieved in the future?	
6	Impact	5	Will there be some recognizable/achievable impact as a result of the benchmarking project in the short term?	
7	Resources	10	Can the benchmarking project get the resources required to succeed?	
8	Info Feasibility	10	Is it reasonably possible to acquire the information called for by the benchmarking project (e.g., couldn't get data in three months from another source)?	
9	Risk	15	Can the benchmarking project be executed?	
10	Business Partner Knowledge of Benchmarking	5	Is the Business Partner familiar with benchmarking? Has there been benchmarking in the area before?	
11	Controversy	5	Politically, is this a controversial project?	

To seek partners to benchmark, Table 13-1 provides a set of questions to help determine the probability of whether the benchmarking exercise is worth the investment in resources. Simply score each question with a number from 1 through 10, multiply that number by the weight, and tally. The resulting number will be in the range of 1 through 10 and will provide you with a starting indicator if you should move forward. Table 13-2 shows a sample approach to tracking lessons learned during a benchmarking initiative. The Hospital "A" has many locations throughout the United States, hence in four different time zones. They wanted to see what articles, topics, processes or tools other healthcare facilities used in addition to suggestions of how to increase the value of their services. Comparing the similar organizations side by side provides a basic way to compare. The greatest risk in external benchmarking is making sure the many facets that make a facility successful are understood by those conducting the benchmarking to ensure they are transferable. Additionally, the information others share may need to be treated as confidential.

Table 13-2: A Sample Approach to Tracking Lessons Learned During a Benchmarking Initiative.

Question	Hospital "A"	Hospital "B"	Hospital "C"
Approximately how many people access the hospital's web site monthly?	35,000	100,000	300,000
How many full-time resources maintain the site?	Still in test phase as other government requirements took priority to this; 1Q target is 1 manager, 20 developers/ business staff, 4-8 variable FTEs; use off-shore development.	20	11.5
What is the long-term strategy for the site?	Patient medical information available 24/7 by means of the Internet.	The site is currently in a 3-4 year plan. They are working to create standard more robust templates.	Increase business value and satisfaction through the use of additional transactions.
How frequently is site content updated?	Intranet front page article will be updated by the CEO's staff each month.	The homepage is updated daily, while the rest of the site is constantly updated.	Daily
What kind of content management is used to maintain the site?	Commercial Content management system.	A system is used which consolidates 25 different content management systems into one.	Public Affairs assigns employees to separate parts of the site, and they are then in charge of keeping its contents up-to-date.

Table 13-2: A Sample Approach to Tracking Lessons Learned During a Benchmarking Initiative. (cont.)

Question	Hospital "A"	Hospital "B"	Hospital "C"
Is it hosted internally or externally?	Externally	Internally	Internally
What "transactional" applications are available to users?	Patient medical information.	Patient medical reports, ability to e-mail physicians' offices.	Patient medical reports, list of visits, billing status, make appointments, webinar education such as "Managing diabetes," request to pick up prescriptions, registration for in-person classes such as weight management, surveys, etc.

The external benchmarking exercise just demonstrated yielded several required changes:

- Initiate an ongoing planning process to better the system and keep users aware of plans to upgrade the system.
- Survey users as to what is important to them.
- Prioritize requests based upon government requirements and end-user needs.

After implementing those lessons learned, the results yielded a web site satisfaction increase and overtime use of the system. Even though most believe 90 percent customer satisfaction is acceptable, the manager was able to increase the value of the web site by refusing to accept 90 percent as good enough and sought to continue increasing its value-add services.

Benchmarking has become embedded in most healthcare organizations as part of the way they stay competitive. But there are a lot of opportunities for benchmarking to go wrong. Here are some of the most common mistakes organizations make when benchmarking, and how to avoid them.

Mistake 1: Confusing Benchmarking with Participating in a Survey

A survey of organizations in a similar industry to healthcare is not really benchmarking, whatever it may be called. Such a survey will provide some interesting numbers, but benchmarking is the process of finding out what is behind the numbers. In other words, a benchmarking survey may tell where the organization ranks, but it won't help improve their position.

Mistake 2: Thinking There are Pre-Existing 'Benchmarks' to Be Found

Just because a survey or study says that a cost of $102 is the "benchmark" cost of a particular transaction, does not mean the organization must perform the transaction for that price. The so-called benchmark may simply not be applicable to the healthcare organization's industry, customers or resource levels. Insist on identifying unique benchmarks and benchmarking partners and finding out from them what is achievable, and then whether it can be achieved by a similar level of performance.

Mistake 3: Forgetting About Service Delivery and Patient Satisfaction

Benchmarking stories abound of organizations that have become so fixated on the cost of providing their product or service they have failed to take the patient into account. Paring down the costs often rebounds in lesser service delivery, so patients may go elsewhere. Take a balanced scorecard approach when developing benchmarking metrics.

Mistake 4: The Process Is too Large and Complex to Be Manageable

A process is a group of tasks. A system is a group of processes. Avoid trying to benchmark a total system—it will be extremely costly, will take ages and thus, may be difficult to remain focused. It is better to select one or several processes that form a part of the total system, work with it initially and then move on to the next part of the system.

Mistake 5: Confusing Benchmarking with Research

Benchmarking presupposes that the healthcare organization is working on an existing process that has been in operation long enough to have some data about its effectiveness and its resource costs. Commencing a new process, such as developing a new employee handbook by collecting other people's handbooks and taking ideas from them, is research, not benchmarking.

Mistake 6: Misalignment

A big mistake is choosing a benchmarking topic that is not aligned with the overall strategy and goals of the organization; or worse, one that cuts across some other initiative the organization is already taking. The executive team at the strategic level needs to oversee the benchmarking project and make sure it is in line with what is happening in the organization as a whole.

Mistake 7: Picking a Topic too Intangible and Difficult to Measure

"Employee communication" is probably the most slippery concept that exists in an organization, but it is often cited as one of the worst problems, so many organizations try to benchmark it. Encourage the benchmarking team to select instead a part of the topic that can be observed and measured; for instance, the process of distributing memos around the organization.

Mistake 8: Not Establishing the Baseline

Another mistake is going out to make benchmarking visits before the organization has analyzed its own process thoroughly. Benchmarking assumes the organization already thoroughly knows its process and its level of performance. After all, that information is what is available to offer benchmarking partners in exchange for the information being sought from them. Make sure the benchmarking team is very clear about what it wants to learn before they approach potential benchmarking partners.

Mistake 9: Not Researching Benchmarking Partners Thoroughly

This is essential in selecting the right benchmarking partners, so time is not wasted. There is a rule of benchmarking etiquette that says organizations should never ask a benchmarking partner a question that the organization should have been able to answer for themselves through researching the literature in the public domain.

Mistake 10: Not Having a Code of Ethics and Contract Agreed With Partners

The healthcare organization's partners should be clear about what they are seeking to learn from them, how that information will be treated, who will have access to it and for what purposes it will be used. Ideally, this should be formally agreed upon.

Robert Camp says it over and over in his book, *Benchmarking: The Search for Industry Best Practices That Lead to Superior Performance*: benchmarking is "the process of consistently researching for new ideas for methods, practices, processes, and of either adopting the practices or adapting the good features, and implementing them to become the best of the best."[2]

COLLABORATION

There are four different aspects in which groups work. Each has different characteristics.

- Connection: the ability to develop relationships with others and to share information. The question becomes what people will do with that information.
- Coordination: the ability to act in concert with one another. This normally accompanies an agreement to share information.
- Cooperation: marked by the desire for mutual gain. Each party has something to contribute so both parties can achieve a positive outcome. They agree to team together and not go forward without each other.
- Collaboration: the ability to multiply each other's strengths to produce a result that no party could have achieved alone.

In its simplest form, collaboration is about working together to achieve a common goal. Collaboration provides insight into how others approached a problem, as well as a forum to share lessons learned or steps taken to improve a process. It is also something more; it is working together to accomplish more than any one person or organization could do alone. It is much more than just trying to find common ground on which to act. It is about bringing out the best in the group and helping them to reach a higher ground. It is about increasing the capability of the whole. It is the ability to multiply each others' strengths to produce results no party could achieve themselves. Newer, never before seen capabilities, opportunities and successes emerge from successful collaboration. Collaboration is a highly disciplined way of moving from idea to action. It lets organizations operate at a constant high level of innovation.

Collaboration may be seen as a relational way of operating between organizations that desire to see change take place. Collaboration should be considered when an organization wants:

- Much more accomplished through the combined effort of the entities then can be accomplished alone.
- To cut down on the tendency to reinvent the wheel, as people and organizations learn from each other.
- To complement its resources used as organizations draw upon each other's resources to accomplish the agreed goals.

Examples of collaboration include government grants that fund research completed by several groups with shared results, internal collaboration utilized when several departments within a healthcare facility want to better a process and thereby, initiate a business measure that will reflect on the entire facility, informing departments such as human resources (HR) to ensure that best practices are implemented throughout an entire organization. Other examples include risk management and clinical leaders working together to increase patient safety.

External partners can be found through professional societies, collaborations, consultant groups and vendors who are aware of several companies looking to develop the same product or process. Partners can also be found through research companies who are aware of senior executives' long-term vision. For small endeavors, partners meet several times to share perspectives and then enter into a contract with milestones, deliverables and responsibility assigned to drive the effort to completion. External collaboration will follow the same general approach outlined earlier. Inter-organizational teams will meet, develop a structure and goals, establish a process and work together to accomplish a mutually desired goal.

For a collaborative effort to be strong, all members must have a strong commitment to a common vision and purpose that drives their work. The organizations that form the collaboration are legally independent entities that sometimes behave as a single, larger entity for their own self-interest and for accomplishing their common purpose. Their unified purpose is the glue and driver for their existence. They are independent members who stand on their own. Each group in the collaboration has something useful to contribute at some point in the process. There are five key elements of effective collaboration[3]:

1. Unifying purpose: Shared commitment to the same goal, not legalism, holds the organization together. This is the glue holding the collaboration together. This is created by a very clearly defined and agreed upon purpose for the collaboration, which extends from the abstract to the concrete.
2. Independent members: Each organization is different. Each retains its independence while cooperating with others on specific tasks. There is a healthy independence for each organization.
3. Voluntary links: They communicate extensively and meet often. No one is forced to participate. There are many criss-crossing relationships. There are expansive relationships among people and extensive connections through technology.
4. Multiple leaders: Different people and organizations lead, depending on what needs to be done. During any given process, more than one person leads.
5. Integrated levels: People work on many levels and within itself and other partner organizations in the collaboration that itself is part of the nuts and bolts work, which is embedded in the larger collaboration of relationships. There are groups within groups nesting internally in many collaboration efforts.

The following outlines an example of internal collaboration:

Business scope. A large healthcare provider realized all of its services in acute, ambulatory, senior services and home care services funded and used several different patient safety incident collection software services. Comparing BI metrics was difficult for the executive team, as data mining capabilities were outdated and in different databases. In addition, it stifled the lessons learned capabilities between divisions.

Business need. Sharing best practices between facilities was nearly impossible with outdated data collection and the inability to summarize data. Next steps were not linked to incidents, so tracking resolution long-term effectiveness could not be proven. Reporting with the current software was cumbersome, awkward and took anywhere from 10 to 30 minutes to complete.

Solution. A browser-based software incident reporting system was installed at their data center. Several months were spent agreeing on the incident reporting and investigation process. Nomenclature was normalized while respecting the regulation within each type of healthcare service. A group was formed with representatives from each facility totaling around 60 members. All were provided the opportunity to design and test the system. A subset of each division participated in the initial pilot. The remaining facilities were deployed throughout the next six months.

Successful results and benefits. Best practice sharing between acute, ambulatory, senior services and home health increased with the use of the common system and lexicon.

SUMMARY

As stated from the start, healthcare organizations need a commitment to excellence and a means of measuring that commitment and its results. Benchmarking provides one method for doing this. Thus benchmarking is defined as the practice of identifying, understanding and adapting the successful business practices and processes used by other healthcare organizations and peer groups to increase business performance. Hand in hand with benchmarking is the act of collaborating. In its simplest form, collaboration is about working together to achieve a common goal.

Table 13-3: Chapter 13 Checklist—Leveraging Benchmarking and External Collaboration.

Item	Completed (Yes/No)
1. Document need that warrants benchmarking and collaborative opportunity.	
2. Identify internally where comparable data may be retrieved and utilized.	
3. Identify externally where comparable data may be retrieved and utilized.	
4. Identify a collaborative partnership.	
5. Establish a common goal between the collaborators.	
6. Set priorities and allocate resources.	

REFERENCES

1. Anderson-Miles E. *Benchmarking in Healthcare Organizations: An Introduction.* Healthcare Financial Management; 1994.
2. Camp R. *Benchmarking: The Search for Industry Best Practices That Lead to Superior Performance.* American Society for Quality Control Press; Milwaukee, Wisconsin: 1989.
3. Rowland S. What is Collaboration? 2008-2011. Available online at: http://www.neighborhoodtransformation.net/pdfs/What_is_Collaboration.pdf. Last accessed November 2011.

SECTION IV

Advanced Components of Business Intelligence

CHAPTER 14

Thresholds, Triggers, Alerts and Process Management

By Ray Hess, MSA ,RRT, FHIMSS

This chapter will review the use of thresholds, triggers and alerts as part of a business intelligence (BI) system. It will look at the value they bring to an organization and go over considerations associated with setting up these tools. The chapter will then look at these same tools in the clinical and business context and show that they too are part of a comprehensive BI system. The chapter will then change the focus to considering workflow management and process automation from a BI perspective. Ultimately the chapter will challenge the reader to look beyond the traditional boundaries of BI and seek to drive outcomes rather than just report them.

There are two questions that need to be addressed before the discussion can be initiated. The first is what are the definitions of these terms? The reader needs to have a simple working definition for each of these items. The second is to answer the question of why these tools should be included in a book on business intelligence. These questions will be briefly addressed here and then fleshed out more thoroughly through the chapter. By the end of the discussion, the reader should see the value of including these elements in their BI deployment plan and have a practical idea of how to move forward with addressing these topics in their unique environment.

For this chapter the following definitions will be used:

Threshold. The setting of values that give an acceptable range for a metric. Exceeding a threshold usually initiates an action. A BI example is changing the color of a dashboard indicator from green to red if the current value is more than 5 percent below the target. A clinical example of a threshold would be reaching a certain number of patients waiting in an emergency department (ED) for inpatient beds. A business example would be the number of uncoded charts hitting a certain level based on a business metric (total charts, days discharged but not billed, or unbilled dollar amount). The term *standard* refers to the exact target value and a *threshold* is usually a range placed around the standard.

Trigger. The executing of a pre-defined business rule when certain conditions occur. Sometimes the condition is exceeding an established threshold. A trigger on a BI system might start a pre-defined process to notify specified managers when certain conditions occur. A clinical example of a trigger is the system-generated ordering of a consult if the history of a certain disease condition is noted. A business example would be the automatic checking for a pre-certification authorization if a patient has certain types of insurance and an order for a test that requires pre-certification based on the contract with that payer.

Alert. The process used by a system to prompt an individual or individuals of a condition or that they need to perform a certain action or activity. A BI example might be an automated e-mail stating that a threshold has been crossed. A clinical example would be the system determining that a patient needs a flu shot and alerting the nurse to give it. A business example would be the prompting of a registrar that there is an outstanding balance that he needs to address with the patient being registered.

Workflow management. The defining and optimizing of the steps that need to occur for a certain process to be accomplished efficiently and effectively. This could be a clinical process, a business process or an operational process. Often workflow management is the result of a formal process improvement activity which seeks to identify and implement the optimal workflow for a given process. In this chapter, workflow management will be considered as defining and improving a specific process or processes.

Process automation. The use of an automated system (Business Process Management System) to electronically manage and direct a process. These systems often use the optimized output from a workflow management initiative. A clinical example is the use of a system to manage congestive heart failure patients and assure that all the core measures are addressed. A business example is a supply chain process that directs restocking based on items used and which automatically reorders these supplies from defined suppliers at a certain threshold.

These defined terms are processes or types of technology that use BI, business rules or clinical rules to alert or direct the activity of the staff. Rules are pre-defined logic algorithms that evaluate data or actions for certain conditions or criteria. They represent some of the most powerful tools available to directly affect change and outcomes. Traditional BI seeks to determine and report what has happened in a work setting. These advanced BI techniques look to determine what is happening, whether it is appropriate, and what needs to happen if it is not appropriate to get it back on course. They then intervene and direct the activity to assure that the proper actions do occur. Advanced BI of this nature *drives* results rather than just *reporting* them.

The premise of this chapter is based on the belief that executives who say they want to be able to see what is happening at all times are only telling a half truth. Executives really want to see what is happening *and* that it is all good. They want to see reality, but want that reality to be working and not showing where key performance indicators are failing. Their real desire is to see that these indicators are all meeting or exceeding expectations. They want any in-depth analysis to be focused on new opportunities and growth, not on root cause analysis to determine the cause of failure. The items detailed in this chapter are primary tools to help assure positive outcomes and happier executives.

The first part of this chapter will look at the use of these tools in a BI system. The second part of the chapter will focus on the use of intelligence to drive results and not just to report them. The use of thresholds, triggers and alerts usually falls into a category known as clinical decision support or the business equivalent. These items are used to evaluate criteria and alert caregivers about information they need to know or actions that they need to take. The implementation team that is working on the BI project should be closely aligned with the teams that are creating the system-generated intelligence that is presented to the line staff and clinicians. Ideally, the key performance indicators (KPIs) on the executive's mind should not only drive the parameters of the BI system but should be directly correlated to the rules that are being developed for clinical and business decision support as well. In the end, the coordination of these, often disparate, processes will reap rewards of improved content and outcomes on BI reports and dashboards.

REAL-TIME INTELLIGENCE

Usually, the fresher the intelligence, the more usable it is from an intervention and issue correction standpoint. Having intelligence in or near real-time allows for the maximum opportunity to address any issues that are occurring. Freshness of information has to do with how fast data can be gleaned from the operational systems and how fast it is reviewed. A known question to ponder asks, "If a tree falls in the woods and nobody hears it, does it make any noise?" In BI, the question is "If a report or dashboard has important information on it, but nobody sees it, is it really business intelligence?" As BI systems grow so does the burden to review and wade through a large number of metrics looking for the nuggets of important information that need addressing. Sadly, too often a downward trend or a problematic issue isn't picked up right away, and valuable time is lost as the business activity continues in the wrong direction. Even advanced systems with visual cues must be monitored by someone. This Achilles' heel is why the prudent BI plan will include the creation of automated processes to electronically evaluate the data for areas of potential concern and raise alerts to specified individuals.

At the beginning of the chapter, three terms were defined: thresholds, triggers and alerts. These three items need to work together to form an active monitoring and alerting process within the BI system. As key metrics are being established and created in the system, the BI team needs to develop the standards or targets for each of those items. These values will need to be reviewed regularly and updated when new goals, targets or benchmarks are set or changing conditions occur. Once the target is defined, the team needs to identify the acceptable threshold range for the element around that target. It is rare that a target will be hit exactly. Therefore, establishing these parameters is very important for the BI process to succeed. Establishing accurate standards is one of the key elements of any BI project. The viewer of any BI report or indicator set needs to know whether the numbers are okay, good or bad.

Here is an illustration of this process. A hospital is tracking the indicator of births per month on a dashboard. The budget is determined to be 300 births per month. That is the number of births needed to meet the business goals of the inpatient obstetrics unit. In reviewing the historical data, the team had identified that there is a normal variation of plus or minus 5 percent. By applying this range, the team decided that in a normal month there should be between 285 and 315 births. Therefore, on the dashboard indicator system, a month that is within that range is colored green (normal), while a level of 284 or lower changes the indicator to red (poor) and 316 or above turns it to blue (exceptional). They decided on a threshold of 15 births above or below the target as the point at which a change in color on the dashboard system would be triggered. This system is configured such that if the low threshold (285) is triggered, an e-mail alert is sent out to key individuals alerting them about the low number. While those individuals may not be able to change the number of births, they may be able to curtail spending and change staffing to maintain profitability goals. The threshold is a value that is determined by the team that triggers the system to do something. If the system's action proactively contacts someone, that action is called an alert. Alerts take many forms, which include visual displays, e-mails, pop-ups on the computer, text pages or automated phone calls.

This illustration provides a simple example of how budgeted targets are evaluated for real-world variation. If the target had no threshold, an alert would fire for any number other than the target. The system would never be "green" unless the exact target was achieved.

Anyone seeking to set up a BI system needs to consider these tools and include them in the implementation. Most commercial systems have functionality to set thresholds and send alerts. The availability of this capability should be part of the criteria used to evaluate any BI system that is being considered for purchase. It is important to understand how the system being implemented handles thresholds, triggers and alerts. These are often best applied to "period to date" indicators, which track how the institution is doing on moving toward a targeted standard in a given period (month, quarter or year). There are several considerations that must be evaluated as they are being implemented.

When a BI team develops its key performance metrics, there is usually an established target that is supplied for each metric. These figures may come from finance, operations, clinical best practices, external benchmarks or regulatory requirements. Therefore, the standard provided to the team is usually fairly straightforward to determine. Setting the threshold is often more challenging. The following is a list of items that should be considered as the team sets standards, thresholds and alerts:

1. Is above or below the target good? A volume indicator like radiology exams is better if it is above the budgeted target, while an expense indicator like supply costs is better if it is below the budgeted target.

2. Can the indicator be *too* good? A metric like percent occupancy is an example of this. A higher occupancy is better, but if it becomes too high (above 90 percent), there starts to be issues with bottlenecks and throughput. So, with a budgeted rate of 80 percent, above is good until it gets too high and, therefore, a secondary threshold needs to be set for 90 percent. Note: many systems cannot set a secondary threshold.

3. Should there be any range off of the standard? On some indicators, there is no buffer on the *poor* side. Budgets are often this way. If the item is over budget, it goes to red immediately.

4. What action should crossing a threshold level trigger? Often violating the threshold limit on the poor side results in an alert action to someone who needs to review the metric. On the positive side, it often does not alert an individual, but may just change a color on a dashboard indicator. When setting up the triggers, the team needs to consider what is actionable by the recipient of the alert. Excessive overtime can often be addressed by the manager, but fewer births (in a given month) cannot unless the system is triggering an alert to reduce staffing levels, etc.

5. Should thresholds be weighted or linear? If there are 30 days in the month, does the threshold on the 15th day represent half the monthly target or do weekend days need to weight differently? An example would be clinical visits for a clinic that is closed on weekends. The budget in this case should be divided by the number of weekdays and the budget applied to weekdays only. This can be a difficult task and is often confusing.

6. How sensitive should the alert trigger be? The team needs to evaluate a trigger that is sensitive enough to alert for issues but that doesn't fire for normal variation. Part of the discussion for this item is how critical the indicator is (more sensitive) and how effective an intervention effort can be when alerted (again more sensitive). If the recipient of the alert cannot affect change to the metric being monitored, the designer must question if the alert

is warranted. Too many alerts may result in fatigue and in people ignoring them. Too few may result in important items being missed.

7. If the indicator system includes drill-down capabilities and the budgeted value is set at the top level, the BI team will have to decide how to allocate the budget number across the drill-down population. This can often be difficult and can be as much art as science. The alerts are usually set to the main indicator and, in most cases, should not be included on any drill-downs.

8. Finally, the BI team must decide who should get the alerts. Usually it needs to be a person with clear knowledge of what the alert is saying and with authority to act, investigate, intervene and correct the alert condition. As a procedural rule, the flag that says something is wrong should get to the metric owner (someone who is responsible for the actions that are shown in the metric) as fast as or faster than the executive. Having an executive receive an alert and call the appropriate director who hasn't yet received it is a sure way to foster very negative attitudes toward the BI system from people who have significant ability to influence the effectiveness of the system. It is more efficient to give the director time to research issues and to be ready to respond to the executive query.

Hopefully this review of how alerts and triggers can be used within a BI system will give the reader a primer for how to set these items up. They can be highly effective in ensuring that metrics that are going off target are identified and that the proper people are concurrently alerted. Properly used, the alerting process can reduce the burden of daily review of indicators and ensure that negative activity is quickly recognized. These tools can be very helpful; however, there is typically a delay from the time the events driving the indicator off course occur until when it drifts far enough to trigger a BI alert. Information at this level usually cannot be identified and passed down through the ranks effectively. The damage is already done. The best that can be hoped for is to identify the issue and resolve it before further deterioration is experienced. Ideally, information concerning actions that need to be taken should be presented directly to the person who has the ability to intervene while it can still be changed. A comprehensive BI plan needs to address providing intelligence to every level of the organization.

Most institutions have teams of clinical or business resources working on clinical decision support and other line-level alerts. A separate team is usually working on the BI system and the metrics being tracked by it. Often these two silos do not collaborate or coordinate their efforts with the BI team. Yet, the clinical and business rules drive the results that are being sought by and reported to management through the BI system. At times, the key performance metrics for a system are not the same as what the clinical and business rules are instructing the staff to do. The rules that are developed at the operational level should be based on the identified mission-critical success factors, which come down from the senior administration and the strategic plan of an organization. This is the ideal setting—both groups working in a coordinated way to achieve the desired outcomes. This chapter will not explain how to set up and use operational alerting systems, but rather focus on how these systems connect to BI.

An example of this concept is emergency department (ED) throughput. This metric is part of Meaningful Use Stage 1 and is now being included in other quality initiatives. New CMS (Centers for Medicare and Medicaid Services) rules have full reimbursement tied to ED length-of-stay performance. A good BI system should be able to give a graphical indicator of the mean ED length of stay and have drill-down or analysis capabilities to see when and possibly why delays are occurring. A good clinical system will have the ability to alert the staff when a patient reaches a certain time threshold, of new test results when they come in and other items that can either delay or expedite throughput. The use of real-time intelligence via clinical alerts seeks to give the information to the clinical team that can affect the metric result while the result is still being formulated. The BI tie-in is that the strategic directives for the institution should help drive the priority and logic of the clinical alerts that are being developed. The alert system can further help to electronically collect data that will assist in the analysis of any bottlenecks or issues. An example of this is being able to count the number of times threshold alerts for delayed patient test results were fired on patients with an ED length of stay greater than the desired target level.

On the business side, there are also many examples. A system that identifies and alerts to the exact co-pay that should be collected, that a patient needs to receive the Important Message from Medicare notice or that there is a potential duplicate medical record being created feeds key business indicators. These examples can affect BI indicators for cash, compliance and billing. This may seem rather intuitive, but coordination of the operational/clinical alerts with the BI targets often does not occur. If something is important enough to measure and track in the executive suite, accomplishing it effectively should be a priority at the point of service. Having the system identify and alert for proper actions via real-time intelligence will help assure positive outcomes. The BI team needs to be sure that the worker alert parameters are in sync with the key BI performance metrics.

One major challenge for effective BI is being able to discover data electronically. Many important elements are not appropriately captured in systems. Alerts and other real-time decision support mechanisms can be configured to capture data for the BI system. Therefore, the BI plan should identify the KPIs that require specific actions for achievement and then direct the clinical and business teams to create the rules and processes that support those indicators. The programmers of those rules should create them in such a way that the metadata about the alert are captured electronically for later extraction and BI use. The entire process is a synergy exercise that if accomplished properly will fluidly feed the BI system with data showing detail and context. The priority and content of the front-line worker alerting should always be driven by the key metrics identified in the BI plan. If the BI metrics and the alerts are out of sync, one needs to be adjusted. What is vital to one should be a focus of the other.

ARRA (American Recovery and Reinvestment Act of 2009) has mandated that certified EHR systems have rules-based clinical decision support alerting capabilities. Almost all current financial systems have some level of line level activity alerting capabilities as well. These capabilities represent the application of clinical or BI directly at the point of care while the opportunity exists to achieve proper actions and therefore improved outcomes. A good BI team will always inventory the tools that are available and know the capabilities of those tools. The system at the individual patient or account level should be able to act as a BI analyst proxy and direct actions. These tools should be exploited for maximal success in any BI project.

Another consideration for optimizing BI when developing clinical or business rules, triggers and alerts is the consistency of the format used to develop these tools. A standardized approach to the building of these alerts and the logging of their data will make it much easier to extract, analyze and combine the data with other information for BI purposes. There should always be key identifiers such as medical record/account numbers and date/time stamps in the alert data. Standardized data elements formatted the same way with consistent language or result options makes later analysis much easier. A simple example of this is multi-option results. If one option is a "decline/not clinically appropriate" choice, the programmer should always put it in the same place and/or have it write to the database the same way. In this example, the programmer could choose to always make the decline option the first option no matter how many options are included in an alert. By doing this, a BI analyst can easily query

Thresholds, Triggers, Alerts and Process Management **163**

the total number of declines percentage in the "alerts" table across multiple alerts. Without it, the analyst would need to compile each alert separately and then combine the results.

Here is a checklist to follow for the BI project relating to clinical and business alerts, thresholds and work lists:

1. First determine the capabilities within the various operational systems for creating rules, alerts, thresholds and work lists. The BI implementation team must understand what the institution has and how it can or is being used.

2. Obtain a list of all current rules, alerts, thresholds and work lists. Most likely, there has been previous work accomplished, possibly significant amounts of it. The reviewer needs to understand not only what has been developed but why. What were the key drivers for the work that has been done?

3. Compare the list in step 2 to the key performance metrics for that area that are being reported to the mid- and senior-level managers by the BI system.
   a. Do they coincide with one another or are the two areas working off different "sheets of music"?
   b. Does the rule logic criteria sync with the BI objective? This question is asking if a clinical or business alert that addresses an identified metric is configured to trigger the same way BI is targeting it. The review should especially focus on whether measures are being met completely or whether the alerts only address part of the desired goals.
   c. Identify the gaps where real-time interventions will assist in achieving desired outcomes. The BI plan will have many indicators/metrics that are being tracked. If there is an opportunity, alerts should be created that target these items.

4. Set up the prioritization process to weigh in favor of the identified key BI metrics or change the key BI metrics to reflect the identified clinical/business alerting priorities. The two should sync or something is wrong.

5. Discuss with the rule/alert programmers the opportunity for capturing key data elements as structured data from the alerting process and have that work included in the scope of any rule/alert development request. These programmers have the ability to greatly improve the quality and quantity of the data available for the BI system—use them.

6. Create a mechanism to have team resources attend each other's meetings or at least exchange meeting minutes. The more that each of these two groups knows about the other, the better the chance of a successful coordination of efforts.

7. Create an educational process that allows everyone to see how their actions fit into achieving the goals of the institution and/or patient care. Have the education focus on the importance of adhering to the alert directives and the need to address them in a timely manner. Help the staff see how they are part of a much larger process and how their actions will directly affect outcomes.

8. Create a process to loop back any updates or requirement changes to the alert management resources. Clinical and business alerts can become outdated or actually direct wrong actions if they are not constantly updated to reflect the most current requirements. This will be an ongoing process that will never go away.

WORKFLOW MANAGEMENT AND OPTIMIZATION

The next logical link in driving positive BI outcomes is through workflow management and process optimization. Workflow management goes beyond individual alerts and directions. It seeks to ensure that the desired process flow is optimized for maximal performance. An example of this is the billing process. Workflow management would seek to oversee and direct the account through the various steps necessary to drop a bill and then remit a claim. These items tie to BI in that they help drive multiple key business indicators. In this example, days in AR (accounts receivable), clean claims, rejected claims and cash are all indicators that are affected by this billing process improvement initiative. On the clinical side, an example is overseeing the flow of an HF (heart failure) patient covering the various items needed to meet the HF core measures.

The focus of this discussion is not to explain how to conduct a workflow management and optimization project, but to show how optimized workflow management interlaces with the BI project and feeds its success. The items being targeted by the process improvement teams should be directly tied to the performance indicators identified by the BI project. If they are not, one of the two sides needs to alter its focus. The workflow that has been defined was deemed to be of importance by someone in the organization. If it is important enough to evaluate, diagram and optimize, it is important enough to be tracked and reported. If it isn't deemed important enough to track, one must ask why was it chosen for improvement. As with triggers and alerts, all defined workflows should be tied to processes that are of strategic importance or which clearly support a fundamental operational objective, such as high-quality consistent care.

Workflow management is usually defined and optimized by a formal process improvement effort. In many institutions, trained management engineers are used to run a process improvement (PI) team using a structured methodology, such as Lean or Six Sigma. These trained process improvement professionals are well-versed in using data and metrics to drive decisions. However, they are usually focused on the deliverables of their particular project. How they collect and display their information represents a significant opportunity for feeding and improving the effectiveness of a BI system. Management engineers understand the imperatives of data-driven activity and represent some of the best advocates for robust BI. They should be consulted in any BI effort.

The BI implementation team needs to meet with the PI team leaders and set up standard methodologies for capturing and reporting data. The PI projects usually follow a standard data collection and analysis process. Data that are captured for analysis or oversight should have standard identifiers included in the data sets and should conform to the standard definitions and data type rules established by the BI team. Ideally, the data should be worked in such a way that the BI analyst can easily link them to other data outside of the particular PI project. The data capture process that is set up for the PI project can often be used for ongoing BI reporting and metric tracking. The PI team usually focuses on data that are used to measure the process for improvement. The BI team may have additional data elements that need to be captured, and these should be added to the requirements list for the PI team, even if the PI project doesn't necessarily need it. A coordinated and structured partnership will result in improved BI on key business, operational and clinical processes. This intelligence can and should flow out of a process improvement project.

The projects the PI teams focus on should always be tied to the objectives that management has identified based on the strategic goals. If they are not, one side needs to reevaluate what they are focused on and why. Additionally, the PI team has an in-depth understanding of the process or processes that they have worked on. The knowledge that they have is extremely valuable and needs to be conveyed to the analysts who are evaluating and reporting the data extracted by the BI tools. Proper collaboration can reduce the BI analysis cycle time significantly and help assure more accurate and focused results. The PI team can provide a wealth of knowledge concerning the processes that are being tracked in BI.

The following is a list of items that should be considered for better collaboration between the BI and PI teams:

1. Key performance metrics used in BI monitoring must always be relayed to the process improvement office. These metrics should help drive the decisions concerning which PI projects to focus on improving.
2. A good PI process is always data-driven. These data need to be discussed with the BI team, and ongoing information capture should be an element of the PI process.
3. The PI team will identify aspects in every process that are key to its success. These elements need to be tracked and should be passed to the BI team for inclusion in its reporting strategy.
4. The PI team should make sure that any project it runs includes all the elements identified in the key performance indicators of the BI team.
5. The data collection methodologies set up by the PI team need to be coordinated with the BI team. Specifically, they must include key identifiers, date/time stamps and any potential drill-down elements that might be used by the BI system.
6. The BI and PI team members should sit in on each other's meetings or at least exchange meeting minutes. Understanding and coordinating with what the other group is doing is very important and can greatly enhance BI deliverables.

CLINICAL AND BUSINESS PROCESS MANAGEMENT

Automation of processes represents the highest level of process control and oversight. The hierarchy started with individual alerts and directives. These types of actions instruct an individual that a specific action needs to occur. The second tier is workflow optimization where an entire process is reviewed and optimized to assure that the steps flow together to achieve the desired outcome. Both of these levels present opportunities for the BI team to improve the monitoring and reporting system that is being developed. The challenge with both of these solution levels is that they are still highly dependent on individuals to complete the necessary tasks in an appropriate and timely manner. While this may seem obvious and an accepted reality, new functionality is now coming into play in the healthcare arena that is changing this landscape: automated process management. In the IT industry, tools that accomplish this task are called Business Process Management (BPM) systems and will be referred to by that name in this chapter. As with the other sections of the chapter, this section is not written to be a primer on BPM but to introduce the concept and show how it can interact with and enhance BI.

BPM engines allow a user to enter a defined workflow process into its system, and then the system manages oversight of that process. The BPM system takes many of the tasks and actions in a defined workflow process and executes them based on pre-specified criteria. This results in the removal of dependency on individuals to act appropriately for the successful completion of task. If the automated flow is specified and coded properly, a BPM system greatly increases the institution's ability to assure that the desired outcomes are achieved. These systems are especially helpful in keeping items from falling through the cracks, assuring that logic is consistently applied to assess defined conditions, to monitor compliance, in reducing waits, assuring communications, and completing handoffs. In short, BPM systems can be a key to achieving the goals established for the project.

The availability of BPM capabilities is starting to filter into the healthcare market. Several major EHR vendors already have BPM capabilities within their system. Furthermore, as healthcare systems' designs move toward service-oriented architecture (SOA), the ability to use a third-party BPM engine is increasing. Using BPM functionality will greatly enhance the control of processes and therefore help achieve the desired outcomes. As a BI team seeks to define the organization's assets that can be used to achieve these outcome targets, BPM should be considered.

There are two primary points where BPM and BI cross. This is the focus of this section. The first has to do with the effective capture and enhancing of data. A BPM engine, by definition, is constantly evaluating data and activity that are occurring. It then implements actions that have been programmed into it for the particular process. It oversees that the activity occurs and then moves on. This is where most BPM processes stop. However, there is a significant opportunity with BPM from a BI perspective. The BPM engine can be programmed to function as a real-time data gatherer. The BPM engine usually reacts to events and activities that are triggered in the operational system. These events carry data with them. The BPM engine can concurrently extract those data, supplement them with other data that it pulls, and store the cleaned data off for future use. This is a primary BI ETL (extract/transform/load) function that can occur continuously for the BI team via the BPM system.

The BPM system can act as the BI scribe for the analyst who will be evaluating the data that are extracted from the operational systems. The BPM logs will show who was contacted, when and what actions occurred. These logs provide a deep wealth of information for anyone trying to reconstruct activities in a clinical or business setting. The BI team should be aware of this capability and work with the BPM team to make sure that this tool is taken advantage of to its fullest extent. The BPM programmer often configures what data are captured from the automated process. This data set should be reviewed to assure that it supports BI analysis requirements. As with the earlier discussions, the BI team needs to move out of its implementation silo and collaborate with other working teams within the institution to coordinate activities and therefore help assure optimal outcomes across the organization.

The second capability that the BPM engine offers the BI team is that of a data quality control agent. This may be the most exciting aspect of a BPM engine from a BI perspective. The engine can be configured to evaluate the data that are being entered into the operational systems as soon as they are entered. If the data are in the wrong format or incomplete, the engine can intervene at that point and ping the user to correct or supplement their entry. Properly configured, this tool can significantly increase the quality, usability and reliability of the data in an operational system. It will also act as a teaching agent for the staff. Whenever the action is incorrect or the documentation is incomplete, the engine can intervene to reinforce the proper behavior immediately.

The BPM engine actually uses the tools already discussed in this chapter. It applies thresholds, triggers actions and alerts to individuals. As the institution moves into advanced process management capabilities, the basic tools are not discarded. These tools are interwoven into more robust and functional system capabilities. These tools can direct and drive outcomes. The further down this automation road that the team travels, the more these individual capabilities are leveraged together for greater and greater capabilities and results. As discussed earlier in this chapter, the BI team needs to review all of the tools being used by the institution to drive success coordinating and leveraging wherever possible. See Case Study 14-1 for an illustration of this concept.

OUTCOME MANAGEMENT AS A GOAL

Most discussions about BI focus on being able to accurately report and analyze data. A robust BI system is one that can pull disparate data sets together, link the data and create robust

CASE STUDY 14-1

Using BPM to Drive the Reduction of Hospital-Acquired Methicillin-resistant Staphylococcus Aureus (MRSA) Infections
By Ray Hess, MSA, RRT, FHIMSS, Vice President, Information Management, The Chester County Hospital

Business Scope\Need

The Chester County Hospital, in reviewing its key business metrics, determined that the hospital-acquired MRSA rate was unacceptably high. The data for analyzing the issue were collected and collated manually, which resulted in a very labor intensive process without solid data to review. Hospital-acquired infection rates are publicly reportable and will not be reimbursed in the future. There was a need for a solid BI oversight process. Data needed to be captured and evaluated to support the efforts to reduce the incidence of hospital-acquired MRSA and to better manage this patient population.

Business Solution

The hospital chose to use a BPM engine to automate the process that was defined by a PI team. The BPM system was also used to manage the infection control database and to drive real-time intelligence to key individuals to assure that the proper actions are taken at the proper time. These alerts drive patient placement, screening testing, results evaluation, and several other business processes for the organization.

Benefits

The BPM engine was used to glean data as they came through the clinical system, evaluate the data and to provide real-time intelligence to key individuals based on analysis of the data. This resulted in 100 percent identification of patients with a history of MRSA and their proper isolation placement. Intelligence was supplied directly to the workers who needed to perform key tasks. This process ensured that the proper actions were taken at the proper times. The system also populated and maintained the infection-control database.

Results

As a result of approaching the BI-identified problem using a BPM engine, the hospital-acquired infection rate for MRSA dropped by 74 percent. The database of patients with MRSA is complete and concurrent with all the data that have been deemed to be important for managing and reporting on these patients. The integrity and value of the data is significantly higher, and all reporting that is done off of this database can be used with greater confidence because of the BPM-based data population and control. Ultimately, the team was able to move on to addressing other infectious organisms using this process instead of continuing to investigate and intervene in the MRSA patient management process.

tools for presenting and analyzing those data, ultimately giving managers the ability to know exactly what is happening in their institution. This chapter presented tools for managing outcomes. Outcomes management is proactively intervening to influence outcomes and is a logical extension of any BI project. It is pushing intelligence to every level of the organization that needs it. It is using all available tools to positively affect results created and displayed in traditional BI systems. And, as stated in the beginning of the chapter, it helps ensure that the goal of the executive BI user is fulfilled. They want to see that things are good when they look at their BI system—not issues. Therefore, a good BI team should include the evaluation of all outcome management opportunities in their project plan.

There is a logical progression to the elements of this chapter. Real-time evaluations by the systems allow individuals to identify and react to any situation that is occurring. These types of interventions can correct an issue before the failure is permanent. Clinically, this might be the offering of flu or pneumonia vaccines (core measure data) to a patient who is deemed to be at risk. Financially, this could be getting a pre-certification approval for a procedure that was about to start without one. Operationally, it might be the re-ordering of certain medications and having a proper inventory. Each of these items would appear in various ways on BI reports. Many hospitals have fought with trying to raise poor CMS metrics or lamented lost revenue because the proper authorization was not obtained. Advanced BI seeks to determine one's destiny rather than resign itself to just reporting history.

The BI team will be seeking approval and support from senior administration for a significant resource intensive project. They will attempt to infuse control and change into the organization. They will be presenting potentially bleak reality to some who do not want to see it. In some cases, their efforts will expose weak and ineffective people and processes. Human nature often tends to shoot the messenger. This is a reality that the BI team may have to work through and manage. By embracing outcomes management as a part of BI, the team can take the high road and be seen as part of the solution, rather than as just reporting a storm. A good accountant tells the client what they owe in taxes; a great accountant helps them to (legally) owe less. That is how the BI team should strive to be seen. The key elements to accomplishing outcomes management include:

1. Knowing what tools are available outside the traditional BI setting. This chapter has only reviewed a few; there may be many more. Look for the tools that leverage real-time intervention to help assure appropriate outcomes.
2. Collaboration with other teams and efforts. BI is designed to track and report the key drivers for the institution. These other teams are working on projects that effect process. The disparate silos and teams need to know one another and what each other is trying to accomplish.
3. Communication of strategic goals. The BI team seeks to report key metrics. Those metrics should be universally understood and focused on at all levels of the organization. If this is not occurring, one (the BI metrics) or the other (the focus of the operational team) needs to change.
4. Education. The BI team should provide educational direction to all levels of the institution. Everyone should know the key objectives that need to be achieved and their part in obtaining them. Not everyone will see the detailed numbers, but they should know what is being targeted and see summaries of how the company is doing whenever possible.
5. The BI team needs to position itself as an agent for change. BI is designed to give key individuals what they need to manage the institution. The BI team should be a driver for helping accomplish the management of key outcomes.

SUMMARY

Advanced BI includes tools that alert the user when elements are going off course. It does not depend on someone finding the issue. These automated analysis and alerting tools ensure that the defined concerns are always raised as soon as they occur within the BI system. Beyond that, the BI team should think outside its traditional box and look at other efforts that are occurring in the institution. Understanding and collaborating with these other teams can greatly enhance the effectiveness of the BI system. Key concepts that should always be included in the BI plan are communication and collaboration. The team needs to link with the people involved in creating the data that ultimately are reported as outcomes.

The BI team's responsibility in all of this is fairly straightforward, but not always easy. They need to first understand the broader opportunity and embrace it themselves. The team cannot fall into the trap of just focusing on the narrower deliverables. The BI team needs to become one of great listeners and communicators. They will need to be evangelists for concepts and levels of collaboration that may be new to the organization. They will need to get people onboard and diplomatically keep them from taking the shortsighted but easier way. In short, the BI team needs to be an instrument of change in the workplace and not just an implementer of a reporting and analysis system.

Table 14-1: Chapter 14 Checklist—Thresholds, Triggers, Alerts and Process Management.

Item	Completed (Yes/No)
1. Evaluate the options and create a plan to utilize the functionality for BI alerts (if applicable).	
2. Define a process to determine standards and thresholds including periodic review.	
3. Establish procedures outlining the expectations for the individual receiving an alert.	
4. Evaluate the CDS capabilities and status within the institution, and collaborate with the team working on them.	
5. Collaborate with the process improvement office on the change in processes.	
6. Discuss the BPM capabilities with the IT team.	
7. Position the alerts, triggers and thresholds to drive outcomes within your organization.	

CHAPTER 15

Real-Time Monitoring and Management

By Ray Hess, MSA, RRT, FHIMSS

Business intelligence (BI) exists to provide critical information to key individuals so that they can effectively run their operation. As this book has discussed up to this point, there are many important elements in effective BI. One premise that any BI team must remember is that the more current the information is, the more valuable it can be to affect change. Real-time data can be used to intervene and correct a problem before it becomes a negative outcome on a report or dashboard. This is an advanced BI concept, and it is key for obtaining superior outcomes. This chapter will focus on the use of real-time intelligence to effectively manage the organization and improve outcomes.

Business intelligence, presented in real-time to key managers, allows for more precise management at all levels of the organization. This chapter will focus on providing information to levels of management much lower than those normally discussed in BI plans. Front-line supervisors need to know exactly what is happening in the area under their control. Their having this knowledge can be as important as the senior team having the information available to them. It can be argued that these front-line supervisors have a better opportunity to intervene and alter outcomes than the senior team when it comes to key outcome metrics. Everyone has their role to play in achieving the strategic goals of the institution. This chapter is predicated on the assumption that triggers and alerts discussed in the previous chapter were initiated. Real-time reporting is often built off of these processes. It can stand alone without these triggers and alerts, but that is not the ideal scenario.

In the previous chapter, the concept of concurrent intervention was introduced. This chapter will continue and expand that discussion. Whereas Chapter 14 focused on individual intervention, this chapter will focus on unit- or issue-focused intelligence across a patient population. This means that instead of looking at an individual alert, reports need to be developed to look at the entire population of patients with a certain condition or characteristic and their statuses. For example, an alert might say to one nurse that one patient needs a flu shot. The real-time report will show all the patients needing flu shots. The alert might say this patient needs a pre-authorization. The report shows all the patients who have not yet received approval for scheduled tests. For supervisors or process owners, this type of information is vital as they try to oversee and manage their particular business or care process.

When configured properly, the real-time monitoring system can yield truly concurrent data. These data can then be used to feed the traditional BI system databases with rich and accurate datasets. This chapter will primarily focus its examples on the clinical arena. It is the area of focus in many of the new regulations including value-based purchasing and accountable care organization (ACO) legislation. The clinical arena is where there is often the greatest opportunity for intervention and which usually has the least developed real-time BI support. The concepts once successfully deployed in clinical areas should be transferable to other business areas within the organization. The goal is the delivery of real-time, data-driven information that can be used in the control and oversight of the institution at every level of management.

THE CHALLENGE OF PRESENTING REAL-TIME REPORTS

This book has already spent a significant amount of time focusing on the challenges of data extraction and transformation. There is a lot of work required to take disparate data elements and convert them into usable information. This makes creating real-time reports a challenge. Real-time reports need to come directly from the operational systems. They cannot be taken from the data warehouse or any other periodically extracted data store. The data that are being used for real-time reports will not have gone through any transformation or vetting process. They are often fraught with issues, and it is hard to extract and transform them to the point of being usable for real-time reporting. There is also a problem with the data in that they often don't have many of the unique identifiers and drill-down categories that are needed to link the data together and which are desired for reporting. Instead, the data are raw and unrefined.

Pulling data from a system that was not designed for reporting is hard to do. Systems developed for online transaction processing (OLTP), such as most clinical operational systems, have databases or record structures optimized for single record retrievals. Reporting systems on the other hand, need to be structured and optimized for retrieval of multiple records. These clinical OLTP systems make it difficult to extract aggregated data. The OLTP clinical systems are designed to return detail on one patient, and not on a group of patients, quickly. For example, a clinical system is designed to pull up a view of the current information for an individual patient. This view will include the patient's diagnosis and other pertinent data. The data pull is accomplished based on the patient identifier, which is the indexed field in the table structure. Pulling that same data into a report for a patient population group, heart failure (HF) patients for example, is problematic. The system isn't designed or indexed to focus on the characteristics signifying HF. To pull these data, the report query would require the system to do non-indexed reads of every record in table (table-level scans) across potentially large volumes of data. This is slow and cumbersome. This type of query goes against what the OLTP clinical system's database was designed and optimized to do.

Furthermore, any extraction that is attempted cannot be allowed to affect the system's performance. This can be a significant danger in a highly tuned OLTP system where sub-second response times are critical to clinical users. Compounding the challenge is the fact that the report must return data quickly. These types of reports cannot be scheduled to run off-shift and be ready for someone in the morning. They need to run real-time on demand and return data almost instantly. Usually the data must return in a few seconds; even 20 to 30 seconds can seem like an eternity to a busy worker.

Real-time data present the current state of the institution. They show where things stand and usually can present data showing potential problems while they still can be fixed. Line supervisors and managers need to know what is happening in their area of responsibility if they hope to manage the area effectively. Reports from the BI system that show what has happened yesterday do not help someone to run the operation today. If the BI system is going to be a tool for driving improved outcomes instead of just reporting them, the real-time data conundrum must be addressed. Concurrent activity monitoring needs to be established to have a greater chance at affecting outcomes in a positive way. The process to establish real-time reporting can also feed the traditional BI activities that occur further upstream. The closer to real-time the report gets, the more granular it must become. Supervisors need specifics and details. They usually do not want to see roll-ups and summary data. Those types of reports can be analyzed back at the office, not on the floor.

The next section in this chapter will review a process for setting up a reporting extraction structure that can work in the online transactional setting. Before embarking on the path described next, the BI team should always review the systems that are installed in the organization for operational and clinical care. Many of the newer systems have embedded functionality that may assist in real-time reporting and oversight. Never reinvent a wheel unless conditions necessitate the action. The BI team should be the example of using intelligence to make informed decisions. Do not be guilty of falling into the trap of being exactly what the BI project is attempting to prevent: uninformed or erroneous decision makers who do not use data to drive their actions. Also remember that there are many approaches to successfully extract and present real-time data. This chapter will only focus on one that will illustrate the process and potential. Other methods can be equally effective.

CONCURRENT ACTIVITY MONITORING STRUCTURES

Since an operational database is not well-suited for reporting real-time data, the BI team needs to develop methodologies to manage and present the data safely. The first thing the team needs to do is an inventory of the systems that are installed in the organization. The team needs to understand the characteristics of their particular systems such as their architecture and database. They also need to look at the tools that are available to them natively within the systems for concurrently managing and reporting data. The team can then develop a plan to address the concurrent activity monitoring challenge. This section will present concepts that have been used successfully, but must be evaluated in each unique setting for appropriateness. In most cases, the concurrent activity monitoring concepts can be applied at some level, but to what degree must be determined by assessing the specific environment in question. This process will involve resources that may not traditionally be part of the BI team. The services of a developer for the rules/Business Process Management (BPM) system and a database administrator (DBA) will be required. Additionally, communication and collaboration across the organization are key components needed to be successful.

Usually clinical systems are driven off of an "event"-based process. The system "raises events" for various actions that occur. An event is an intra-system alert that is raised when actions occur. Examples of actions that can raise events include when new orders are written, when there are new test results, and when new assessments are saved. The event is how the system knows something has happened. The developers have architected the software to react to these events in pre-defined, appropriate ways. This type of system architecture, using events and "services" to activate a process or return data, is called service-oriented architecture (SOA). The system has defined services, which can be called or subscribed to. In some cases, events and services return data sets for a particular element of activity or action. This book will not discuss this type of design, but it may be something worth reviewing if this is how the institution's systems are architected. Events usually carry key pieces of data associated with the activity that the event is alerting about. Clinical decision support (CDS) systems, rules-based systems and BPM systems are designed to listen for these events, evaluate the data, and take actions based on the programmed logic and what the data show. The developer sets up the logic in the system to trigger an action or alert if criteria are met. Once the action is completed, the process ends and the system goes back to listening for the next event. In our earlier example of a patient needing a flu shot, an "admission assessment save" event would trigger a rule to evaluate the patient's medical history for high-risk criteria. If the patient is deemed to be a "high-risk" patient, the rule would then raise an alert to give the flu shot.

Many CDS systems have capabilities to interact with databases. Usually this takes the form of read-only queries to pull data sets for evaluation. This database interaction is often accomplished by using one of several connection methods such as an object database connectivity (ODBC) driver that links to the particular type of database the operational system uses. These drivers allow external processes to query the system's database.

WARNING: It is usually a very bad idea to try to circumvent the system's programming and alter the operational database directly. This chapter is not suggesting that such an action be considered; it should not. The operational database should be considered off-limits for anything other than reading the data stored there. If the operational system uses a relational database like SQL Server or Oracle, then an ODBC driver exists, and the database data should be available for pulling data. If the CDS can use an ODBC driver or another form of database connectivity, then all the pieces are in place for attempting to create a concurrent reporting structure that can be used by the institution.

There are several steps in setting up the process of real-time reporting out of an OLTP system. The first will involve having the DBA create a separate database for holding the data that will be used for real-time reporting. The location of this database will depend on the system, its structure, and security permissions. It can exist on the same database instance that the clinical system uses or, if that isn't appropriate, on any database that is accessible over the network by the CDS's database connectivity drivers. Once the new "reporting" database is established, the DBA will need to create a series of relationally structured tables in it once the reporting database has been designed from table requirements. The requirements for these tables will come from the analysis phase of this project, which will be discussed in the next few paragraphs. Examples of how this works are given later in this section. A real-time reporting database should be designed with tables that require as few joins as possible to other tables. This will require a de-normalized design, where data fields may need to be replicated in multiple tables, for performance purposes; quite different from an OLTP database design. Also, the tables should contain only specific columns that are needed, so they will be kept as small as possible. There will need to be at least one table with simple demographic identifiers for the patients that are in house: name, room, physician, medical record number, etc. Other tables will house specific data for whatever issue/population is being reported.

The BI team needs to determine what items need to be tracked real-time. These are items that have inconsistent outcomes, are mission critical, or that can be corrected with concurrent intervention. Usually there is already some type of CDS-alerting process configured to direct the staff members concerning specific actions that need to be taken. These items should always be part of the key metrics defined by an analysis of the organization's strategic goals. The team needs to determine what data elements are important to know real-time and who needs to know them. To determine what is important, the BI team needs to meet with the line supervisors or function owners and discuss how they conduct their operation and what information they need and use. These required elements, when analyzed by the DBA, will be designed into physical tables and columns in the newly created tables previously discussed.

The BI team should also determine how the information is optimally displayed during these interviews. A report writer will be needed to create the reports once they are specified. The process for concurrent monitoring reports should be similar to developing any report with several qualifications. These reports should be detailed reports and should not present summary data. Summary data should be given in a standard BI report system after the normal extraction process. These real-time data reports will hold the pertinent data but no excess data. They are designed to show a snapshot in time and no more. The supervisors need key data elements showing current conditions. They don't have time to wade through a lot of superfluous information, and the process should not have any unnecessary overhead. These reports are not used for drill-down or trending; that capability is handled elsewhere with other BI tools.

The key to the real-time reporting strategy being presented here is that the CDS can, as it evaluates an event, be used to take the data associated with that event and maintain the tables in the newly created real-time database. The CDS does an extract/transformation/load (ETL) process on the individual event, taking the appropriate data for that event and moving them to the new database. This can occur in the same logic flow that it uses to raise individual alerts and triggers. If the data meet a criteria to alert a worker, they meet a criteria to be placed in the summary table for that type of data as well. The process will add, update and delete data as appropriate. The tables in the reporting database should only hold information on current patients and current activity. The CDS can usually handle this added micro ETL role if it is configured correctly. In the flu shot example, every patient who needs a flu shot is added to the table. When a medication event is raised showing that the vaccine was given, the system would delete that row.

Accomplishing this feat will require close collaboration with the rules programmer and may possibly require the DBA to get involved as well. The process is fairly straightforward. When an event represents a targeted activity, the rule will complete its normal evaluation and then update the relational tables as appropriate. The key data elements are inserted or updated in a table row representing the patient whose data was associated with the event. Each CDSS/BPM event process will maintain its row in the table, so that the table will have a complete dataset of all patients with the defined condition. In this way, the relational tables will always reflect the current state of affairs for any targeted activity. In essence, this process will extract the pertinent data and perform a single patient ETL. The CDS/rules/BPM system becomes a tool to convert hierarchical data into reportable relational data. It becomes the device that manages the mini-reporting database.

The previous example of HF patients can be used to illustrate this process. An event is raised when an admission assessment is completed. On the assessment, a patient is identified as an HF patient. The CDS raises an alert to the HF team that a new patient has been admitted and that patient needs certain actions completed. It also takes the data and writes them to the "HF" table in the relational data store. As additional events are raised for test results and other HF-specific actions, the patient's row in the table is updated by the CDS as it performs its normal evaluation functions. When the patient is discharged (another event), the CDS either deletes or moves the row out of the table to another table for traditional BI extraction. A concurrent report is created that reports off of the HF table and can easily and quickly show all the HF patients in-house and their current status regarding key metrics.

Figure 15-1 shows a schematic of this process using a BPM engine for the ETL function. The figure shows a clinical system that raises events through the normal course of the day. These events are received and evaluated by the BPM system. When the logic dictates, the system raises alerts and conducts actions based on its configuration and programming. It also extracts the defined dataset and places it into the relational tables. The BPM system, by reading other events, will add, update or remove the data from the tables as well. If a patient

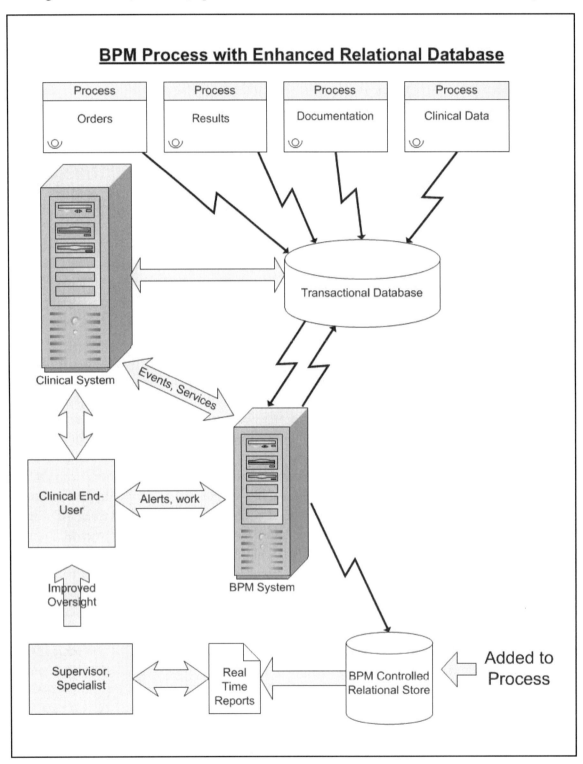

Figure 15-1: A Schematic of a BPM-Controlled Relational Data Store. (From *2010 BPM and Workflow Handbook;* Future Strategies Inc., Used with permission.)

is discharged, that event will trigger a "delete data from the tables" action if configured to do so. The report writer has created a series of simple reports that are accessible through the institution's reporting system, which present the content of these tables. Key personnel use these reports to oversee the operation and assure that the appropriate actions are being taken by their staff.

The tables in the BPM-controlled relational database (lower right of Figure 15-1) will reflect current state information for patients in-house. Usually, data that need to be tracked beyond a patient's discharge will be extracted to the traditional BI database and reported from that venue. Figure 15-2 represents a simple example of this process in action. The CDS or BPM system is configured to listen for critical lab results. These are important because of a requirement of The Joint Commission for the nurse to document that the physician was notified on all critical lab results and what action was taken. The first image in Figure 15-2 shows the individual alert that goes to the nurse stating that a clinical note is needed on a lab result. This particular example gives the nurse a one click option for the system to add a note on his/ her behalf. This type of alert was discussed in Chapter 14.

In this example, the BPM system has also written the data to a table in the real-time reporting relational database. This table holds data of interest for managing critical lab results. Another event listener in the BPM system is listening for completed clinical notes and evaluating whether the clinical note is associated with a critical lab. If the note is associated with a critical lab, the data are entered into the critical lab table by the BPM system. The second image in Figure 15-2 shows a small portion of a real-time report of critical labs for a floor and highlights those without clinical notes. The nurse manager for a unit pulls this report up for his/her floor and can see all the critical labs for patients on the floor and whether the nurse has placed the appropriate documentation in the chart. This report actually shows the result and the note detail. It has date/time stamps and allows the manager to oversee all aspects of the critical lab evaluation and documentation process. Patient-specific identifying information has been removed from the image to ensure Health Insurance Portability and Accountability Act (HIPAA) privacy. The report is normally color coded to draw the manager's eyes to results that have not yet been addressed.

The third image in Figure 15-2 shows a summary report that is easily produced from these data. This report is created from data in the real-time tables. One consideration that should be evaluated when setting this type of system up is, rather than deleting the table data when a patient is discharged, move the data to a separate holding table. Once the data are in a holding table, they can be picked up by the normal ETL process and moved into the normal data warehouse. These data are a rich source of accurate information for the BI system to use. This summary percentage report was extremely easy to create from the real-time data store. It would be extremely difficult to produce from the clinical system. It gives the quality management and nursing administration the information they need to assess compliance to the JCAHO (formerly, the Joint Commission on Accreditation of Healthcare Organizations, now The Joint Commission) measure.

Other reports can be set up to give drill-down, trending and other analysis details in the traditional BI system. This example was added to present the potential.

Figures 15-3, 15-4 and 15-5 show how this same real-time reporting concept has been applied to IVs, Foley catheters and pressure wounds. In each case, an individual event that triggered an evaluation for an alert to an individual clinician was modified to capture pertinent data and place them in the appropriate table. This has allowed the report writing team to create a series of reports that present these data for a population instead of just for an individual.

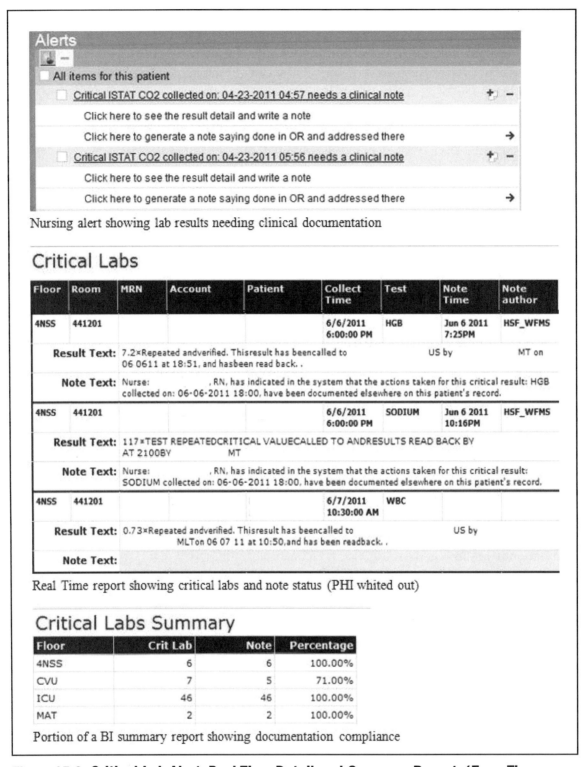

Nursing alert showing lab results needing clinical documentation

Real Time report showing critical labs and note status (PHI whited out)

Portion of a BI summary report showing documentation compliance

Figure 15-2: Critical Lab Alert, Real-Time Detail and Summary Report. (From The Chester County Hospital and Health System Clinical Reporting System. Used with permission.)

The IV report in Figure 15-3 shows every IV in the institution. It is populated with data from the nursing assessment. When the assessment is signed by the nurse, an event is raised. The system evaluates the IV data and, if there is a change, updates the IV table. All the key IV data are now in one small table for almost instantaneous reporting. The Foley Catheter report (Figure

pt name	floor	bed	IV Number	central line	site	type	date inserted	appearance	Pre Hosp Insert	Account	MRN
	WW2	025602	IV1	0	R Outer Forearm	Peripheral IV	Jun 10, 2011	None	0		
	WW2	025701	IV1	0	L Antecubital	Peripheral IV	Jun 12, 2011	No pain, no erythema	0		
	WW2	025702	IV1	0	R Inner Forearm	Peripheral IV	Jun 10, 2011	No pain, no erythema	0		
	WW2	025801	IV2	1	L Upper Arm	PICC	Apr 20, 2011	No pain, no erythema	0		
	WW2	025901	IV1	0	R Dorsal Hand	Peripheral IV	Jun 11, 2011	No pain, no erythema	0		
	WW2	026001	IV1	0	R Wrist	Peripheral IV	Jun 11, 2011	No pain, no erythema	0		
	WW2	026002	IV1	0	L Antecubital	Peripheral IV	Jun 08, 2011		0		

Figure 15-3: Portion of a Real-Time IV Report Showing All IVs and Their Status. (From The Chester County Hospital and Health System Clinical Reporting System. Used with permission.)

15-4) and the pressure wound report (Figure 15-5) are other examples of the process in use. In each case, system events launch a single patient ETL data management process.

The IV team, quality management, and wound care team use these reports to oversee an entire population of patients with specific conditions. These reports give them a concise snapshot of their area of responsibility. They can drive compliance because they have the information needed to know the current state of all patients in-house with the disease or conditions they are responsible to manage. This is concurrent activity monitoring, and it can drive outcomes by giving the information to the appropriate individuals while it can be modified. These issue "owners" have responsibility to see that their patient population is properly managed, and these reports allow this to happen. This process, while considered advanced BI,

Med-Surg Foley Status

Floor	Bed	Patient	Insert Date	Hours	Attending Dr	Last Clinically Checked	Hrs Since Checked	Account	MRN
TELE	331102		06/10/2011 23:01	39			0		
WW1	016502		06/06/2011 07:30			6/12/2011 10:49:00 AM	4		
WW1	017301		06/11/2011 15:40	23			0		
WW1	017401		06/09/2011 01:22	85					
WW2	025401		06/10/2011 19:00	43			0		

Figure 15-4: Portion of a Real-Time Report Showing Every Foley Catheter In-House. (From The Chester County Hospital and Health System Clinical Reporting System. Used with permission.)

Wound Care Report

Floor	Bed	MRN	First Name	Last Name	Current Braden	Old Braden	Po A	Current Wound	Site No	Site	Type	Stage	Prev Strat
TELE	331501				14	11	No	Yes	Site 1	Sacrum	Pressure Sore	1	Yes
WW1	015201				15	13	No	Yes	Site 1	Sacrum	Pressure Sore	1	Yes
WW1	015401				12	14	Yes	Yes	Site 1	Sacrum	Pressure Sore	1	Yes
WW1	015401				12	14	Yes	Yes	Site 2	left foot	Pressure Sore	2	
WW1	015901				13	13	Yes	Yes	Site 1	Right Heel	Pressure Sore	Deep Tissue Injury	Yes

Figure 15-5: Portion of a Wound Care Report Showing Every Pressure Sore In-House. (From The Chester County Hospital and Health System Clinical Reporting System. Used with permission.)

provides so much potential that every BI project should at least evaluate the environment for this type of activity.

The reports just presented are examples of the types of data that can be collated and presented for activity monitoring and oversight. The BI team will need to work with the individuals using the report to determine the level of granularity necessary to make the report effect. There is a balancing act that must be maintained in this consideration. Too much data will put strain on the extraction process being conducted by the rules/BPM system, can possibly effect system performance, and can prolong report loading times. Ideally, these reports should load in less than five seconds. They need to provide the essential detail needed for line management.

The team will need to be careful to avoid the temptation to put more in these reports than is needed for the specified functions. Other reporting requirements should be handled in the BI system, not in the real-time oversight process. The BI team should carefully evaluate each case and avoid the temptation of over-saturating the user. Start small and expand. It is a much safer approach. Often it is best for this type of BI process to design one table for each element being tracked and reported. This table is usually tied to an alerting process and shows the detail for the patients involved. The CDS rule is conducting ETL for one process on one patient at a time.

The implementation team will need to decide how open or restricted the access to these reports should be. There are good arguments and concerns on both sides of the issue. A more open system will be accessible to a greater number of people and the line staff can start to see the bigger picture and may take greater ownership of issues. On the other hand, some of the data may be sensitive and allow staff to assess the effectiveness of their peers. This could result in individual staff members trying to interfere with the management process and potentially violating hospital policies or state regulations. Ultimately, a corporate culture for openness needs to be assessed and, where possible, followed in setting up these reports. Whatever the level of security that is implemented, the team should strive to have the reports available to the user using their existing log-on and within their operational system. The less people need to move out of their normal workflow, the more likely they are to use these tools and make them part of their daily routine. This process needs to be part of the bigger process for system oversight and security control. In all cases, the synchronization of the processes makes adherence, maintenance and management easier. All of this will result in greater use and therefore improve outcomes.

REPORTING AND CONTROL HIERARCHY

The process described in this chapter needs to feed into the overall BI master plan. This requirement cannot be overstated. There needs to be a comprehensive plan and each piece of the plan needs to have a defined role with expectations and limits. Many projects get into trouble because the interactions of the pieces are not properly laid out and/or the pieces do not complement each other. The purpose of a particular plan element should be spelled out and at some level be both unique and necessary. If something can be done at multiple levels in diverse ways, there is a danger of divergent outcomes being reported. This is not saying that there cannot be multiple tools that can perform a similar function but that their scope needs to be defined and controlled. An analytical tool should not try to be a dashboard, nor should a dashboard try to be a report writer. The process at one level of the BI hierarchy should be consistent with and complementary to other processes in other levels.

The process discussed in this chapter should present real-time data to the individuals who need it. It should not try to give trends, drill-downs or predictive capabilities. Tools for those purposes are needed, but not at the concurrent monitoring level. However, the process in this chapter should feed those tools and support and complement their functions. The BI team needs to review their palate of tools and determine which tool is best equipped for which function or functions. The tools should then be configured for their particular role. The BI structure should be developed in such a way that the various layers and tools feed one another. The data should flow in a cohesive fashion across the BI system, and it should always be compatible and consistent with the other functions in the BI system. The BI team is responsible to assure that this happens. Too often the team gets caught up in the details of configuring each piece and forgets to assure that the bigger picture is accomplished.

While most BI projects realize the need to coordinate the tools, they can fail to see the need to coordinate the responsibilities of the individuals who use the tools at each level. To leverage BI maximally, each player must know their role and fulfill it. The roles of these individuals must include how they need to use the BI system, what they need to do with the information provided by the BI system and how to feed their actions back into the system. Tiered personnel responsibility should parallel the tiered-system functionality. In the case of the real-time monitoring process, supervisors need to know the expectations that are being added to their responsibilities. For example, they may be expected to review the reports at least twice a shift and act on any unaddressed issues. For the process to work properly, this review needs to occur. Based on what is learned from the review, actions need to be taken promptly. The expectations for use of the BI system (at all levels) should be built into the plan and agreed upon by senior administration. After successful piloting of the tools, they then need to be given to the users, and they need to be held accountable for their use. A comprehensive BI system only reaches its highest level of effectiveness when it is used properly, and its use is part of everyone's job expectations.

OPTIMIZING THE 'SYSTEM' TO ACHIEVE CONSISTENT MANAGEMENT AND OUTCOMES

The purpose of developing a real-time monitoring process is to achieve improved oversight and, therefore, better outcomes. It is BI in its purest form, the use of information to drive decisions and actions. There is often a danger in losing sight of that goal. The BI project exists to provide the information needed to manage the institution, achieve goals and improve outcomes. It does not exist to promote BI for BI's sake. While this may seem obvious, it is often lost in the trenches. The BI team needs to keep in constant communication with the individuals who will be using the system. The users are the experts in what they do and why. Getting time with these individuals can be difficult. It is often easier to use proxies and not take the time to involve the staff. Furthermore, line-level individuals may not see the bigger picture and understand what is being done or why. It takes time to educate and work with someone and, sadly, BI teams sometimes minimize or skip these parts of the process. The system that is being developed exists to assist these users. What they think and need must be understood if the BI team hopes to have their product used optimally.

Another danger is failing to re-test and adapt the system once it has been used for a while. The BI team wants to get its project done and sometimes is tempted not to keep refining the delivered system as needed. It develops specifications, builds to those requirements and launches a product. Success feels good and the team is happy and wants to move on. However, the BI system is only a success if the staff at all levels use it and, more importantly, if it helps them accomplish their tasks. They can be forced to use something, but it is only truly successful if they feel it works and that it is helping them. User adoptions is key to BI success. Once the system is built and released, the real testing occurs. Whether incomplete specifications were obtained, the staff did not give an accurate specification or specifications have changed: the only constant is change. The team needs to be prepared to alter the system as often and as much as necessary. The worker is being asked to adapt to use a tool and that tool needs to be honed as much as possible to support the user. The staff is being asked to alter their activities based on what the system is telling them needs to be done. The BI team needs to be willing to alter their system based on what the users are telling them isn't working or complete.

Properly implemented BI changes the way a company does business. Properly implemented, BI shows where change needs to occur and drives it. Properly implemented BI is a game changer. So what is needed to achieve these lofty goals? Much of this book is focused on the system and how to develop it. This small section is written to remind the reader that the BI system needs to be an integrated part of the larger operational "ecosystem." It needs to fit the culture and/or the culture needs to adjust to use BI effectively. The most obvious example of this revolves around the requirement for use and action. Using BI tools should be part of the job requirements for individuals. Knowing the tools and their uses should be part of every orientation. Configuring the system to support the environment and, therefore, being able to use the system to change the environment is possible. The goal is consistent oversight and improved outcomes. BI is a key.

SUMMARY

In this chapter, the concept of real-time monitoring and reporting has been discussed. This chapter primarily focused on the clinical world, but the concepts are transferable to other business settings as well. Business intelligence is most effective when it can provide information that identifies potential issues and guides the corrective action. Real-time activity monitoring is a key tool in the BI arsenal, and its use should be considered in any comprehensive BI plan.

This chapter provides one example of a process that will allow the BI initiative to achieve higher levels of impact and penetration within the organization. There are many different tools and techniques that can be used to achieve this objective. It can be done; the team needs to figure out how. There are a few organizations where this type of intervention will not be accepted. Unfortunately, in those organizations, the power of BI will be significantly curtailed, and the value of the project will most likely never be fully recognized. However, this is a rare scenario. Most institutions will embrace the new BI-driven process if it is properly designed, configured and tested. That is the challenge, and it has a rich pay-off for the BI team that can accomplish the task.

Table 15-1: Chapter 15 Checklist—Real-Time Monitoring and Management.

Item	Completed (Yes/No)
1. Complete an inventory of the systems that are installed in the organization.	
2. Develop a plan to address the concurrent activity monitoring challenge.	
3. Determine the access options for all databases in use.	
4. Create reporting structure (database and tables).	
5. Determine all items that need monitored in real-time.	
6. Create real-time reports on specifications from the end users.	
7. Review and approve user access levels.	
8. Determine and communicate end user real-time report responsibilities.	
9. Determine the scope of use for each of the BI tools, its part in the master BI plan.	
10. Create an ongoing system use, review and follow-up process.	

CHAPTER 16

Modeling, Simulation, Forecasting and Predictive Analytics

By Anna Fredricks and Susan D. Noack

In preceding chapters, the focus has been on detailing the basic components and building blocks of business intelligence (BI), and how healthcare organizations approach, build and leverage these new capabilities for their institutions. For most organizations, migrating to data-driven decision making is not only an evolving competency, it is becoming a necessity for staying competitive and efficient in today's healthcare industry. Business intelligence supports this need, and for every successful project completed, the requests for new information and more sophisticated analysis grows.

Advanced analytics is about taking the next step, developing not only greater expertise to gain insight, but applying analytics to support the business: to become pro-active to change, resilient to threats and predictive toward outcomes. In the healthcare industry, and in the practice of medicine, the opportunities for applying advanced analytics are unbounded. Where, when and how an organization expands their analytics capabilities to more advanced techniques will vary, based upon the priorities of the institution and the advocates for the issues to be solved. The rest is in the data.

So rather than a "how to" approach, this chapter is intended to illustrate through case study examples the near unlimited potential of applying advanced analytics to solve critical healthcare business needs. Applying advanced BI within your organization follows the same approach and techniques offered throughout this book, and therefore, the reader is encouraged to revisit the previous relevant chapters as necessary.

THE PROMISE OF ADVANCED ANALYTICS

Modeling, simulation, forecasting and predictive analytics technologies utilize large volumes of historical data to project current and future outcomes. Many companies in most industries around the world are using these more sophisticated techniques to gain timely insights and optimize results. Advanced analytics require the collection of vast amounts of data and the analysis of those data to better determine future outcomes. Key analytic capabilities include:

- Modeling to create representations of situations and scenarios to determine a future state of an activity or action, or to test and model a system whose behavior will change over time, with the result to predict reaction to external forces and other stresses.

- Simulation to show how processes react under different circumstances, by using data on existing processes and then defining scenarios to measure the impact of changes on process results.

- Forecasting to leverage in-depth understanding of the current environment in relationship to historical trends, peers and the overall market to make statements about the future—commonly used to forecast financial status and expense.

- Predictive analytics to leverage data mining techniques to ascertain the probability of future states by identifying trends and correlations in data, performing analysis to determine whether correlations are statistically significant and predicting outcomes under specific conditions.

Although these capabilities may sound complicated to the uninitiated, some healthcare organizations are already using advanced analytics to improve administrative, operational and financial management. However, until recently, most organizations weren't able to leverage data and analytics to improve the quality of patient care and treatment outcomes because individual and aggregate clinical data were not readily accessible.

This situation is changing rapidly with the adoption of electronic health records (EHR), which provide a longitudinal record of patient health information. By applying advanced analytics to these data, healthcare organizations can be more proactive across all functional areas, from evaluating disease conditions and gathering evidence to improve treatment processes to better understanding expense trends and improving operational efficiencies. Data and analytics can provide insights into potential outcomes of different scenarios and predict which options will yield the best results.

Yet much of healthcare today is still based on manual, labor-intensive processes performed by individuals who routinely make decisions based on their own unique training and personal experience. The transition to standardized information, evidence-based knowledge and shared decision making will be challenging. For many organizations, it will require a profound change—both in the way care providers and operational teams think and work and how information systems are designed. This shift will be necessary for organizations to significantly improve healthcare processes and enhance performance across key domains including quality, safety and cost.

Organizations can improve operations and the systematic allocation and utilization of resources by providing access to more data and developing analytic capabilities—in particular, advanced analytic capabilities. For example, by deploying technologies to analyze, model and project the flow of patients through a care delivery process, institutions will be able to better manage staffing to support fluctuating patient volumes and, in doing so, increase efficiencies and reduce costs. More patient data and evidence-based, aggregate clinical information will enable care providers to have a higher level of confidence in the decisions they make and will help improve patient outcomes.

We are at a turning point for most healthcare institutions. For the first time, decision makers are able to access aggregate clinical, financial and operational data. By applying modeling, forecasting, simulations and predictive analytics to integrated enterprise data, institutions will be able to gain insight into potential workflow, process and treatment improvements.

The use of advanced analytics will continue to grow and diversify, as more healthcare providers implement EHRs and gain access to additional internal and external data sources. New methods and tools will enable information to be embedded into clinical and business processes to help make insights more understandable and actionable. Looking ahead, the tools most valued today will change over time as users become dependent on new and different tools to do their jobs.

According to a recent study by MIT (Massachusetts Institute of Technology) Sloan Management Review in collaboration with the IBM (International Business Machines) Institute for Business Value, which surveyed a global sample of nearly 3,000 cross-industry executive managers and analysts, new methods and tools to embed information into business processes–use cases, analytics solutions, optimization, workflows and simulations–are making insights more understandable and actionable. Respondents identified trend analysis, forecasting and standardized reporting as the most important tools they use today. However, they also identified tools that will have greater value in 24 months. The downswings in "as-is" methods accompanied by corresponding upswings in "to-be" methods were dramatic (see Figure 16-1).

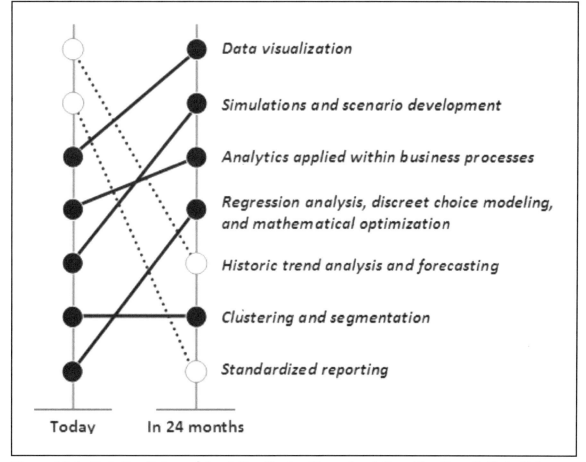

Figure 16-1: Relative Value of Analytics Tools. (From Analytics: The New Path to Value, a joint MIT Sloan Management Review and IBM Institute for Business Value study. Copyright © Massachusetts Institute of Technology 2010. Used with permission.) Respondents were asked to "Select the type of analytics creating the most value in your organization today, and which types you believe will create the greatest value 24 months from now. (Select up to three in each time frame.)"

CONTINUING THE BI JOURNEY: ADVANCED ANALYTICS

The key for most organizations will be to determine how best to begin or expand their analytic journey and to determine both how and when to apply advanced analytics to their decision-making processes. When looking at healthcare organizations that have already progressed their BI skills to more advanced techniques within their analytics initiatives, four best practices emerge:

- Begin the journey with the pressing issues that have relevance to the strategic objectives of your organization.
- Leverage the data that are readily accessible *today* in your organization and determine how advanced analytics technologies can be applied to help achieve those most pressing business objectives.
- Invest in developing in-house proficiency in analytics, as the ability to leverage new forms of data for innovative business value is an iterative process, dependent on both trust and knowledge of the data, which are crucial to achieving organizational objectives.
- Create a vision for applying advanced analytics to both operational and clinical processes, and support that vision by sharing results frequently to illustrate the incremental progress achieved toward measurable business and treatment improvements.

The advanced data software, techniques and technologies that are available today enable healthcare organizations to bring together historical operational, financial and clinical data; analyze those data and provide better information to support key objectives. With these new systems in place, healthcare organizations can:

- Reduce operating costs by identifying, implementing and monitoring operational process efficiencies.
- Improve patient safety and clinical outcomes by optimizing and aligning clinical processes to improve quality.
- Identify opportunities for improving workflow and treatment processes by providing insights into the correlations among cost, quality and safety.
- Increase accountability, collaboration and equitable access to care by enabling easy access to reliable cost and quality information.

Operational forecasting of expected activities for inpatient and outpatient facilities can deliver significant cost and quality-of-care benefits. For inpatient care, most organizations will begin these efforts by focusing on the emergency department (ED), which must be prepared to diagnose and treat a broad spectrum of illnesses and injuries for an unplanned number of patients. By modeling patient volumes and workflow, and the types of resources required to treat them, facilities will be able to more dynamically redirect resources where they are needed to optimize utilization and throughput and ultimately improve patient care and satisfaction.

Outpatient care can also benefit from better forecasting and modeling technologies. One area where improvements can be significant is open-access scheduling of patients with acute and sub-acute conditions. Today, most outpatient facilities schedule appointments in advance, which ensures a constant flow of patients throughout the day, yet this process does not easily accommodate same-day appointments for conditions that require immediate attention. As a result, many of those patients currently seek care in the ED. Advanced analytics technologies applied to open-access scheduling in outpatient facilities can help optimize load balancing efficiencies and enable services for a broader range of patients.

Advanced analytics software with capabilities to model, forecast and predict are already helping healthcare institutions to improve operational workflows, and their contributions will only increase as more organizations adopt them. Organizations equipped with these new insights can re-engineer processes to improve staffing efficiencies and resource utilization, more accurately predict patient flows, implement open access outpatient scheduling and identify expense trends with a much higher level of confidence than they could before. See Case Study 16-1 for an example.

BEYOND OPERATIONS: APPLYING ADVANCED ANALYTICS TO SUPPORT CLINICAL PROCESSES

Advanced analytics play an important role to enable clinical process initiatives and to predict outcomes for treatments. One of the major challenges in healthcare is in determining how to better align the utilization of clinical resources with need. To do this effectively, care coordination initiatives need to be able to stratify a population based on need, which requires the ability to predict or project outcomes and make accurate prognoses. By leveraging more sophisticated data and substantiated proof, organizations can make evidence-based decisions to support their care processes and quality of outcomes.

Care providers can achieve new levels of understanding to keep people healthier and improve treatment effectiveness when they have access to detailed views of patient information; data pertaining to conditions across groups; demographic trends; and the best treatment options based on analyses of prior outcomes and patient-specific conditions. Early results include evidence-based, personalized care that is administered more quickly, accurately and effectively based on pertinent, accessible information to the individual patient.

Using advanced analytics, care providers can more accurately forecast and predict prognoses for individual patients, so care can be managed in a more rational, personal and effective way. At the same time, they can model patient scenarios across organizations to ensure that the right mix of resources is available to care for each person. With access to better information and coordination, care providers are able to match the level of resource needed to a patient's actual requirements and avoid over-treatment or under-treatment.

This journey to evidence-based medicine frequently starts with grassroots efforts in the healthcare delivery system, often led by the providers who are closest to both the diagnosis and the treatment. By applying practice-based research, treatment design and care protocols are improved and the traditional medical research knowledge foundation is augmented. Analytics are being applied to the most critical issues whereby you measure both performance and success of the treatment practice. (See Case Study 16-2).

TRANSFORMING HEALTHCARE WITH NEW INSIGHTS

One of the impacts of contemporary medicine has been the evolution of acute illnesses into chronic conditions. However, these conditions require ongoing management, increasing demand for health services and associated costs. Most healthcare systems have not yet successfully implemented new models to efficiently manage the longitudinal care that many of these chronic conditions require.

Healthcare systems can improve outcomes for chronic disease patients by incorporating the use of leading evidence-based practices to treat groups of patients with similar diseases and demographics. Evidence is generated through the analysis of population-level data that were not previously available. With access to these new insights, the quality of care and outcomes across groups of people with the same conditions can improve significantly.

One aspect of creating a successful model of care delivery for chronic conditions is to be able to quantitatively assess a patient's progress over time. With the adoption of EHRs, access to relevant clinical data and the availability of advanced analytics capabilities, providers can:

CASE STUDY 16-1

Business Intelligence and Analytics Reduce Wait Times, Improve Operations

We use the example of Cardiff and Vale University Health Board in Wales, which is using forecasting and modeling to enhance operations, reduce patient wait times and provide managers and clinicians with more information and analysis to better prioritize patient care and treatment plans. Building upon its success, the organization is expanding its use of analytics to realize additional improvements, including more efficient service for accident and emergency patients and better patient-level costing evaluations. (From "Cardiff and Vale University Health Board improves operations with IBM Cognos 8 Business Intelligence," April 2010. Used by permission.) The case study features commentary from Alan Roderick, Head of Performance & Information.

Business Scope/Need

Cardiff and Vale University Health Board manages nine hospitals and 17 health centers in Wales and provides services in health centers run by its National Health Service (NHS) partners. At a time when the NHS is under more pressure than ever before to meet government targets and keep costs under control, having ready access to the information that can improve organizational efficiency is critical. With the goal to reduce patient wait times and improve efficiency, Cardiff and Vale needed to provide senior managers and clinicians with faster and simpler access to patient and organizational data and the ability to analyze and report on this information.

Business Solution

Cardiff and Vale established a project board that included technical and clinical representatives tasked with overseeing the development of the new systems and approach. The first step was to implement a data warehouse to serve as the central repository for data from multiple systems across the Health Board. The data included patient information and management data, along with information on pathology, radiology, pharmacy, prosthetics, care pathways, inpatients and outpatients, diagnostics, therapy plans and mental health.

With the warehouse in place, the Health Board deployed BI software to turn reporting into a self-service system for managers and clinicians, and enable the IT staff to have easy access to information and analytics as required. With the analytics platform in place, the IT staff was able to perform faster manipulation of data for *ad-hoc* analysis in response to requests for more complex analysis and to create dashboards and scorecards to continually review performance.

Benefits

Managers and the IT staff now have access to near real-time views of information to which they apply analytics to forecast activity and make decisions more quickly than before. Cardiff and Vale has realized the following benefits:
- Wait times are managed more effectively.
- Patient service and care are improved.
- Decisions are based on the latest information.

Results

The deployment of BI and analytics has allowed the Health Board to achieve a number of organizational efficiencies, service and care improvements. One of the most immediate results is a reduction in wait times across the organization, improving patient care and helping it meet the Welsh government's targets for referral to treatment time. In addition, the new system allows Health Board managers and clinicians to view analysis and make decisions quickly about how to prioritize patient care and treatment plans.

Going forward, the Health Board is expanding its use of analytics to other areas such as incorporating all accident and emergency data to improve trauma services offered—to make it easier to monitor progress and to evaluate and model patient-level costing by building up an image of the number of tests required, the diagnosis process and operations, admissions, discharge and drug information for specific complaints.

Improving Outcomes with Evidence-Based Predictive Analytics

This case study features Centerstone Research Institute, a clinical research institute that is applying predictive analytics to patient-generated data to enable more accurate diagnosis and treatment decisions. (From "A Model of Health Centerstone Research Institute mines patient data with IBM SPSS predictive modeling to optimize treatment and enhance clinical outcomes," October 2010. Used by permission.) The case study features commentary from Tom Doub, PhD, COO, and Casey Bennett, PhD, Lead Data Architect & Analyst.

Business Scope/Need

Centerstone Research Institute (CRI) works within Centerstone's network of more than 130 non-profit community mental health locations in Indiana and Tennessee to conduct clinically relevant research for the benefit of individuals with mental illness. Like healthcare providers and nonprofits throughout the country, Centerstone has been challenged with funding cuts, lower reimbursement schedules and increased demand for mental health services. CRI wanted to use practice-based evidence to provide clinicians with actionable information, to improve patient outcomes and to contain costs.

Business Solution

CRI created a data-mining solution, leveraging predictive analytics software to analyze multi-variable patient treatment information to provide individualized predictions of patient outcomes and help clinicians optimize treatments for mental health disorders. The system utilizes predictive models to analyze the effectiveness of various medications and modalities to determine which are the most beneficial. The system enables clinicians to use patient-generated data as a tool to predict outcomes, including data gathered at every session.

The system integrates data from patient interviews and clinical databases into sophisticated predictive models that analyze 14 variables across more than 9,000 patients, including socio-economic status, demographic information and a range of diagnostic and clinical data. Researchers also incorporate multiple sets of outcome measures from internal EHRs and a statewide outcomes collection system. The result is a set of predictions about the effectiveness of various treatment options for each patient based on his or her unique characteristics.

Benefits

By leveraging advanced and predictive analytics, CRI is able to use direct feedback from patients to steadily improve Centerstone's knowledge base and help clinicians understand which treatments have the highest likelihood of success. The predictive analytics system has enabled CRI and Centerstone to realize the following benefits:

- Treatment results within the study are understood within months instead of years.
- Care is highly personalized based on actual patient experiences with medications and modalities.
- Analytics support development of client-directed, outcome-informed (CDOI) clinical treatment models.
- Clinicians can access a growing repository of clinical intelligence.

Results

By applying predictive analytics to patient-generated data, Centerstone is able to make more accurate diagnosis and treatment decisions resulting in more personalized medicine, better patient outcomes and lower healthcare costs. During its pilot programs, the system yielded a 50 percent improvement in choosing the correct course of treatment. Overall, Centerstone has boosted its ability to choose the most appropriate treatment option for a given patient between 70 percent and 75 percent. By eliminating less effective courses of treatment and rapidly understanding treatment efficacy, Centerstone has lowered its operating costs, which will enable Centerstone clinics to better withstand fluctuations in federal funding and insurance reimbursements.

- Measure outcomes more accurately.
- Identify trends across groups of patients.
- Ensure that treatment regimens meet quality of care standards.
- Identify disparities by segment.
- Track patient status in real-time.
- Correlate financial results with health outcomes.

Leveraging advanced analytics to new and expanding data stores made possible by EHRs is helping organizations meet the Institute of Medicine's (IOM) quality of care guidelines to make healthcare safe, effective, patient-centered, timely, efficient and equitable. (See Case Study 16-3.)

CASE STUDY 16-3

Advanced Data Analysis and Reporting Improves Outcomes and Care Quality

This case study profiles Southeast Texas Medical Associates (SETMA), a physician organization that is using analytics to meet IOM objectives. In this example, a Texas-based primary healthcare group is using advanced analytics to audit and improve care quality and patient health. Using practice-level research and honing their own abilities with BI technologies, SETMA is leveraging analytics to enable their providers to track and analyze patient metrics to ensure that quality of care is continuously improving. (From "Business intelligence and reporting at SETMA: Improving quality, outcomes and clinical practices," September 2010. Used by permission.) The case study features commentary from James L. Holly, MD, CEO and Managing Partner.

Business Scope/Need

Southeast Texas Medical Associates (SETMA), a private primary healthcare group based in Texas, is a multi-specialty practice with a secure electronic medical record system for all patients. The practice's goal was to improve care quality and patient health by better utilizing data to audit and improve care processes. Although SETMA had been capturing quality metrics for more than 13 years, drilling down into those data to analyze results was too time-consuming to be effective. The practice was looking for a way to analyze complex information quickly and deliver daily reports on every patient and every provider and on populations of patients.

Business Solution

SETMA launched an initiative to leverage data from its electronic patient record and equip the practice with analytic tools for clinical data analysis, performance measurement and reporting. The practice wanted to be able to enable real-time auditing and tracking by individual patients, and the analysis of results by populations of patients. To start, SETMA engaged a partner to design and develop an enterprise data warehouse to serve as the foundation for enabling the reporting, dashboarding and analytical capabilities. Business intelligence (BI) software was deployed to apply statistical analysis to treatment data, evaluate the validity of its treatment methods and identify disparities, gaps and opportunities for improvements in care.

Dashboards were created to allow providers to contrast their performance with results from other clinics or selected groups of providers. In addition, a series of structured healthcare performance audits were produced to enable SETMA to report to providers, staff and the public about the quality of care patients are receiving.

Benefits

By leveraging analytic capabilities, SETMA is able to audit its care practices and processes across its population of patients and at the point of service with each patient. Clinicians now have access to data before, during and after patient care encounters, quickly compare data about individual patients with an entire population and share data with patients during examinations.

By providing real-time views into patient-specific information measured against more than 300 quality metrics, clinicians and patients both better understand what they can do to improve health outcomes. The system:

- Monitors whether evidence-based standards of care are being employed.
- Increases the attention providers and patients give to processes and outcomes.
- Evaluates performance every day, on every patient, at every encounter.
- Identifies trends across panels of patients to improve care policies and outcomes.

Results

SETMA is able to track and analyze patient metrics to ensure that quality of care is continuously improving. The system provides the same analytics capabilities that would typically require an entire department of 30 analysts to produce. Disease-specific dashboards allow physicians to quickly analyze patients who are treated to goal versus those who are not, allowing providers to recognize differences between the two groups and take steps to ensure that more patients achieve treatment goals.

SETMA has also been able to reduce the rate of preventable patient hospital readmissions by analyzing characteristics of hospital patients who did not require re-admissions and detecting patterns across populations. In the future, SETMA plans to improve operational results by combining the analysis of care outcomes with financial metrics. The practice hopes to find ways to decrease costs while maintaining or improving the quality of care and increasing patient satisfaction.

CREATING A VISION

As we look to the future, advanced analytics will play a critical role for proactive intervention and personalized healthcare. Personalized healthcare adapts methodologies of care to the biological and social profile of an individual and marries evidence and best practices to specific biological variations. Personalized healthcare models care options specific to each patient by combining population-based characteristics a patient shares with others that have the same condition with their own individual characteristics and biology. Some of these techniques are already in use in genomics and will be applied to protonomics and metabanomics in the near future. The incorporation of new types of data such as unstructured, image and high-volume monitoring data for evidence creation, will also be leveraged.

We use the example of how real-time, continuous capture data collected from patient monitors can be used for intervention and potential disease disruption. Today data from medical monitors are often stored but not examined, due to the high volume. See Case Study 16-4 to explore a first-of-a-kind project, a Canadian children's hospital and clinical researchers are examining how high-volume streaming data can provide insight to disease progression.

SUMMARY: ACCELERATING THE JOURNEY TO BETTER, SUSTAINABLE OUTCOMES

Despite opportunities that are close at hand, the analytic journey will vary based upon the data available and the priorities of each organization. From the previously mentioned MIT study, researchers found that it is the inability of an organization to understand how analytics and advanced capabilities can solve real business challenges that is the most daunting obstacle to widespread adoption. With management attention focused on other priorities, valuable analytics opportunities can be crowded out by business as usual. The single greatest opportunity—and challenge—to speed adoption of analytics is to embed analytics into daily opera-

Continuous Analysis of Streaming Data Improves Patient Outcomes

This case study explores a first-of-a-kind project, a Canadian children's hospital—The Hospital for Sick Children—the University of Ontario Institute of Technology and clinical researchers who are examining how high-volume streaming data can provide insight to disease progression. Clinicians are studying data to develop models for interventional care that enable disease prevention even before symptoms are detectable. Through its use of predictive analytics, the organization is able to detect subtle warning signs of complications in the hospital's neonatal intensive care unit (NICU), work to help increase success rates and potentially save lives. The case study features commentary from Dr. Andrew James, Staff Neonatologist and Associate Clinical Director, NICU, The Hospital for Sick Children, and Dr. Carolyn McGregor, Canada Research Chair in Health Information, University of Ontario Institute of Technology. (From University of Ontario Institute of Technology Leveraging key data to provide proactive patient care; December 2010. Used by permission.)

Business Scope/Need

The Hospital for Sick Children (SickKids) is Canada's most research-intensive hospital and the largest center dedicated to improving children's health in the country. As innovators in child health, SickKids improves the health of children by integrating care, research and teaching. SickKids wanted to better detect subtle warning signs of complications in the hospital's NICU.

To provide its clinicians with greater insight into the moment-by-moment conditions of neonatal babies, SickKids partnered with the University of Ontario Institute of Technology (UOIT) and with IBM to find a way to make better use of the real-time information produced by numerous monitoring devices. The team decided to focus first on early detection of nosocomial infections by watching several physiological data streams and other indications.

Solution

The team worked with a first-of-its-kind, stream-computing platform, developed by IBM Research, which captures and analyzes real-time data from medical monitors. The platform, based on IBM InfoSphere™ Streams information processing architecture, enables near-real-time decision support through the continuous analysis of streaming data using sophisticated, targeted algorithms.

The first step for the team was to create and fine-tune an algorithm to detect the telltale signs of nosocomial infection. This algorithm ingests several physiological data streams that include blood pressures, respiration rates, pulse oximetry and electrocardiograms. The system uses common bedside monitoring systems to capture a patient's vital-sign data sampled up to 1,000 times per second. The data are processed using clinical models built to reflect the team's best understanding of the condition. These rules can be changed or updated as the team learns more about the infection or to account for variations in individual patients.

The system is currently integrated with SickKids' clinical information system, allowing streaming data to combine with a variety of data inputs commonly collected in patient records (e.g., lab results, observational notes). In the future, the platform and its early-warning capabilities may be applied to detect other conditions that manifest themselves in physiological data streams.

Benefits

The use of near real-time decision support technologies will enable clinicians to detect medically significant events even before patients exhibit symptoms. The system integrates monitoring-device data and clinician knowledge for more robust results, continuously analyzes data to spot subtle trends and provides near-real-time decision support.

Results

The team from SickKids and UOIT analyzed real-time streams of data and created algorithms to detect the early warning indicators of nosocomial infection in neonatal infants up to 24 hours before they exhibit symptoms. Early warning may give caregivers the ability to take the initiative, deal with potential complications and ultimately improve outcomes. By providing proactive treatment before the condition worsens, the work being done at SickKids has the potential to increase treatment success rates and save lives.

tions. The study found that organizations that use analytics to answer big, make-it-or-break-it challenges have the greatest opportunity to meet their goals.

For the healthcare industry, the adoption of analytics including the advanced capabilities of modeling, simulation, forecasting and predictive analytics technologies, provides real promise for accelerating improvements in quality and costs. These technologies enable insight to increase efficiencies in the areas of administrative, operational and financial management, and to improve treatment outcomes, prognoses and longitudinal care. To progress the analytic journey within your own organization, consider these common elements for success:

- How and when your organization will incorporate advanced analytics into data-driven decision making will depend on their ability to access data and to provide the empowered support and focus of their analysts to the most pressing issues of the institution.
- Work with the data that are available today and get started; as deployment of EHRs continues, more clinical data about individuals and segments of the population, within and outside an organization, will become available and accessible to benefit clinical studies. With advanced capabilities applied to these data, better models, forecasts, simulations and predictions can be developed which will enhance care, increase longevity and improve outcomes overall.
- Develop an in-house proficiency in analytics; this will be important, as over time, the knowledge of your own data and the ability to leverage new forms of data, with constant iteration and exploration, will become crucial to achieving organizational objectives. Formulation of a roadmap for both governance and management of data will enable an organization to proceed along its analytic journey.
- The insights derived from advanced analytics will most likely impact how people work and may result in changes in workflows and processes. To support adoption within your organization, share project results and successes widely. New process changes should be accompanied by hard evidence and outcomes about how patients, care providers, medical research and administrative teams will benefit.

As the journey progresses, advanced analytics will be central to optimization and transformation of the healthcare delivery system by supporting the continuous learning and examination of evidence, processes, treatments and outcomes.

Table 16-1: Chapter 16 Checklist—Modeling, Simulation, Forecasting and Predictive Analytics.

Item	Completed (Yes/No)
1. Identify and document the need for advanced analytics.	
2. Outline the anticipated goal and outcome of the analytics. This will drive the approach to be used.	
3. Identify the source of data and reliability of the date to be used for the advanced reviewed.	
4. Identify in-house resources who can support advanced analytics.	
5. Outline anticipated outcome and evaluate change in processes.	
6. Modify advanced analytics programs on routine basis to provide for further drill-down and clarification.	

CHAPTER 17

Summary

By Cynthia McKinney, MBA, FHIMSS, PMP; Ray Hess, MSA, RRT, FHIMSS; and Michael Whitecar, MIS, LCDR (ret.), MSC, USN

Business intelligence (BI) is much more than another IT project or reporting system. BI is an important cog in a healthcare organization's machinery. It helps to guide and direct the organization to achieve its goals and objectives. Anyone embarking on the BI journey needs to first understand their healthcare system, its specific needs and the requirements for success. The BI project needs to be an organizational project and not just a departmental one.

Business intelligence has many aspects and it should be used in all facets of healthcare, including financial, operational and clinical functions. Members of the C-suite and all of management need this information to run the organization effectively. BI will also be a key component for any organization that is moving into the new realities of value-based reimbursement and accountable care.

Properly configuring the project team and governance structure are critical in achieving established BI goals. The team must have representation from key stakeholders in the process. The entire project needs to be directed by a solid charter that lays out the parameters for the effort. Early identification and involvement of "champions" will greatly enhance the probability of a successful project. The team needs to understand how things work in their institution and set up metrics and/or best practice targets for the project. All of these things should be part of properly configuring the project before it gets started.

After establishing the committee and governance model, the next important step is a systematic assessment of the environment. This assessment needs to include processes, culture, people, resources and technology. The committee must always remember that technology is only one piece of a much larger puzzle. Do not let it drive the project. Understanding the environment is a key to success. It will help discover risks and issues that may derail the process. The team must determine what processes will be affected and the impact on those processes. Managing change is a systematic and controlled fashion and is necessary.

Now the team is ready to start evaluating the data. Data evaluation needs to be comprehensive. Elements that need to be evaluated include integrity, completeness, consistency and accessibility. The team needs to determine the metadata about the data and what elements are not available in a functional format. A plan needs to be developed to address any deficiencies and holes that are identified. The information in a BI system is only as good as the data that feed it.

Once the data are evaluated, the next step in the process is to design a framework for the management and presentation of the data. This starts with evaluating the data source and then moves in to determining data integration needs. The BI team will be responsible to set up any data storage requirements, as well as data analysis structures and, finally, the presentation layer. All of this is done in the context of previously determined principles like governance and metadata management, as well as security and system performance. All of these items fall into a category of operational or general concerns that need to be evaluated and addressed during the implementation.

A major key to the success of a BI project is the data design process. In this process, the source data are analyzed and a transformation methodology created. This process, if properly done, greatly helps ensure that the information being reported is accurate and appropriate. While this deliverable is very technical, the end user still needs to be engaged to make sure that the ETL (extraction, transfer and load) process meets the needs of the intended users.

Once the BI system is set-up there needs to be ongoing evaluation and an established feedback mechanism. This needs to be created so that the effectiveness of the BI solution can be monitored and adapted as necessary. A formal structure with defined feedback loops can be very helpful to the organization. The BI project team should not see BI as a finite project, but as an ongoing, living process that needs to be incorporated into the corporate culture.

The concept of change management is very important for BI. How the organization embraces the system is one consideration. What the organization does with the information and how it will be used to improve the processes is another. A change management framework provides structure to support the use, adoption and value of BI. The team needs to help establish this framework for the enterprise.

There are many tools in the BI toolbox. A good understanding of each and its role is critical to any BI implementation. The dashboard is a key component that gives visual representations of the current status of an organization's key performance metrics. This tool is often used at the executive level for quick review of the current status. The BI team needs to make sure that any dashboards are properly set-up and need to know as well what items are appropriate, and not appropriate, for placement in a dashboard.

Reports are the foundational core of any BI system. They represent the primary way that information is delivered to the organization. There are four layers of reporting complexity, and the BI team needs to understand the advantages and limitations of each level. There is no universal reporting strategy. Each institution needs to assess their specific needs and resources and then create a plan that is best for them.

Along with reports which target the general end user, BI offers analysts the ability to drill through the data to more granular or more summarized levels. By understanding and developing this concept, the BI team can provide great power to the users trying to understand and utilize the data. There are multiple ways to allow this to occur and multiple tools that support this type of analysis.

The BI team should also consider where the application of benchmarking data may help the organization to assess their process. External benchmarking with peer organizations or against published standards provides an objective lens for the evaluation of a process. If a process is found to need improvement, collaboration with other like-minded organizations can often provide valuable insight and more predictable improvement outcomes.

When developing an advanced BI system, the project team needs to understand and use capabilities within the system to evaluate the data and alert appropriate users concerning issues that are occurring. This should be a part of any BI installation and can be extended to real-time directives, which allow front line staff the opportunity to address needs before they become failures on a report or dashboard. Wherever possible, the systems that exist in the organization should be leveraged to support BI and positive outcomes.

The BI project team should also consider how they can develop real-time reporting capabilities for key end users. This type of report is a pivotal piece in trying to manage key processes effectively. The real-time process can also be used to collect and evaluate data that will be used in more traditional BI settings. There is great power in developing this capability.

As the BI system implementation is complete and the staff is getting used to the functionality of the new system, the project team should consider advanced capabilities, such as modeling, forecasting, simulation and predictive analytics. These techniques allow the analyst to use existing data to project future outcomes with statistical accuracy. There are many opportunities for an organization that successfully implements and uses these tools.

Business intelligence is more than a system. It is a comprehensive methodology and management philosophy, using information to drive key decisions and operations within the organization. Anyone who is attempting to walk the road of BI should consider all of these elements and include them as appropriate. The business intelligence sub-committee of the Management Engineering-Process Improvement community at HIMSS wishes the reader well as he/she embarks on this important and exciting journey.

Chapter Checklists

Item	Completed (Y/N)
Chapter 1: Why Does Your Organization Need Business Intelligence?	
1. Understand the key drivers specific to your organization.	
2. Create awareness and the overall value of improved information among key executives and stakeholders.	
3. Develop consensus on the key information requirements to support the organization's priorities.	
4. Assess the organization's business intelligence readiness.	
5. Develop a shared vision and strategy for the role of business intelligence.	
Chapter 2: A Case for Business Intelligence across the Continuum of Care	
6. Identify specific opportunities or problem areas where better information will significantly improve business and/or clinical results.	
7. Engage clinician and management champions.	
8. Identify and enlist the support of key stakeholders, subject-matter experts and other participants needed to address the problem/ opportunity.	
9. Determine what BI information and capabilities will be needed to determine the root cause and evaluate alternative solutions.	
10. Conduct analysis of current state and alternative solutions.	

Item	Completed (Y/N)
11. Evaluate analysis results and implement preferred alternative(s).	
12. Evaluate results for validation and implement continuous improvement results where appropriate.	
Chapter 3: Getting Started within Your Organization	
13. Know the definition and development needs of establishing a BI committee governed by a charter formulated by executive management.	
14. Establish the appropriate level of governance for your BI project.	
15. Identify stakeholders and BI champions, and seek for committee membership.	
16. Define the inner workings of business and clinical processes utilizing tools, such as the discovery matrix, to assist with prioritizing initiatives and recognizing low-hanging fruit.	
17. Establish and institutionalize industry best practices supporting project management and identify a project manager.	
Chapter 4: Assess Your Environment	
18. Create a picture of the environment labeled with processes, location of data sources and other resources to facilitate the asset inventory.	
19. Complete inventory of technologies, resources, processes, culture and environment.	
20. Complete inventory of processes and complete analysis—and adjust as needed.	
21. Develop and implement a feedback mechanism.	
22. Complete inventory of people resources, outlining skills, knowledge and experience required.	
23. All the required information has been located, and it is understood how the information will be stored and retrieved.	
24. Technologies are in place to allow information to be shareable throughout the organization and available in a variety of formats.	
25. Tools are available along with the resources and skill sets to present the information.	
26. There is a clear understanding by the stakeholders how the business rules will be developed and applied.	
Chapter 5: Understanding the Data	
27. Possess strong understanding of business need for business intelligence.	
28. Clearly understand the goals and objectives.	
29. Identify business owners/experts to assist with use cases and metadata.	

Item	Completed (Y/N)
30. Identify technical staff to assist with use cases and metadata.	
31. Develop use cases scenarios/stories for each indicator.	
32. Define metadata for each Key Performance Indicator.	
33. Map out process to understand input and outputs.	
Chapter 6: Design the Framework	
34. Understand all of the elements of BI architecture.	
35. Determine what data are needed for your BI solution and where they can be obtained.	
36. Determine the framework for evaluating and managing the data throughout the BI process.	
37. Develop a plan for extracting the data from the disparate systems and then integrating them into one usable source.	
38. Establish methodology to store your data.	
39. Determine what tools will be used for data analysis and how each tool will be applied.	
40. Evaluate and understand presentation tools.	
41. Develop/evaluate security, performance, metadata management and governance into the BI plan.	
Chapter 7: From Design and Build to Implementation and Validation	
42. Determine appropriate scope for the first BI release.	
43. Create source-to-target mapping document.	
44. Possess working knowledge of data profiling.	
45. Complete data-profiling process.	
46. Develop working design for your target database.	
47. Develop and document the ETL process.	
48. Document issues that can plague ETL and evaluate the risk.	
49. Create and approve the front-end design.	
50. Develop the testing plan.	
51. Create the training strategy.	
Chapter 8: Post-Implementation	
52. Establish a feedback loop to receive and respond to communication from the recipients of the BI information.	
53. Tailor the necessary processes to optimize use of BI.	
54. Tailor the BI strategy if needed due to unexpected cultural reaction.	

Item	Completed (Y/N)
55. Define post-implementation responsibilities.	
56. Document procedures to allow for repeatability and consistency.	
57. Develop a toolkit to communicate the standards of the BI framework, how results are measured and how the metrics are calculated.	
58. Evaluate the governance structure to maximize support of BI.	
59. Implement a Dashboard Review Board (DRB) to ensure post-implementation compliance.	
Chapter 9: Change Management and Adoption	
60. Ensure senior management is onboard and supports the change required throughout the organization.	
61. Develop a change management plan.	
62. Monitored activities have been implemented to support the change to determine its effectiveness and its shortfalls.	
63. Establish a reward and recognition program to identify those individuals who are successfully contributing to the need for change.	
64. Develop a communication plan to clearly articulate the reason for change, the benefits of change, and what's in it for "me."	
65. Create policies that ensure BI processes that get built continue to get utilized for ongoing management reporting.	
Chapter 10: Presenting Results through Dashboards	
66. Define the purpose of the dashboard.	
67. Identify the key stakeholders and ownership of each KPI.	
68. Outline the look and feel of each dashboard (e.g. trends, alerts).	
69. Outline the frequency of update.	
70. Develop prioritization criteria to develop each dashboard.	
71. Identify the source of data and complete validation.	
72. Establish targets for each indicator.	
73. Develop dashboard appearance: analog, gauge, digital readout.	
Chapter 11: Communicating through Robust Reporting	
74. Define the BI reporting requirements unique to your organizational characteristics, staffing and strategic needs.	
75. Evaluate staffing. Starting incrementally, the healthcare organization begins with any appropriate level of maturity and moves on to the next level. Even if there are short-term pressures, avoid the temptation to go back to the previous level (i.e., Level 2) after achieving a higher level (i.e., Level 3).	

Item	Completed (Y/N)
76. Determine the scope and purpose of reports across the healthcare organization; the journey becomes easier if the project team has determined these requirements.	
77. Choose and use the appropriate report type, frequency and media to communicate the BI results.	
78. Present text and charts in the most effective way possible for the intended audience; do not allow the reporting tool to determine the choices.	
79. Decide on a reporting tool only after completing at least the vast majority, if not all, of the analyses described earlier in Level 4.	
80. Create bi-directional reports; use reports to institute and drive a culture of data consumption and analysis.	
81. Track report usage patterns, and make the necessary changes in order to drive user acceptance and buy-in.	
82. Don't forget about hierarchies and drill paths; the most visually pleasing report is useless if it does not provide support for hierarchies. Hierarchies are critical for organizing data and serve as a foundation for drill-up/down behaviors.	
83. Create a cross-functional reporting team, and identify who will fill the critical role of report analyst.	
Chapter 12: Further Diagnosing with Drill-Down Capabilities	
84. Research the drilling capabilities of the chosen BI solution.	
85. Determine which tools will be used.	
86. Set up drilling functionality.	
87. Establish budgeted numbers distribution plan across drilled views.	
88. Set up trending analysis tools.	
89. Create multi-dimensional models.	
Chapter 13: Leveraging Benchmarking and External Collaboration	
90. Document need that warrants benchmarking and collaborative opportunity.	
91. Identify internally where comparable data may be retrieved and utilized.	
92. Identify externally where comparable data may be retired and utilized.	
93. Identify a collaborative partnership.	
94. Establish a common goal between the collaborators.	
95. Set priorities and allocate resources.	

Item	Completed (Y/N)
Chapter 14: Thresholds, Triggers, Alerts and Process Management	
96. Evaluate the options and create a plan to utilize the functionality for BI Alerts (if applicable).	
97. Define a process to determine standards and thresholds including periodic review.	
98. Establish procedures outlining the expectations for the individual receiving an alert.	
99. Evaluate the CDS capabilities and status within the institution, and collaborate with the team working on them.	
100. Collaborate with the process improvement office on the change in processes.	
101. Discuss the BPM (business process management) capabilities with the IT Team.	
102. Position the alerts, triggers and thresholds to drive outcomes within your organization.	
Chapter 15: Real-Time Monitoring and Management	
103. Complete an inventory of the systems that are installed in the organization.	
104. Develop a plan to address the concurrent activity monitoring challenge.	
105. Determine the access options for all databases in use.	
106. Create reporting structure (database and tables).	
107. Determine all items that need monitored in real-time.	
108. Create real-time reports on specifications from the end users.	
109. Review and approve user access levels.	
110. Determine and communicate end user real-time report responsibilities.	
111. Determine the scope of use for each of the BI tools and its part in the master BI plan.	
112. Create an ongoing system use, review and follow-up process.	
Chapter 16: Modeling, Simulation, Forecasting and Predictive Analytics	
113. Identify and document the need for advanced analytics.	
114. Outline the anticipated goal and outcome of the analytics. This will drive the approach to be used.	
115. Identify the source of data and reliability of the data to be used for the advanced reviewed.	
116. Identify in-house resources who can support advanced analytics.	

Item	Completed (Y/N)
117. Outline anticipated outcome and evaluate change in processes.	
118. Modify advanced analytics programs on routine basis to provide for further drill-down and clarification.	

Index